Concepts a
in the Law of
CONTRACTS

SEVENTH EDITION

By

MARVIN A. CHIRELSTEIN
Professor of Law, Columbia University

CONCEPTS AND INSIGHTS SERIES®

FOUNDATION PRESS

© 2013 By MARVIN CHIRELSTEIN
    610 Opperman Drive
    St. Paul, MN 55123
    1–800–313–9378
Printed in the United States of America

ISBN 978–1–60930–330–3

Mat #41412257

To Ellen

PREFACE

My purpose in writing a brief Contracts primer is to offer first-year law students a reliable overview of the major themes and leading cases in the field. As the modest size of this book must suggest, I have made no effort to be comprehensive or to prepare a work that could possibly or even remotely qualify as a treatise. Very much more of the law of Contracts is omitted than included, and indeed two major topics—the Statute of Frauds and Assignment and Delegation—are touched upon only in passing. Some will feel that too much has been left out, but my own view is that omitting things is a good way to learn this or any other legal subject. At all events, my hope (and my hunch) is that less will actually turn out to be, if not more, then at least quite sufficient from the standpoint of a student reader.

* * *

A virtual avalanche of newly edited Contracts casebooks has come down upon us during the past year, with most exceeding in length and coverage anything previously seen by workers in the field. How well this serves the interests of first-year law students I am not sure, but my own perverse impulse has been to make this primer even shorter than it was in earlier editions. I have not quite succeeded. A few new cases–new to the primer, I mean–have been added along with some further explanatory material that may be of value to some readers. As before, my aim is to stress conceptual elements and case analysis rather than legal detail.

I am grateful to Barbara Aronstein Black for comments and advice.

MARVIN A. CHIRELSTEIN

Columbia University
June, 2013

TABLE OF CONTENTS

TABLE OF CONTENTS

Concepts and Case Analysis
in the Law of
CONTRACTS

Chapter 1

BACKGROUND ELEMENTS: THE CONTRACT CURVE AND EXPECTATION DAMAGES

Exchanging one thing for another—money for goods and services, typically—is a major preoccupation for most of us and for better or worse absorbs the greater part of our active lives. This being so, it is not surprising that Contracts—which is essentially the law of exchange—should have the status of a foundation course in law school. Any exchange relationship, even the simplest transaction at retail, is based on an agreement between the parties, and we naturally expect—though without thinking about it unless we have to—that legal rules in some way provide assurance that the agreement will be honored. Contract law is supposed to implement that expectation. In the process it chiefly asks and answers the following questions: first, whether the parties have behaved in such a way as to create legally recognizable expectations in one another; second, if they have, how those expectations should be characterized and understood; third, whether the understanding thus arrived at was faithfully carried out by the parties or somehow thwarted; and finally, if thwarted, what if anything the law should do about it. These questions can, of course, be presented in a fairly subtle way and they may prove irritatingly difficult to answer. They are not very numerous, however, and quite often the difficulty arises less from the need to solve a complex legal issue than from uncertainty about what the parties really *did* expect and understand in the particular case under consideration. Judicial opinions, even the "great" opinions that have been chewed over for generations, are sometimes rather dream-like and opaque when it comes to explaining why the parties acted or expressed themselves as they did, and it is that "opacity," I believe, not the legal rules as such, that creates problems in many instances.

But before approaching the cases themselves, it may be worthwhile to say something about the economic framework in which contract law arises, admitting in advance that "economics," here, pretty well reduces to a set of truisms that are largely obvious to begin with. One such truism is that people enter into exchange relationships with one another—trading this for that—for the sole and sufficient reason that it makes them feel better off to do so. Thus, imagine a world consisting of only two commodities—apples

1

and oranges—and only two consumers—A and B—each with different preferences but each wanting to consume *some* quantity of both
commodities. We can be quite sure that, unless already satisfied
with the allocation of those commodities, A and B will at once
commence to negotiate a trade, with A giving up some of his apples,
say, in exchange for some of B's oranges and B doing the opposite.
The effect, it is important to note, should be to make *both* parties
feel richer than previously—not just A, not just B, but both. The
trading process is not a poker game in which one player wins what
another loses; rather, it is a kind of joint undertaking which
increases the wealth of both parties and from which both emerge
with a measure of enhanced utility. This is true, moreover, even
though A and B are essentially in conflict, each seeking to drive the
hardest bargain he can against the other and each having and
cherishing the mentality of a shark. The act of making an exchange
will (in the generality of cases) lead not only to individual but to
mutual advantage despite a thoroughly self-centered outlook on the
part of the traders. That being so, it would be unfortunate, even
wasteful in economic terms, if the exchange did not take place.

All this is slightly banal, I admit, but it does describe the
formal setting in which contracts calling for the exchange of one
thing for another are made. A and B *both* trade up, so to speak,
until one or the other feels that no further trading will lead to his
advantage. They are not of course unique. The same formulation
can be extended to a society more nearly resembling the real
world—that is, a society in which there are many commodities and
many consumers, including, I should add, not only consumers of
outputs—households that eat up the apples and oranges—but consumers of inputs—business firms that buy and use labor and raw
materials in producing goods and services. Once more, all of these
individuals and entities will "naturally" engage in trading one
thing for another—buying and selling, getting and spending—up to
the point where such activity produces no further *mutual* advantage and the allocation of available resources—people as well as
things—is classically "efficient."

Stressing economic efficiency leads to yet another important
question (though, again, pretty easily answered). Thus, why should
the law—as of course it does—go to the trouble of enforcing
contract obligations between private parties? Why should our costly
legal apparatus be used (in some way not yet specified) to *compel*
people to keep their promises? As already noted, A and B are *both*
presumed to be made better off by trading goods and services. If
that is so, why shouldn't they be expected to keep their promises
voluntarily—why add the element of legal compulsion to an ar-

rangement which the parties entered into *without* compulsion and which each evidently regards as being in his own best interest?

The answer, of course, is that if all transactions took place instantaneously, as in the case of an everyday retail purchase, the need for enforcement rules would be slight. If you buy a book at the bookstore, the transaction is complete once the cashier has counted your money and you put the book under your arm. But retail sales are really the exception, although of course not without their own special problems. In most other situations, including almost all commercial dealings, the agreed-upon exchange is noninstantaneous; rather, it is intended to occur at some date in the future or is expected to take considerable time to carry out. An example of the former would be an agreement to pay $X for Y tons of steel to be delivered in ninety days. An example of the latter would be an agreement to build a factory for a stated price, construction to be completed in two years. In both cases vital terms are agreed to by the parties today, while performance—full payment on the buyer's side perhaps, and certainly delivery or construction on the seller's— is necessarily deferred.

Given a lapse of time between agreement and performance, it is possible that one of the two parties will come to regret the deal. Their agreement represents the parties' best estimates of future market conditions, but those estimates will almost never be perfectly accurate and it is easy to imagine that buyer or seller, owner or builder, will subsequently find that actual market prices have moved in a direction that makes performance in accordance with the terms originally agreed upon unprofitable. Considerations of reputation and standing might even then deter the disadvantaged party from breaking his promise, but if the financial loss that he confronts becomes substantial he might well prefer to tolerate the other party's hard feelings and back out of the deal altogether. Clearly, however, both parties *intended* to be bound by their agreement and would have found it difficult or impossible to carry on business in the first place without being able to count on the enforcement of their claims to performance. The steel buyer, for example, might have made an agreement to resupply the steel (perhaps after further processing) at a fixed price to a customer of his own; the builder would surely have made fixed-price agreements with various material suppliers and sub-contractors when calculating his costs for the factory building. Planning at all stages will have been carried forward on the assumption that the promises made by other actors will be kept or (if not) enforced. Unless that assumption *can* be made the process of exchange will obviously be discouraged or greatly complicated. While the legal system could leave each party to protect himself against breach by the other through the medium of insurance, bonding, hedging or the like, it is not easy to think of any self-protective device (other than violence or taking human hostages) that does not itself entail a contractual commitment by which the affected parties expect to be bound.

Accepting that legal enforcement is desirable, the next and in a sense the last really important question is what form such enforcement should take. One possibility would be physical compulsion: a person committing breach of contract would be ordered to perform and would be *made* to do so by threat of fine or imprisonment. Actually, the law does compel performance in certain situations, but these are isolated and relatively few in number. More generally, the common law deals and has always dealt with contract breach not by forced compliance but by compensating the injured party for his loss through an award of money damages. Our rule, briefly stated, is that the injured party may recover from the party in breach a dollar sum sufficient to put him in as good a position as he would have occupied had the contract been performed in full. This principle—easily the most important single idea in the whole contracts field—is referred to by convention as the "expectation damage" rule, and of course it is the injured party's "expectations" that are being compensated.

To illustrate the rule as simply as possible, assume that Buyer and Seller contract for the sale of 1,000 barrels of oil (carefully specified as to grade or whatever) at a price of $50 a barrel, payment and delivery in 90 days. On the payment/delivery date, as it happens, oil is selling at only $44 a barrel and Buyer refuses to go through with the transaction. How much can Seller, the injured party, recover? A possible answer—but wrong—is $50,000. To be sure, $50,000 is the aggregate purchase price due under the contract, and clearly Buyer has breached. If, however, we give appropriate recognition to the fact that there is an active market for oil, Seller would obviously be over-compensated if we awarded him an amount equal to the full purchase price. Having learned from Buyer that the agreement is being dishonored, Seller is free, if he chooses, to sell his 1,000 barrels on the market to any buyer at the prevailing $44 price. Assume he does. If he were *also* entitled to recover $50,000 from Buyer, Seller's total receipts would be $94,000 and the breach of contract would have been a piece of rare good fortune from his standpoint. Aimed at compensating, but not over-compensating Seller for Buyer's breach, the expectation damage rule limits Seller's claim to the difference between the contract price—$50—and the market value of the goods at the contract date—$44—or $6 a barrel. In effect, Seller is required to "mitigate" damages by accepting the best price then available in the market. Whether or not he really sells the oil doesn't matter for this purpose: since he could if he wished, he is presumed to have done so. The proceeds of such sale, actual or presumed, are then applied to Buyer's account, that is, are treated as if received by Seller from Buyer himself. It follows that Seller's claim against Buyer under the prevailing common law damage rule is limited to $6,000, the sum "needed" to satisfy Seller's original expectation. That expectation, of course, was to receive $50 a barrel for 1,000 barrels of oil.

The concept just described is a simple one, I know, but to make sure of it I might ask the following: In applying the expectation damage rule, should it matter whether Seller *later* disposes of his oil for more or less than its market value at the contract date? Suppose after shrewd calculation he decides to retain the oil in the hope that the market, which is apparently volatile, will go back up to $50 in the near future? And suppose it quickly does, so that Seller actually *gets* his $50 a barrel, say two weeks afterwards. Or suppose it drops still further and the oil is finally sold by Seller for only $40. Should either of these events make a difference in computing Seller's damage claim? The answer is no. Seller is not required to dispose of his oil at $44, but if he doesn't he is on his own both legally and in economic terms. The entitlements and obligations of the parties—and in particular Seller's rights against Buyer—are cut off and determined at the date set by the contract. The reason is plain. Market forecasts made by the parties when the contract was entered into were keyed to a date exactly 90 days forward, no later. Seller proved to be the better forecaster (this time). But Seller's decision to hold his oil off the market *after* that date—to retain his long position hoping for a price jump—is obviously a decision made solely for his own interest; the consequences, good or bad, are his alone. Hence, Buyer's breach gives Seller a claim to $6,000 in damages—no more, no less—without regard to subsequent events.

This very brief description of the expectation damage rule has focused on proper compensation to Seller, the injured party, but the implications for Buyer are equally notable. Given the rule, Buyer's act in breaching the contract gains him nothing in my illustrative case. From Buyer's standpoint the obligation to pay Seller $6,000 in damages leaves Buyer no better off than he would be if he completed the contract by paying Seller $50,000 as promised, took delivery, and then simply sold the oil in the market for $44,000. Whatever he does, whether he fulfills the contract or breaches, Buyer is poorer by $6,000. Accordingly, unless he thinks he has some legal defense to offer, Buyer might as well grit his teeth and carry out his obligations in accordance with the contract.

And very probably he would, which may suggest to the reader that the principal impact of the expectation damage rule is *prospective* rather than backward-looking and remedial. Viewed from the beginning rather than the end of the contracting process, it is obvious that both parties then considered themselves better off by (a) agreeing to exchange cash for oil and (b) fixing the price at $50 a barrel. Each party undoubtedly felt that the agreement was to his advantage despite an awareness that his market prediction might turn out badly. Why or how the two parties reached their respective conclusions about the future price of oil we don't know, but for our purposes it is enough to state that each of them must have regarded the promised exchange as advantageous from the standpoint of his own wealth position. Buyer evidently feared that oil prices would be higher in 90 days, maybe a lot higher, Seller just the opposite. Apparently, each party thought it desirable to avoid or at least minimize his risk by substituting a single known quantity and price figure—1,000 barrels of oil at $50 a barrel—for the range of possible market prices 90 days in the future. Plainly, however, the expected benefit could be realized by the parties only if their agreement was seen to be fully reciprocal, that is, only if it was evident to both—at the outset—that neither could lose through one-sided compliance. If the legal rules permitted either party to breach without compensation to the other, then, probably, the best course to follow would be to avoid agreement altogether—regretfully, to be sure, because, as noted, the proposed exchange, including the fixed-price feature, was otherwise thought by each to be to his advantage.

But, of course, contracts calling for a forward exchange are entered into every day, and most are routinely performed, even though as to any single transaction one party is likely to prove a better forecaster of future market developments than the other. The reason for this is that the expectation damage rule operates to deprive the "loser"—Buyer on this occasion—of any benefit from indulging in non-cooperative conduct and, reciprocally, gives the "winner" his due. The gamble is fair to both parties; neither can renege after the cards are dealt. In this respect the rule has a consistent and important role in making cooperative relations feasible[1] and in promoting what was described above as "efficient" resource allocation.

1. Birmingham, *Legal and Moral Duty in Game Theory: Common Law* *Contract and Chinese Analogies,* 18 Buffalo L.Rev. 99, 105 (1969).

The foregoing, I hope, adequately explains the expectation damage rule in its simplest and most fundamental aspect, but I should caution that the subject of contract remedies is far more complex and extensive than my simple illustration suggests. If, for example, the transaction between a buyer and seller involved some product or service for which no active trading market existed, measuring damages by reference to daily price quotations would not be possible. In some situations, also, buyer and seller might have different expectations of benefit, so that the convenient element of symmetry would be lacking. Finally, my illustration entirely neglects the possibility that the parties may have incurred out-of-pocket costs in *reliance* on the contract—again, perhaps, in differing amounts—for which the injured party would presumably seek recovery as well. How should all or any of these circumstances be handled in fashioning a well-calibrated damage rule? These and other detailed remedy problems are examined in Chapter 8.

Calculation of damages is the final and culminating event in any contract litigation. Before reaching the damage question, as noted earlier, one needs first to determine whether a "contract" actually exists between the parties, one that the law recognizes and will enforce, then what the contract means, then whether the acts or omissions complained of by the plaintiff constitute a breach. Issues of this sort make up the bulk (the word is used advisedly) of most Contracts courses and are taken up at appropriate points in the Chapters that follow. Probably, though, the student's perspective will be clearer at each of these stages if he or she has some idea in advance of what is ultimately at stake for the parties, and this suggests that an overview of damages and remedies may be a suitable starting point in this field.

Having praised the expectation damage rule as instrumental to the welfare-maximizing function of exchange, I should add, or concede, that in general contract law has nothing much to do with the larger question of who gets what in this world. The economist's model of efficiency is one in which all mutually beneficial trades have been carried out and executed, with the happy consequence that further changes that would benefit *all* individuals are impossible, at least until circumstances change. But beware the syllogism: the fact that no further changes can be made that will make everybody happy does not mean that everybody *is* happy. A given society's resources may, for example, be allocated in such a way that 10% of the population owns 90% of all the apples and oranges and everything else, while 90% of the population must live on the 10% that is left. This seems inequitable, to put it mildly, but resource allocation is "efficient" in economic terms if there are no further opportunities to exchange goods and services in a way that will make someone better off without making someone else worse off (if, in effect, no further gains from trade can be achieved). By contrast, a redistributive measure that produced a greater degree of equality in the ownership of resources would neither be compelled nor justified under a pure efficiency standard. Those made worse off would obviously suffer a loss of well-being unless they are altruists, and would therefore be unlikely to regard such a measure as anything but a forced exaction (otherwise known as a tax). Shifting wealth from one person (or group of people) to another—making the latter better off but the former worse off—lacks the element of *mutual* benefit with which the efficiency standard is usually identified.

We might, nevertheless, and probably would conclude that the distribution of resources in the society just described was inhumane and unfair and decide that something should be done about it. Plainly, however, the process of trading one thing for another, which assumes the pursuit of purely selfish motives, will not serve well as an instrument of "reform" unless we are sure that the people in the rich minority will be consistently wrong in their predictions about the economic future, like Buyer in my illustration. But that is implausible. It follows, I think, that Contracts, the law of *voluntary* exchange, has relatively little to say about equity and fairness in the large. Rather, its focus is on that multitude of commonplace, small-scale transactions by means of which private individuals seek to advance their personal well-being, each individual acting strictly in his own interest.

All this is pretty cold-blooded. Not liking it very much, some writers argue that contract law, with its emphasis on enforcement, is essentially a reactionary force, one that operates to preserve the status quo by treating the act of voluntary exchange as sacrosanct and inviolable, even though in some cases the parties to a contract may be unequal in bargaining power and education. Where such inequality exists (it is said) enforcement on the usual basis is unjustified and rules of amelioration should be developed. From the other end, some assert that strict enforcement of contracts is really a way of showing respect for the dignity and freedom of other individuals by taking them at their word. Hence, arguably, judicial or legislative interventions in the name of fairness—for example, excusing certain people from performance when it appears that the obligations they have assumed are especially harsh—amounts to creating one class of caretakers and another class of sheep. These viewpoints, which inevitably involve the proponent's ethical values,

8

are brought into sharper focus in connection with the subject of unconscionability, which is taken up in Chapter 4.

One further (and concluding) set of observations should be made concerning the purpose and function of legal rules in the Contracts field. As has been seen, contracts are voluntary arrangements created by the parties themselves to carry out their own particular aims. People exchange things with one another because they want to not because they have to, and in fashioning the terms of exchange—who is obliged to do what for whom—they are likewise free, within broad limits, to invent their own rules of conduct and to structure their relationship in the way that best suits their personal interests. As usual, the structure finally adopted will be the product of negotiation—sometimes protracted, sometimes instantaneous—with each party seeking his own advantage but with both parties, presumably, feeling better off as a result of the exchange.

The role of legal rules in this setting—whether we speak of statutory rules, as in the case of the Uniform Commercial Code, or of common law rules—is important but, in a sense, subordinate. If the parties to a contract had the time and the vision to negotiate and articulate every element that could conceivably bear upon their relationship, weighing every contingency and imagining all possible future states of the world, there would be little need for contract rules as such. The resulting agreement, under these idealized circumstances, would be complete and self-contained; there would be no gaps of meaning and no ambiguity of language or expression, and hence nothing would be left for judicial interpolation or surmise. The courts, then, would function solely as an enforcement mechanism, automatically converting known obligations and entitlements into legal judgments.

The difficulty, of course, is that no contract, however detailed, can or will be wholly comprehensive. Apart from limitations on human foresight, the cost in time and money of sorting out all possible contingencies and then drafting the relevant contract provisions would be prohibitive even for large transactions, and the resulting contract would be as thick as the proverbial phone-book (actually, some are). For the smaller, routine transactions of daily business or personal life, anything more complex and time-consuming than a one- or two-page purchase order is obviously impractical.

Having this circumstance in mind, the primary function of legal rules becomes apparent. Thus, the presence of standing rules on which the parties can rely in the absence of a fully articulated agreement makes it unnecessary to burden every contractual undertaking with the costly process just referred to. By saying nothing in their agreement to the contrary, the contracting parties will be deemed to have adopted the legal rules supplied by statute or common law just as if those rules had been agreed to and written into the contract itself. In effect, the parties can go forward on the assumption that they have a complete contract *without* the need to reach express agreement on each and every question that might have bearing on their relationship. The legal rules serve to fill in the gaps.

This, in turn, means that the legal rules themselves—if they are to play their gap-filling role in a useful fashion—should reflect the arrangements that the contracting parties, in the generality of cases, would have wanted and chosen had they actually gone to the trouble and expense of reaching an agreed position on the particular point at issue. If it were otherwise, that is, if the standing rules of contract law ran contrary to the arrangements likely to be chosen in most cases by the contracting parties themselves, then in order to escape those rules the parties would have to incur additional negotiation and drafting costs, which they would obviously prefer to avoid. Over time, presumably, such ill-fitting rules would come to be viewed as obstacles to agreement and would be changed or discarded.

But how do we know just what arrangements the parties *would* have chosen and agreed to? How can the law, long afterwards, go back and, putting itself in the parties' place, reconstruct a hypothetical bargain between them? The answer is: it can't. All that can really be done by courts and legislatures is to make the very general assumption that the parties to a contract, acting in their own interest, would normally seek to maximize their *combined* benefits under the contract by allocating risks and responsibilities in the least costly manner. If, for example, it appears that Party A would usually be in a position to deal with a particular risk or responsibility more cheaply and efficiently than Party B, then it is reasonable to assume that the parties would have allocated that risk or responsibility to Party A had they actually taken time to reach agreement on the matter. Minimizing the *joint* costs of performance means that the net value of the contractual pie will be larger. With more to divide up, each of the parties would be likely to get a bigger slice than otherwise. It follows that the "default" rule—the rule supplied by contract law in default of express agreement—should be fashioned with that objective in view.[2]

2. On this important topic, *see, e.g.,* Ayres & Gertner, *Filling Gaps in Incom-* *plete Contracts: An Economic Theory of* *Default Rules,* 99 Yale L.J. 87 (1989);

Once again, however, we should be aware that the legal rules in this field are not obligatory elements of every contract. The parties are by no means bound to adopt those rules, and if their particular interests dictate otherwise, then, in general, they are free to create their own "rules" by explicit contractual provision. Their freedom in this regard is not unlimited—in a very few instances the legal rules are mandatory—but for the most part the parties can either accept or "contract around" the standing rules at will.

Barnett, *The Sound of Silence: Default Rules and Contractual Consent,* 78 Va. L.Rev. 821 (1992); Goetz & Scott, *The Limits of Expanded Choice: An Analysis of the Interactions Between Express and Implied Terms,* 73 Calif.L.Rev. 261 (1985); Speidel, *Restatement Second: Omitted Terms and Contract Method,* 67 Cornell L.Rev. 785 (1982).

Chapter 2

CONSIDERATION AND THE
BARGAINED–FOR
EXCHANGE

Chapter 1 makes the not very surprising point that the chief function of contract law is to provide a framework for the enforcement of promises. Since, however, the law cannot be concerned, even by implication, with every promise that people make in their daily lives, the first question that has to be faced is how to distinguish between those promises that merit enforcement by legal means and those that don't. The answer is largely (but, as it turns out, not exclusively) to be found in the common-law requirement of "consideration", which, in simplest terms, denotes the receipt by the promisor of "something of value" from the promisee. As already observed, contract law is centrally concerned with the everyday business of exchange—apples for oranges and all that—and hence legal enforcement is chiefly addressed to undertakings that arise in that context.

Section 17 of the Restatement* expresses the general understanding on this well-worn topic by stating that, except where special rules apply, the formation of a contract requires "a bargain" to which the contracting parties give assent, and "a consideration", which can take the form of either a return promise or an actual performance. Thus, most contractual arrangements that are made in a business setting involve an exchange of promises to do something in the future: Seller promises to deliver certain merchandise in 30 days; in return, Buyer promises to pay Seller $X when the merchandise is delivered. Here, the consideration for each party's promise is the promise made by the other. Once promises are exchanged, there is a "contract" and both parties are bound to perform accordingly. Less commonly, perhaps, consideration for a promise may consist *solely* of a "performance" by the promisee. C promises to pay D $10 if D mows C's lawn. D is not asked to say "I promise" but just to go ahead and mow. C's promise to pay becomes binding if and when the service is rendered by D (or, at least, commenced). In conventional terminology, contracts of the first sort—those involving an exchange of promises—are referred to

* All Restatement references are to the Restatement of the Law, Second, of Contracts.

12

as "bilateral"; contracts of the second kind—those involving an exchange of a promise for a performance—are called "unilateral". As suggested in Chapter 3, the distinction between bilateral and unilateral contracts has legal and conceptual consequences that go beyond mere terminology, but for the moment we can simply note that the requirement of consideration may be met either by promising or by doing, depending on the context.

As stated, the aim of the consideration requirement, speaking very generally, is to tie legal enforcement to the common act of trading one thing for another. On the other hand, the ways in which people deal with each other are infinitely various and idiosyncratic, and for that reason it seems unlikely that any single doctrinal idea can succeed in being both broad enough and particular enough to cover every situation that arises. Consider, for example, a voluntary promise to pay retirement benefits. Thus, X Corporation, acting through its board of directors, promises to pay Z, a long-time employee, a monthly pension when Z retires. Taking X at its word, Z does retire after a short time and makes no effort to find another job. X pays the pension for a few years but then, having undergone a change in management, stops. Can Z enforce X's promise at that point? One certainly hopes so. To be sure, X was merely being generous when it promised to pay the pension, and it received nothing measurable or tangible from Z in return. Yet it seems entirely plain that a failure to enforce Z's claim would work a fearful injustice, since Z, we can assume, is now too old and infirm to do anything but starve. To avoid this dire result, we (or a sympathetic court) could indulge in a little factual or semantic manipulation and find that Z's "early retirement" really was a valid consideration for X's promise. But if that is too farfetched, then we might frankly recognize that the consideration requirement operates too narrowly to promote fair outcomes in these and similar circumstances and conclude that an alternative basis for the enforcement of promises—here, obviously, the promisee's "induced reliance"—needs to be adopted.

As noted, Restatement Section 17 provides that a "contract" requires a "bargain" and a "consideration" *except* where "special rules" apply. It is, of course, the exceptions and the special-rule occasions that are of interest, and hence the discussion that follows is largely concerned with those cases in which the requirement of consideration does *not* apply or has been modified. To keep perspective, however, we should remind ourselves that these "exceptional" situations are just that, and that in the common run of business and consumer dealings the element of consideration is present virtually by definition. I should add that the aim of this Chapter is merely to outline the traditional bases for the enforcement of promises in contract law—consideration, promissory estoppel, and moral obligation—and not by any means to canvass or exhaust the entire subject of consideration and its alternatives. Particular applications are to be found elsewhere—in Chapter 3, for example, in connection with firm offers and revocation, in Chapter 4 in connection with contract modification and duress, and in Chapter 5 in connection with exclusive agency agreements and requirements contracts. In each of those contexts, as it happens, the formal nature of the consideration requirement has sometimes made it harder, rather than easier, to reach sensible results, and not infrequently it has had to be subordinated to other legal criteria.

A final introductory note may be in order. It has often been observed that lay persons—non-lawyers—sometimes seem to think that an agreement has to be in writing in order to be legally binding. That, of course, is not true. A spoken promise may be no less effective as a matter of law than a written promise, and indeed most, or at least many, of the transactions that people enter into in daily life—small-scale retail purchases, short-term employment arrangements—are based on "contracts" and entail binding promises even though there is no "writing" that embodies the parties' understanding. Going further, Restatement Section 19 confirms that a promise may be expressed "in acts", that is, without words, and indeed, as indicated in the next Chapter, the commencement of performance may by itself constitute a "return promise" that is sufficient to create a bilateral contract.

The point should not, of course, be overstressed. Almost any exchange that involves substantial outlays or complexity of detail is likely to be reduced to writing and to be signed by the parties, although in many instances the cost of formalization is held to a minimum through the use of standardized contract forms. As a safeguard against spurious claims, moreover, the Statute of Frauds, applicable with minor variations in every State, forbids the enforcement of certain classes of contracts—among others, sales of land, suretyships, and service contracts not to be performed within one year—unless evidenced by a "written memorandum". UCC 2–201 contains a like restriction applicable to sales of "goods" for a price of $500 or more. Neither the Statute nor the UCC means that oral agreements within the affected classes cannot be made and performed—they are not in any sense illegal—but only that enforcement may be unavailable if one party or the other refuses to fulfil her obligations. A sizable body of relatively uninteresting jurisprudence has grown up around the Statute of Frauds, much of it aimed at confining and limiting the application of the Statute. Some of this is adverted to at various points, but the Statute and its case-law progeny are not otherwise systematically discussed in this volume.

A. Promises to Make a Gift

Donative promises—parent, for example, promising to give child a new car when child graduates from college—would appear to fall entirely outside the "bargain" configuration that underlies the formation of a binding contract. The parent's promise may create a happy expectation in the child, but the parent is obviously free—without, as a legal matter, risking anything more than the child's hard feelings—to change her mind. For the reason, I suppose, that a disappointed donee suffers relatively little in the way of measurable damages, the general rule is that a promise to make a gift in the future is not enforceable.

But suppose that the promisor demands specific conduct from the promisee as a condition of the gift; or suppose the promisee, counting on the promisor to keep her word, incurs irreversible obligations of her own. A promisor who reneges under these circumstances can certainly be criticized for having behaved in a misleading fashion. The question here, however, is whether, apart from recriminations and other forms of personal revenge, the promisee has any strictly legal recourse. Are there situations in which the promise to make a future gift is actually treated as enforceable, either on the ground that promisor and promisee have in some sense struck a "bargain" or because the promisee has made commitments in reliance on the promisor's good faith?

In *Hamer v. Sidway,*[1] Uncle William promised to give young Willie, his nephew and namesake, the sum of $5,000 if the lad, then 15 years old, would refrain from smoking, drinking and gambling until he reached the age of 21. Willie evidently did refrain and on reaching his majority wrote to his Uncle requesting the promised sum. In a letter of reply, Uncle William stated that he would carry out his promise by placing $5,000 in a bank account for Willie's benefit and would keep the fund "on interest" until he thought his nephew capable of using it wisely. "I would hate very much," wrote Uncle, a self-made man, "to have you start out in some adventure that you thought all right and lose this money in one year." Getting the money in the first place, he explained, "cost me a heap of hard work...." Willie apparently made no objection to this decision, at

---

1. 124 N.Y. 538, 27 N.E. 256 (1891).

least none that was recorded, and Uncle went ahead and established the bank account.

A dozen years then passed into history, during which time (as recounted by the court below) Willie borrowed from Uncle, but lost and never repaid, some $13,000 in money and merchandise. Willie finally declared bankruptcy, though without disclosing to his creditors any interest in the $5,000 bank account, having previously (so he said) transferred that interest to his wife. Uncle died at the end of this period, and the plaintiff, to whom Willie's claim was hastily reassigned, demanded that the defendant, as executor of Uncle's estate, pay over the $5,000 account (plus accumulated interest) to her. Defendant refused on the asserted ground, among others, that as Uncle had received no consideration for his original promise to Willie, no contract existed which the assignee of Willie's wife could now enforce.

Reversing the lower court, which had characterized the proceeding as an assault on the estate by dissatisfied relatives, the New York Court of Appeals held for the plaintiff. In promising to "pay" Willie $5,000 for being abstemious until he reached age 21, Uncle had in fact induced Willie to "forbear" from doing things he had a legal right to do. Willie *used* to smoke and drink occasionally, it appeared, but he stopped like a good fellow when offered a monetary inducement by his uncle. Under settled law, said the Court, surrendering one's freedom of action is sufficient consideration for a promise; in effect, Willie "performed", even though performance consisted of a forbearance rather than an affirmative act. It was of course true that Uncle, intending Willie's good more than his own, received no tangible benefit himself. But the courts do not, as a general rule, inquire into the "adequacy" of consideration—that being a matter for the private judgment of the parties—and if Uncle thought it worth $5,000 to get Willie to avoid bad habits, then there was "nothing ... that would permit a determination that the uncle was not benefited in a legal sense."

Solely from the standpoint of doctrine—and putting aside one's less than favorable view of young Willie himself—the decision in *Hamer v. Sidway* is generally regarded as correct. There *was* a bargained-for consideration of sorts, and apparently Uncle got the result he sought. As compared with other things Uncle might have bought with his money, I suppose good behavior on Willie's part ranked reasonably high, and there can be little doubt that Uncle, if asked, would have *wanted* Willie to believe that the money would finally be his. In social terms, the transaction was a bit unusual—senior family members do not typically "buy" good conduct from juniors—and we might doubt whether it is really worthwhile to invoke costly legal processes in support of Uncle's moral standards. On the other hand, if a donor-promisor actually wishes to make his gift the subject of a "deal", and particularly if the amount involved is not trivial, then, arguably, there may be no more reason in this context than in a commercial setting to deny the parties an opportunity to capture benefits through trade.

But suppose the underlying arrangement lacks the "bargain" feature said to be present in the *Hamer* case, or that the element of benefit to the promisor is simply too remote to be recognized. Is the absence of consideration always fatal from the standpoint of a disappointed donee-promisee, or are there other grounds on which the enforcement of a future gift-promise might be justified? In *Ricketts v. Scothorn,*[2] a kindly grandfather, eager to make life easier for a granddaughter who was slaving away in a shop at a salary of $10 a week, gave the granddaughter his demand note for $2,000 with annual interest at 6%. Grandfather expressed the hope that the yearly interest would enable granddaughter to quit her miserable job if she chose. While quitting the job was not a requirement or condition of the gift, granddaughter did abandon her employment at that point, although she went back to work a year later, apparently because grandfather was unable to keep up the interest payments. At grandfather's death, granddaughter demanded that his estate pay the principal amount of the note and on being refused brought suit against the executor.

Drawing on decisions involving the enforcement of pledges to charity, the Supreme Court of Nebraska held for the plaintiff. The Court conceded, indeed it emphasized, that there was no consideration to support the grandfather's promise. Ordinarily, it said, a mere promise to make a gift in the future is not enforceable. But where a donee, relying in good faith on the donor's promise, is led thereby to spend money, incur debts or take some other costly and irreversible step, the donor may be "estopped" on grounds of equity

---

2. 57 Neb. 51, 77 N.W. 365 (1898). *Compare* Kirksey v. Kirksey, 8 Ala. 131 (1845), another casebook standby in the field of family gifts. Having learned of his brother's death, the defendant wrote to his bereaved sister-in-law inviting her to give up her current residence and come with her children to live in a more comfortable house on his ample property. His reason: "I feel like I want you and the children to do well." The plaintiff accepted the invitation and happily moved into the comfortable house, but after two years the defendant changed his mind and forced the plaintiff to pack up and move to a miserable hut "in the woods". Subsequently, he threw her out altogether. The explanation for this apparent cruelty is unknown (to us), but I suppose we might guess that the two former in-laws at some point formed a "relationship", that the relationship later broke down, and that the defendant then took steps to eliminate all ties.

In any event, the Court, holding that the defendant's promise was a mere gratuity and lacked consideration, refused to award the plaintiff damages for breach despite the obvious elements of inducement and reliance.

and fairness from asserting "want of consideration". This is true, at least, where the promisor's object is reasonably clear at the time the promise is made. In the case of a charitable pledge, the promisor's aim might be to support the construction of a facility— say a hospital wing—or to fund a research project. In the present case, the donor's object was to free his granddaughter from the obligation to continue her employment, and in fact she did give up her job at his suggestion. "Having intentionally influenced the plaintiff to alter her position for the worse on the faith of the note being paid when due, it would be grossly inequitable to permit the maker, or his executor, to resist payment on the ground that the promise was given without consideration. The petition charges the elements of an equitable estoppel, and the evidence conclusively establishes them."

The concept of "estoppel" based on the promisor's representations to the promisee—now generally referred to as promissory estoppel—is reflected, with refinements and enlargements, in Section 90 of the Restatement, discussed in more detail below. Briefly, Section 90 provides that a promise which is expected by the promisor to induce the promisee to take some action, and which does induce such action, is binding and enforceable if necessary to avoid injustice. Reliance by the promisee may thus be sufficient to create an enforcement right against the promisor, even though the transaction does not involve a "bargain" between the parties and even though the promisor receives no "consideration". Grandfather Ricketts sought neither a return promise nor a performance from his granddaughter; his promise was nonreciprocal in the sense that it imposed no obligation on the promisee. Grandfather did, however, intend and expect that granddaughter would quit her job and opt for a life of leisure. She understood his purpose and she opted, confident of his support. There was no element of exchange, but there was foreseeable reliance, and that, in the Court's view, justified enforcement.

Taken together, the *Hamer* and *Ricketts* cases suggest a threefold classification of family gift-promises, which can be illustrated as follows:

(1) A promises to pay B, her niece, $10,000 if B, now employed as a bartender, will quit her job and go to law-school, payment to be made on graduation day. A, a lawyer herself, thinks law is a nobler profession than tending bar and wants B to continue in the family tradition.

(2) A is told that B is sick of tending bar and wishes to go to law-school but will have to borrow heavily to meet expenses. Eager

to forward B's ambitions, A promises that when B graduates she, A, will pay off B's student loans up to a limit of $10,000.

(3) A, glad that B wants to give up bartending and go to law-school, promises to give B $10,000 as a graduation present.

Assume in each instance that B does go to law-school and graduates, but that A refuses to come across with the $10,000. If the matter is actually litigated, I suppose we might expect the following results: enforcement of A's promise in Case (1), because, as in *Hamer v. Sidway,* there was a "bargain" and a "consideration"; enforcement in Case (2), because, as in *Ricketts,* A's promise should reasonably have been expected to induce, and did induce, action on B's part that involved a significant cost; but no enforcement in Case (3), because A merely promised B a gratuity and was always free to change her mind.

To be sure, the outcomes just suggested assume that we can tell with some degree of confidence just which of the three cases is actually up for decision. A has put nothing in writing, however, and hence the parties' understanding would have to be derived by reconstructing the conversation that took place between them when they discussed the matter across the kitchen table. The quality of the evidence, therefore, is likely to be rather doubtful—especially so if, as in *Hamer* and *Ricketts,* A is no longer among the living at the time of the trial—and there is the obvious possibility of selective recall. But even if we knew exactly what had been said, the fact is that the three cases, although distinguishable in formal terms, are really very much alike at bottom. Quite simply, A wished to help B to a better future, and B persuaded herself that law-school was marginally preferable to mixing drinks. Whether viewed as a "bargain", an "inducement", or a "gratuity", all that was really involved was A's desire to act generously towards B and B's confidence in A's good will. Essentially, and in common understanding, the relationship between the parties was based not on legal commitment, but on trust and family feeling. The notion that B would ever regard herself as rendering a service to A for which she could later claim compensation is, despite *Hamer,* quite absurd; and while B doubtless hoped that A would continue in a generous frame of mind, the possibility that A might be unwilling—or, as in *Ricketts,* unable—to make the promised gift would surely have been considered by B and would temper her reliance.

In any event, and although approved by the Restatement, the decisions in *Hamer* and *Ricketts* appear to be fairly singular. The courts, perhaps concerned about the risk of false claims, have seldom enforced donative promises in a family setting, being unwilling, on the whole, either to construe such promises as bargained-for or to find significant reliance on the part of the promisee. The two decisions themselves, really, are little more than casebook curiosities and can probably be explained on the ground that neither of the promisors actually revoked or withdrew the future gift-promise during his lifetime. The litigation in both cases was not (as it would be in the hypotheticals above) between a promisee and a promisor attempting to resist enforcement, but between the promisee and the promisor's executor, the latter acting on behalf of other relatives named in the promisor's Will. In practical terms the question was not whether the promisor himself should be made to pay, but how to divide the promisor's estate among his quarreling descendants. Doctrinal issues aside, I think it may have appeared to the respective courts that each of the promisors (certainly Grandfather Ricketts, but probably Uncle William as well) went to his final rest wanting and intending that his gift to the plaintiff be completed ahead of other bequests; indeed, both promisors may actually have assumed that their gifts *had* been completed during life—in Uncle's case by placing the money in a designated bank account, in Grandfather's by delivery of a demand note to the donee. Possibly (even probably) the court in each case felt that it was effectuating the decedent's true testamentary purpose by enforcing his promise, and it may well have been *that* perception, rather than the element of consideration or of reliance (both pretty much trumped-up and artificial), that ultimately led to the results described.

Given the strictures of the consideration requirement, some writers have argued that donor-promisors who specifically wish to be liable to their donee-promisees ought to be free, by purely formal means, to *render* their promises enforceable.[3] If Uncle William actually wants to obligate himself (or his estate) to his nephew, why make things difficult by requiring the nephew to show, later on, that Uncle's promise had been supported by consideration? In earlier times the seal served the purpose just mentioned, because a promise made under seal, even though it was a gift-promise and without consideration, was generally regarded as binding. This, perhaps unfortunately, is no longer true: the legal efficacy of hot wax and engraved signet rings has been eliminated by decision or statute in most states, although legal stationers can still provide you with gummed wafers and red ribbons if you want them. Actually, however, the place of the seal has been taken by yet another type of formal observance, namely, the recital of nominal

3. Posner, *Gratuitous Promises in Economics and Law,* 6 J.Legal Studies 411 (1977).

consideration. Thus, in exchange for "one dollar in hand paid, receipt whereof is hereby acknowledged", X makes a promise of some sort to Y. As already noted, apart from allegations of fraud or legal incapacity, the courts do not ordinarily inquire into the adequacy of consideration. It is the *existence* of a bargain that matters, not whether the bargain is equal or unequal from the standpoint of an objective observer. Accordingly, it is at least arguable that a future gift promise is enforceable if it is in writing and is given the form of a bargain, even though there is no consideration for the promise in fact.

But should the law treat mere formality (whether by seal or recital) as sufficient to support a gift promise? The answer, one would think, depends on why we hesitate about enforcing future gift promises in the first place. If our reason is a worry about false claims, misunderstandings and the like, then the affixing of a seal or a recital of nominal consideration might be taken as proof that the donor's promise had been made in a conscious and deliberate frame of mind, although the existence of a signed "writing" by itself seems sufficient to show that. On the other hand, if our reason for withholding enforcement is that we think donee-promisees are unlikely to be much harmed when unrelied-upon gift promises are not kept, or if we feel that donors really *ought* to be free to change their minds (e.g., because later the donor either goes broke or loses her affection for the donee), then mere formality at the time the promise is made would appear to be insufficient if not irrelevant.[4]

Without quite knowing where to look for a definitive statement of policy on donative promises, I take some comfort from the rather confident hunch that the whole problem, despite its casebook prominence, cannot really be very important. As in *Ricketts,* promises that are relied upon by the donee to her detriment will be enforced on that ground even though consideration is lacking, so that donees who are truly harmed by the donor's failure to keep her word are to that extent protected. But even where there is no credible reliance factor, donors who wish to make gifts which the donee will *receive* in the future can easily do so by transferring their property in trust for the donee's benefit. The trust instrument would direct the trustee to distribute the property to the donee on the occurrence of some future event—when the donee reaches age 21, say, or graduates from law-school—but to return the property to the donor if the future event fails to occur. The donor's intention

---

4. *See* Eisenberg, *Donative Promises,* 47 U.Chi.L.Rev. 1 (1979); Goetz & Scott, *Enforcing Promises: An Examination of* *the Basis of Contract,* 89 Yale L.J. 1261 (1980).

to make a future gift would be largely realized by this device, yet the transfer in trust would be regarded as a *present* gift—completed when the property is transferred to the trustee—and the question of consideration would not arise.

B.   Reliance and Promissory Estoppel

Whatever one thinks of the *Ricketts* decision, it has long seemed evident that the bargain-theory of consideration operates too narrowly and too inflexibly to do equity in all circumstances. One way to put the point is to say that there appears to be a mixed set of "interactive dealings" that stands midway between conventional swap transactions, in which consideration is present by definition, and wholly nonreciprocal gift-promises, in which consideration is plainly lacking. What characterizes such dealings, as suggested, is a promise on one side and a cost—but neither a "return promise" nor a "performance"—on the other. An automatic application of the consideration requirement under these circumstances would preclude enforcement and would excuse the promisor from financial accountability. Yet it is obvious that the promise and the cost are causally related—there is at least an inference of reciprocity—and simple fairness suggests that the law would be deficient in reflecting reasonable expectations unless a remedy of some sort were made available to the promisee.

As already mentioned, the task of supplying flexibility in this area is largely entrusted to the doctrine of promissory estoppel, which treats the promisee's "reliance" as an independent and sufficient basis for enforcement. The Restatement continues to adhere to the requirement of a bargained-for consideration in general terms. By way of exception, however, Section 90 provides that—

> "(1) A promise which the promisor should reasonably expect to induce action or forbearance on the part of the promisee or a third person and which does induce such action or forbearance is binding if injustice can be avoided only by enforcement of the promise. The remedy granted for breach may be limited as justice requires."

In effect, a promisee acting in reliance can obtain enforcement even though consideration for the promise is lacking, although the promisee's remedy may be "limited"—meaning, presumably, that the promisee's recovery may be less in amount than the customary measure of expectation damages.

The doctrine of promissory estoppel has been applied to charitable subscriptions, to cases involving gratuitous bailments in which the bailee undertakes to preserve or insure the property delivered to her care, to oral promises to convey land on which the promisee then enters and makes improvements, and, as indicated, occasionally to family gifts.

The courts have divided on the voluntary payment of retirement benefits to employees, the best known case on that topic being *Feinberg v. Pfeiffer Co.*[5], a case with simple facts though some minor mysteries. Mrs. Feinberg, having served as Pfeiffer's chief bookkeeper and assistant treasurer for 37 years, and being in her middle 50's, one day received some welcome news from Mr. Lippman, Pfeiffer's chief executive and principal shareholder. The Board of Directors, she was told, in recognition of her "long and faithful service .... devo[tion] .... exceptional ability and skill ...," had voted to increase her salary from $350 to $400 a month. In addition, on her retirement—*whenever* she might choose to retire—the company would pay her $200 a month for the rest of her life. "[This] retirement plan," said the Board resolution, "is merely being adopted ... to afford Mrs. Feinberg security for the future and in the hope that her active services will continue with the corporation for many years to come." The Board's action, we may assume, was taken at Mr. Lippman's direction—probably without an actual meeting of the Board.

Though somewhat underpaid, Mrs. Feinberg's work as bookkeeper and assistant treasurer was apparently much appreciated, as indicated by the fact that she received annual bonuses running as high as $2,000. In addition—and surprisingly, since Pfeiffer was a family-owned concern—she was given and allowed to acquire by purchase 70 shares of stock (1%) in the corporation itself, entitling her to annual dividends along with the family shareholders.

At all events, Mrs. Feinberg continued to work for Pfeiffer for another year and a half, and then formally retired, following which the company began paying her $200 on the first day of each month as promised. Unfortunately for Mrs. Feinberg, Mr. Lippman died a few years later and was succeeded as head of the company by his son-in-law, Mr. Harris. Advised by his lawyer and accountant that Mrs. Feinberg's pension was a "gift" and not a contractual obligation supported by consideration, Harris cut the payments down to $100 a month and indicated that at some point soon they would be stopped entirely. Mrs. Feinberg sued Pfeiffer.

5. Feinberg v. Pfeiffer Co., 322 S.W.2d 163 (Mo.App.1959).

The Missouri Court agreed with Pfeiffer that there had been no consideration for the company's promise to pay Mrs. Feinberg $200 a month for life. Her "long and faithful service" obviously lay in the past. She had been paid her salary plus bonuses in full compensation for those services and had no legal claim to additional compensation in the form of a pension. That much Mrs. Feinberg had to concede. She did, however, argue that there were two other elements that did create an enforceable contract: first, that she continued working for the company for an additional year and a half; and second, her "change of position," that is, her retirement and relinquishment of gainful employment in reliance on Pfeiffer's promise.

The first alleged element—that she continued working for the company—found no support in the evidence, said the Court. Mrs. Feinberg made no promise to continue her employment, and indeed the Board resolution made it clear that the pension would be paid even if she retired at once. But the second element—choosing to retire early in reliance on Pfeiffer's promise to pay her $200 a month—was sufficient to establish her legal right to the pension under the doctrine of promissory estoppel and Section 90. "At the time she retired," said the Court, "she was 57 [!] years of age. At the time the payments were discontinued she was over 63 years of age. It is common knowledge that it is virtually impossible for a woman of that age to find satisfactory employment ..." The implication, presumably, was that Mrs. Feinberg would have continued working until she dropped had it not been for the company's promise to fund her retirement. Hence Section 90 gave her the enforceable right she sought.

Mrs. Feinberg is lucky, in a sense, that she chose to retire so soon after the Board resolution was adopted. Suppose instead that, liking her job and wanting full pay, she continued to work for Pfeiffer until age 70, the age at which Pfeiffer employees normally retire or are required to retire. Her retirement then would simply be a consequence of age, but would not have been "induced" by Pfeiffer's "promise" of a pension. The Section 90 claim would presumably be lost or, at least, much harder to maintain. Unsupported by consideration (as the Court found), the pension might then be denied—just when she needed it most. That outcome seems illogical, certainly unintended. I think the fault, to call it that, lies in the tone or mood of the Board resolution itself. The Board's language, "... long and faithful service .... served the corporation devotedly ....", has a donative, even a testamentary flavor and no doubt reflected Mr. Lippman's personal feelings for his loyal servant, loved by him and pitied, and now approaching old age and loss of income. So it *was* a future gift—the cruel Mr. Harris, along with his cruel lawyer and cruel accountant, was quite right. What the Board resolution should have said, obviously, was something like: "In order to retain the valuable services of Mrs. Feinberg, whose threatened departure for other employment at this time would be damaging to the company, and to induce her to remain in her present position as assistant treasurer, etc., etc." Expressed in those terms, as it easily could have been, the requirement of consideration would be met, at least formally, and the case might never have arisen.

While Section 90 authorizes the enforcement of a promise solely on the basis of the promisee's reliance, the question of whether, in the first place, there has been a communication that actually *qualifies* as a promise may itself present some difficulty. In *East Providence Credit Union v. Geremia,*[6] the plaintiff-bank made a standard car-purchase loan to the defendants, the loan being secured by a chattel mortgage on the car itself. The loan agreement required the defendants to carry collision insurance, naming the bank as payee, and provided that if defendants failed to keep the policy in force by paying the premiums when due, the bank could pay such premiums and add the amount thereof, with interest, to the principal of the defendants' debt.

Having received notice that defendants' insurance was about to be cancelled for non-payment of premiums, the bank sent the defendants a nasty form letter that said:

"We are in receipt of a cancellation notice on your Policy. If we are not notified of a renewal Policy within 10 days, we shall be forced to renew the policy for you and apply this amount to your loan."

Defendants reacted by calling the bank and telling a clerk that they were broke and that the bank should therefore go ahead and pay the premium. A few weeks later, and at a time when the defendants still owed the bank about $1,000 on the original loan, the car was totally demolished in an accident. Had the insurance policy still been in effect, the proceeds would have been paid to the bank and would presumably have satisfied the defendants' debt in full. In fact, however, the bank never did pay the overdue premium and the policy was cancelled before the accident. The loan then being in default, the bank applied to principal some $200 which the defendants had in a savings account and sued for the $800 balance. Insisting that they owed nothing because the bank had bound itself

6.   103 R.I. 597, 239 A.2d 725 (1968).

to renew the policy in a timely fashion, defendants counterclaimed for their $200 savings account.

The Supreme Court of Rhode Island, though saying relatively little about the particular facts of the case itself, enthusiastically adopted Section 90 as the law of the State and held for the defendants. The doctrine of promissory estoppel, said the Court, provides "a much needed remedy to alleviate the plight of those who suffer a serious injustice as a result of their good-faith reliance on the unfulfilled promises of others." Citing an Arkansas decision in which promissory estoppel was praised as "an attempt by the courts to keep remedies abreast of increased moral consciousness of honesty and fair representations in all business dealings", the Court declared that it gladly subscribed to "those sentiments." As a sort of back-up or reinforcement, however, the Court also found that there really *had* been a consideration for the bank's promise, because the loan agreement gave the bank the right to add the renewal premium to the principal of the defendants' loan and to charge additional interest on the recomputed balance.

Was the decision in the *East Providence* case correct or merely compassionate? The Court's holding, and particularly its application of the promissory estoppel doctrine, seems justified *if* we accept what appear to have been its factual premises, namely, (a) that the bank really did "promise" to renew the policy and (b) that the defendants "relied" on that promise in some material way. But did the bank actually promise anything? The language of the bank's form letter—"If we are not notified ..., we shall be forced to ..."—sounds more like a threat than a promise to me, and I think anyone receiving such a letter would at once understand that the sender's purpose was not to make a commitment but to enforce an obligation. In effect, the letter warned the defendants that, unless they did as *they* had promised, the bank would feel compelled to protect its own interest in the loan collateral at their expense. To construe that warning as a "promise"—one that entitled the defendants to hop in their car and drive about without even checking to *see* if the insurance problem had been taken care of—is to convert what was supposed to be a club into a boomerang. The bank probably did plan to renew the policy and simply slipped up. Pretty plainly, however, it had no intention either of obligating itself to renew or of inducing reliance in the defendants, and the phrase "we shall be forced to ..." hardly justified the latter in believing otherwise.

The question raised in the *East Providence* case—whether there has been a "promise" and a justified reliance within the meaning of Section 90—comes up again, as will be seen, in connection with the important subject of offer-and-acceptance. Thus, A offers to sell Blackacre to B at a stated price. B spends time and money investigating the proposal, but before she can accept A withdraws the offer. Does Section 90 afford B a remedy in these circumstances, or should we consider that B simply took a risk when she failed to accept A's offer at the time it was made? Going further, suppose C tells D that she will offer D a franchise to sell certain merchandise if D can raise a stated amount of investment capital. D raises the capital by selling various assets that she owns, but C then decides that D's funds are insufficient and refuses to make the franchise available. Again, does D have enforcement rights against C under the rule of Section 90, or should D have nailed the matter down in some way at the very beginning? These and related issues receive an airing in Chapter 3.

C. Illusory Promises

Suppose S for seller offers to sell B for buyer at $1,000 a ton as many tons of widgets, not exceeding 10 tons, as B may choose to order within the next 90 days. B accepts, agreeing to buy at that price as many tons of widgets (up to 10) as he may order from S within the 90–day period. The market price of widgets promptly jumps to $1,500 a ton and B orders 10 tons from S at the $1,000 contract price, only wishing he could order more. S, however, claiming that his promise to sell for $1,000 lacked consideration in the form of a return promise from B, refuses to fill the order at anything less than the current market price of $1,500. Pretty clearly, S is legally justified in refusing to sell for $1,000. Under the terms of the "agreement," B was completely free either to order or not to order up to 10 tons of widgets from S and hence quite obviously promised S nothing. Contracts to buy and sell in the future at a fixed price are intended and expected to protect each of the contracting parties against an adverse market change. Since B had no obligation to buy from S but could buy from some other seller if the price of widgets dropped, it appears that B's promise was no promise at all and that the agreement was entirely hollow. Presumably for that reason, the common law, supported by the Restatement,[7] would regard B's promise as "illusory" on the facts given and would treat the purported contract as unenforceable.

On the other hand, not much is needed to change B's promise into real consideration. Had B promised, at the price stated, to order *exclusively* from S all the widgets up to 10 tons that B might require during the next 90 days, or to order from S up to 10 but not

---

7. Restatement Section 77, *Example* 1 et seq.

less than 3 tons of widgets within that period, then, no doubt, having accepted some limitation on his future action or having obligated himself to buy some quantity of widgets from S, B's promise would constitute "consideration" even though B was free to take less than the full amount of S's commitment or, if for some reason he "required" no widgets, none at all.[8]

But these are easy cases. *Mattei v. Hopper*,[9] something of a classic in the illusory promise field, is closer to the borderline. In *Mattei*, the plaintiff, a shopping-center developer, after extended negotiations entered into a contract (called a "deposit receipt") with defendant for the purchase of defendant's land at a price of $57,500. The land was adjacent to the tract on which the shopping center was to be built and would presumably serve as a parking area for customers. The contract of sale gave the plaintiff-purchaser 120 days to produce his check and close the sale, but it also gave the plaintiff an "out" by providing that the plaintiff's obligation to close was conditional or contingent on his "obtaining leases satisfactory to the purchaser," that is, to Mattei himself. The plaintiff then began the process of securing leases from potential shopping-center tenants. Before the 120–day period had passed, however, and while the plaintiff was still engaged in arranging leases, the defendant notified the plaintiff that the deal was off, at least at the price agreed to. The plaintiff in due time informed the defendant that satisfactory leases had been obtained, but defendant refused to tender her deed and plaintiff sued for damages.

Reversing the trial court, which found for the defendant on the ground that the "satisfactory to the purchaser" clause rendered the plaintiff's promise illusory, the Supreme Court of California held that such promise was genuine and substantial despite the "satisfactory" condition, and therefore constituted valuable consideration for the defendant's promise to sell her property. The Court conceded that the determination of whether leases were or were not satisfactory lay within the sole judgment of the plaintiff, but it then reasoned that the exercise of that judgment was subject to a "good faith" obligation on the plaintiff's part which made his promise to purchase the seller's property enforceable even though conditional. Stretching somewhat for authority, the Court pointed to decided cases in which a buyer in similar circumstances, declaring himself dissatisfied, had successfully defended a decision *not* to buy on the ground that his judgment had been made in good faith rather than arbitrarily. None of those decisions, said the Court, had found the

8. *See* UCC 2–306(1).   **9.** 51 Cal.2d 119, 330 P.2d 625 (1958).

contract at issue invalid because of lack of mutuality. To be sure, the question of illusory promise was not "expressly" considered by the courts in the cases cited, and indeed that question could hardly have been raised by a buyer in his own defense. Nevertheless, the implication was that the "satisfaction" clause did not make the buyer's promise illusory where, as here, the buyer's satisfaction or dissatisfaction was dependent upon an exercise of judgment in "good faith."

Just what "good faith" consisted of in *Mattei* was not gone into very much, but evidently Mattei was able to show that he had in fact obtained a portfolio of satisfactory leases within the 120-day period. That, in turn, was taken to be proof that he had acted in "good faith" to meet his contractual obligation to the seller.

Was "satisfactory" solely a matter of Mattei's good-faith judgment or did the term have an objective reference of some sort even though not expressed in the agreement? Mattei's business aim was to build a shopping center. To do that Mattei would need a construction loan from a bank, and a large loan at that. To obtain such financing Mattei would have to present the bank-lender with lease commitments sufficient in amount and duration to give the bank assurance that the loan would be repaid (or could be refinanced) once the shopping center was built. If he failed in that effort, the shopping center project would simply collapse. In a sense, therefore, the "satisfactory" clause was similar or equivalent to the standard mortgage-availability clause that appears in many home-sale contracts. A home-buyer's obligation to a home-seller is conditioned, often, on the availability of mortgage financing for some portion of the purchase price, and the buyer agrees to use due diligence in attempting to obtain a mortgage loan. No one doubts that "due diligence" is an objective requirement and that the home-buyer's promise is enforceable by the seller if willing mortgage-lenders can (with due diligence) be identified. Mattei's promise to Hopper was similarly subject to a financing contingency, one that extended not merely to Hopper's property but to the entire project, of which Hopper's land was a part. The term "satisfactory," thus, referred not to some element of personal satisfaction on Mattei's part, but to the ultimate judgment of a bank-lender as to whether the leases secured by Mattei would support a loan. If the bank said yes, then such leases would be deemed "satisfactory to the purchaser" and the land sale would promptly close.

Hopper undoubtedly understood all this perfectly well. Aware that Mattei was eager to carry out his development plans as rapidly as possible, Hopper (or her counsel) thought it unnecessary to include a due diligence obligation in the "deposit receipt" or to spell out in further detail the obvious purpose of the "satisfactory" clause. The Court, I suppose, could have read the financing contingency and due diligence elements into the contract, but "good faith," always available as a default term, was sensibly employed to the same effect.

What is, and what isn't, an illusory promise also arises in connection with agreements in which one party makes a flexible commitment to the other—for example, to use his "best efforts" to market the promisee's product or to accomplish some other commercial objective. The term "best efforts" is obviously somewhat unspecific and appears to leave the level of commitment pretty much up to the promisor himself. Is a promise of that sort to be treated as "consideration," or does such an agreement lack mutuality of obligation? The question is briefly discussed in Section B of Chapter 5, below.

D. Moral Obligation and Past Consideration

Promissory estoppel—the concept of reliance-based enforcement—represents the principal exception to the standard requirement of consideration, but not the only exception. Yet another class of promises that sometimes appear to call for enforcement despite the absence of consideration (at least of present consideration) consists of promises made in recognition of a benefit received in the past. As a general proposition, a person who performs unrequested services for another does not thereby acquire a right to compensation or restitution, even though the performance entailed a cost to the former and a benefit to the latter. In effect, if you do somebody a favor, you cannot convert your generosity into an enforceable contract claim; services that were intended to be voluntary and gratuitous remain so as a matter of legal presumption. There are, of course, limits to this "rule". Thus, a doctor who gives emergency treatment to an accident victim is assumed to be responding to the latter's request and can therefore recover the fair value of her professional services[10]. In general, however, one who makes a gift, including a gift of services, cannot afterwards withdraw her gift by reconstituting herself a creditor.

But suppose that the beneficiary of the voluntary service—grateful, perhaps embarrassed—subsequently *promises* to compensate the volunteer for the value of the benefit received. Should that promise be treated as binding on a sort of hindsight view of events, or should it simply be regarded as a future-gift promise—returning

---

10. Cotnam v. Wisdom, 83 Ark. 601,
104 S.W. 164 (1907).

the favor, so to speak—and hence, on general principles, be held unenforceable if the promisor later changes her mind?

In *Mills v. Wyman*,[11] the plaintiff, as an act of kindness, gave shelter, food and some sort of medical attention to the defendant's son, who, having returned from a "voyage at sea," was found by the plaintiff wandering the lonely streets of Hartford ill and destitute. The son, age 25, died after a couple of weeks and the plaintiff then wrote to the defendant (who lived in Massachusetts) telling him what had happened and requesting reimbursement for the plaintiff's added expenses. Although he had no legal obligation to pay his son's bills, the son being an adult, the defendant instantly wrote back promising to reimburse the plaintiff in the amount requested. Later, however, apparently after some reflection (and perhaps after making further inquiries), the defendant changed his mind and refused to pay. His reason for refusing—whether just cold-hearted stinginess or something else—we never learn.

At all events, the Supreme Court of Massachusetts, with evident regret, held for the defendant on the ground that there had been no legal consideration for the defendant's promise. The defendant obviously hadn't asked the plaintiff to care for his son—the plaintiff had "acted the part of the good Samaritan" and had simply volunteered his services. Accordingly, there was no present consideration for the defendant's promise. While past consideration might sometimes be sufficient—as, for example, where a debtor promises to pay a debt previously contracted but now discharged in bankruptcy or barred by the statute of limitations—here there was no pre-existing obligation because the son was of full age and lived independently of his father's family. Having received nothing from the plaintiff, the defendant's promise must be regarded as gratuitous, a promise to make a gift. The defendant's moral duty to keep his promise would be recognized by everyone; but as there could be no legal enforcement absent some "gain" to the promisor, the matter would have to be left "to the interior forum, as the tribunal of conscience has been aptly called". There was, in the Court's view, an overriding need to protect the security of those "honest and fair-minded men, who may inconsiderately make promises without any equivalent", even if the consequence here was to relieve a promisor whose behavior should be regarded as "disgraceful".

The decision in *Mills* can be (always is) contrasted with that in *Webb v. McGowin*,[12] where the promisor himself was the beneficiary

---

11. 20 Mass. (3 Pick.) 207 (1825).

12. 27 Ala.App. 82, 168 So. 196 (1935).

of the plaintiff's rescue efforts. According to the allegations in the complaint, Webb, a workman employed by a lumber mill, had been on the point of dropping a huge pine block from an upper floor of the mill to the ground below when he perceived that the falling block would be likely to crush McGowin, who had suddenly appeared from nowhere and now stood directly beneath him. To prevent this catastrophe, Webb elected to go over the side along with the block, in that way diverting the block away from McGowin but sustaining crippling injuries to himself. Subsequently, and allegedly in consideration of the plaintiff's act of self-sacrifice, McGowin, who also happened to be president of the company, promised to pay Webb $15 every two weeks for the rest of his life. McGowin did make such payments on a regular basis during his own lifetime, but following McGowin's death his executors refused to continue the payments, claiming that McGowin's promise to Webb had been without consideration.

Reversing the lower court, which had granted the defendant-executors' motion to dismiss, the Alabama Court of Appeals held that the plaintiff's allegations of fact sufficed to state a legal basis for the enforcement of McGowin's promise. Admittedly, McGowin had no strictly legal obligation to Webb at the time he made his promise: having behaved as a "volunteer", Webb evidently had no claim against McGowin for restitution, and it was not suggested that McGowin had himself caused Webb's injuries through any act of personal negligence. In that sense McGowin's promise was gratuitous. Plainly, however, McGowin had realized a material benefit in being saved by Webb from death or serious harm; equally plainly in view of Webb's resulting disability, McGowin had a moral obligation to compensate Webb for his loss. While he could have ignored it, McGowin chose instead to affirm and ratify that obligation by promising to pay Webb a lifetime annuity. "Material benefit" plus "moral obligation" added up to a "valid consideration", and hence McGowin's promise was enforceable even though made after the event.

Taken together, *Webb v. McGowin* and *Mills v. Wyman* obviously suggest that moral obligation may support a promise in the absence of traditional consideration, but only if the promisor has been personally benefited or enriched by the promisee's sacrifice and there is, as a consequence, a just and reasonable claim for compensation. No clearer case of an enrichment-and-sacrifice can be imagined than that in *Webb v. McGowin* (at least that alleged[13]).

---

13. The executors apparently settled with Webb instead of going to trial. It is, of course, just possible that Webb's injuries were the result of an ordinary, if

The decision in *Mills*, by contrast, though painful (unless, again, there was more to the story than we are told[14]), presumably can be accepted on the ground that the defendant's promise was simply a shock-reaction to the news of his son's death and was given without forethought or deliberation. Actually, "moral obligation" does not appear to have been a logically necessary criterion in either case. Thus, moral obligation by itself entitled the respective plaintiffs to nothing whatever *until* a promise had been made. But once there *was* a promise moral obligation became irrelevant, because the decisive question then, indeed the only question, was whether the promisor had received a personal benefit for which the plaintiff could justly demand compensation.

Restatement Section 86 (which is grouped under the heading "Contracts Without Consideration") provides that "A promise made in recognition of a benefit previously received by the promisor from the promisee is binding to the extent necessary to prevent injustice." The court's decision in *Webb v. McGowin* is expressly approved by the Restatement—McGowin obviously received a life-saving "benefit." So is the contrary decision in *Mills v. Wyman*—no "benefit" to Wyman, because Wyman had no legal duty to support his adult son[15]. Section 86 does not make reference to "past consideration" or to "moral obligation." Rather, the aim of the Section is strictly restitutionary: compensation for "a benefit previously received...."

Webb recovers under Section 86 even though his claim is based solely on his own testimony. Mills does not, even though he is prepared (I assume) to substantiate his expenditures.

Section 5–1105 of the General Obligations Law of New York can be contrasted with the Restatement:

"A promise in writing and signed by the promisor .... shall not be denied effect as a valid contractual obligation on the ground that consideration for the promise is past or executed, if the consideration is expressed in writing and is proved to have been given or performed and would be a valid consideration but for the time when it was given or performed."

The *McGowin* and *Wyman* cases would apparently *both* come out the opposite way under the New York statute. *McGowin* would

dreadful, workplace accident; that McGowin simply took pity on a disabled employee to whom no other compensation was available; and that the life-saving "story" was exactly that (McGowin no longer being available to confirm or deny).

14. There is: see, Watson, *In the Tribunal of Conscience: Mills v. Wyman Reconsidered*, 71 Tulane L.Rev. 1749 (1997).

15. Restatement Section 86, *Examples* 1, 7.

be reversed because of the absence of a signed writing by the alleged promisor. Webb's tale of the falling pine boulder would fail to satisfy the "expressed in writing" requirement of the statute (possibly for good reason). By contrast, Wyman did make his promise in writing (the letter to Mills), and Mills' caretaking expenses would certainly be "consideration" if requested by Wyman at the time Mills found his son in need. Guarding against false claims, the New York statute would require Mills to furnish proof of his expenditures, presumably in the form of bills and receipts. If he does furnish proof, he recovers—and I think quite properly.

Rescue cases like *Webb* and *Mills* are uncommon, as has been observed,[16] and perhaps we ought to try to test the benefit-received principle in a more conventional setting. Under ordinary circumstances, someone seeking to purchase a service would offer—that is, promise—to pay the service-provider a stated sum for the service that she wants. The offer to pay, made after due deliberation, invites a consideration in the form of a performance (or perhaps a promise to perform), and once the consideration has been supplied by the promisee there is a "contract" and the promisor is bound. But suppose the process is *reversed* in time, with the performance actually preceding the promise to pay. D mows C's lawn while C is away on vacation and then asks C to pay her whatever C thinks the service is worth. D presumably has no legal claim on C at this point because C never requested the service and obviously cannot return it as if it were a misdelivered package. But suppose C, feeling somewhat cornered, promises to pay D $10 on the following Tuesday. Subsequently, C changes her mind and refuses to pay. Is C's promise binding even though she was under no legal obligation to D when she made it, or should the promise be treated as gratuitous and unenforceable even though the lawn was, in fact, neatly mowed?

The answer, probably, is that enforcement would be denied. To be sure, C has received a benefit and $10 appears to be a reasonable price for the service. But D's act in imposing the service on C without C's request is obviously a high-pressure sales tactic which one hesitates to reward or encourage. Section 86 of the Restatement provides that a promise made in recognition of a benefit previously received is binding to the extent necessary to prevent injustice *unless* the benefit was conferred "as a gift or for other reasons the promisor has not been unjustly enriched". Reflecting the decision in *Drake v. Bell*,[17] the explanatory comment indicates

---

16. S.D. Henderson, *Promises Grounded in the Past: The Idea of Unjust Enrichment and the Law of Contracts,* 57 Va.L.Rev. 1115 (1971).

17. 26 Misc. 237, 55 N.Y.S. 945 (1899).

that C's promise would be binding if D, having been employed to mow a neighbor's lawn, had simply mowed C's lawn by mistake. In that circumstance, D's motives are innocent and the benefit-received principle justifies treating C's subsequent promise to pay as a kind of ratification or approval of the transaction. The pure "imposition" case similarly involves a promise and a benefit-received. In the end, however, I suppose we can conclude that an imposed-upon promisor would be regarded as having been victimized rather than *unjustly* enriched, while the promisee would be viewed as having taken a conscious risk that her unrequested service might earn her nothing. It follows, I think, that neither the courts nor the Restatement would treat a promise made under these conditions as binding.

I should add that the foregoing by no means exhausts the subject of restitution, unjust enrichment and "quasi-contractual" relief. The topic comes up again, and in a more significant context, under the general heading of Remedies in Chapter 8.

Chapter 3

CONTRACT FORMATION

The formation of an enforceable contract involves a two-step procedure with which everyone is instinctively familiar. Thus, we make it known that our legal services are available for a fee. Clients, one hopes, offer to employ us. If they do, we pretty readily accept. We ourselves are besieged by people wanting to sell us things; we succumb and offer to buy, and *they* accept. The critical process elements—offer and acceptance—are learned quickly and early on by almost everyone, and at the level of daily conduct they require little more than an exercise of intuitive preferences.

On occasion, however, the question of whether an "offer" has been made that the law will recognize as such, and if so whether it has been "accepted", becomes the subject of dispute. The reason, most often, is that one party or the other has changed his mind. Having taken steps that seem to evidence an intention to offer or accept, the individual or the firm suddenly has second thoughts: the price initially proposed now seems too high or too low, or the terms of sale now seem too generous or too burdensome, or perhaps a better deal is proposed by someone else. Since an enforceable obligation attaches only if there has been an "offer" and an "acceptance" in legal terms, one avenue of escape may be to argue that the putative transaction is lacking in either or both of those vital supports. The problem, then, in general, is to determine whether the reluctant party went so far in the direction of the other party, whether by word or conduct, as to generate an irreversible undertaking. The answer, I think, while partly to be found in the doctrinal elements discussed in Section A of this Chapter, ultimately depends on how the circumstances of the particular case are perceived and interpreted by a court or a jury.

The problem just mentioned—whether the parties have in fact struck a deal—is greatly complicated by the long-standing common law rule that an offeror may revoke his offer at any time prior to its acceptance by the offeree. Except as limited by the doctrine of promissory estoppel and, in some instances, by statute, the offeror is free, in effect, to terminate the offeree's power to accept by exercising his own power of revocation. Such termination may result also if the offeree takes action that can be interpreted, even if not really intended, as a rejection of the original offer—for example, by making a counteroffer in reply. The consequence of all this, as the discussion in Section B should suggest, is to raise vexing questions about which party acted first, what was meant or understood by the words used or the action taken, and so on.

In this connection, and before getting involved in details, it may be worthwhile to remind oneself, very briefly, that the offer and acceptance rules do have a larger purpose. As noted in Chapter 1, the principal function of contract law is to provide an enabling framework within which private parties can carry out a mutually beneficial exchange of goods and services—A and B, again, trading apples for oranges. But the fact that the parties can improve their respective wealth positions by making an exchange does *not* mean, even theoretically, that there is only one single point at which the mutually beneficial swap must or should take place. Rather, there exists a number of possible trading points—a range of "efficient outcomes"—at any one of which an exchange will be beneficial to both. If the subject-matter of the exchange is a commodity that trades in an active market, then, of course, the current market price is the only price at which the commodity would be bought or sold. But if the subject-matter is nonfungible—that is, a service or good or property interest that has special characteristics and lacks an active market—the price on which the parties may finally agree will obviously have to be bargained out between them. A will of course prefer that the rate of exchange be more favorable to him while B will prefer the contrary, and it is this circumstance that inevitably prompts the two parties to commit a certain amount of time to the tedious process of haggling. Which of them is the better haggler we cannot know in advance, but at some stage in the process each of the parties should reach the conclusion that the returns to additional bargaining are too small to justify further struggle. They will then, presumably, make a deal. In a very general sense, the role of contract law in this context is (a) to distinguish the culminating moment of agreement from all the bargaining activity that has gone before and (b) to protect the agreement thus arrived at from any effort by either party to start the bargaining process up again.

Apart from the need for a recognizable offer and acceptance, there is a kind of overriding legal requirement that the parties to a contract evidence by some discernable means their intention actually to be bound by the terms of their agreement. It must appear (in the scriptural language of Restatement Section 17) that there has been "a manifestation of mutual assent." Assent would normally be "manifested" by the execution of a written document, or by an oral expression of agreement, or perhaps simply by commencement of the performance that the offer calls for. As one possible complication, however, suppose a contract is entered into purely in jest (at least by one of the parties) or as a dare or in a mood of drunken boasting. Should the law take account of personal intent in this connection, or should it take the spoken or the written word as literally meant? In *Lucy v. Zehmer,*[1] the defendant claimed (a) that he was drunk, (b) that he was kidding, and (c) that the plaintiff knew the defendant was (a) and (b) when the defendant agreed to sell the plaintiff his farm for $50,000. A 12–word contract of sale was drawn up on the back of a counter check and signed by both parties. Arguing that the whole thing had been intended and understood as a joke, the defendant later refused to transfer the farm and the plaintiff sued for specific performance.

Reversing the trial court, the Supreme Court of Virginia held for the plaintiff. The Court seemed to believe that the defendant hadn't been all *that* drunk (it was defendant who wrote out the contract) and had really meant his offer as a dare—forcing Lucy to admit that he couldn't *raise* $50,000—rather than a joke. But even if Zehmer truly did intend the contract to be a joke, Lucy apparently never got the point and instead considered the execution of the contract to be a serious commitment that was binding on Zehmer as well as on himself. He scurried about the very next day, so he said, and arranged (with his brother) to put up half the purchase price, then engaged an attorney to examine title, and thereafter advised the defendant in writing that he was ready to close the deal. Since the plaintiff reasonably thought that the defendant was serious, and since the language of the contract was plain and unmistakable, the parties' mutual promises were enforceable despite Zehmer's "undisclosed intention" to regard these doings as buffoonery.

The trial court in *Zehmer* took a different view of the parties' conduct and apparently considered that Lucy actually knew, or had reason to know, that Zehmer was joking about the farm sale. If Lucy had been aware that Zehmer was joking (assuming Zehmer *was* joking), then clearly there should have been no contract. While the law normally treats a promisor as having been sincere in his spoken or written utterances, it would be absurd and ritualistic to hold a party to his promise if both he *and* the promisee understood the matter to be a joke. The larger object of the law, after all, is to provide a basis or framework in which the exchange of goods and services can be made with some assurance by persons who more or less consciously expect to be better off as a consequence. No reason whatever can be suggested for enforcing a "contract" that neither

1.   196 Va. 493, 84 S.E.2d 516 (1954).

party intended or expected to be fulfilled, though it is presumably fair enough to impose the burden of proof on the alleged joker. A slightly harder question—that presented by *Lucy v. Zehmer* if, with the Court, we assume a somewhat humorless Lucy—is what to do when the promisor's joke is taken seriously by the promisee. At that point, I suppose, we might as well draw down the corners of our mouths and hold the promisor. It is not so much a matter of being tough-minded and "objective" in our approach to the language of the contract as it is a need to resolve the clash between the two parties' individual expectations.[2]

However comical, the *Zehmer* case does raise a theoretical issue that deserves brief comment. What if Zehmer had acted even quicker to retract his assent to the sale, perhaps even before Lucy left the tavern? Would instantaneous retraction have made a difference, or was it too late from Zehmer's standpoint once he signed that infamous countercheck? The answer, I think, is that a retraction, even if virtually instantaneous, would be legally ineffective; Zehmer would be bound by his promise the moment he made it. The reason usually given for such a strict rule is that we want the promisee (Lucy), who may be planning to act the moment the contract has been signed, to be free of the risk that his time and money will be wasted if the promisor suddenly and unexpectedly retracts. The alternative, presumably, would be to permit retraction (at least for a limited period) unless the promisee furnished *proof* of his reliance prior to the retraction. But proving reliance may be difficult and itself the subject of dispute, even litigation. Lucy claimed to have taken certain steps the very next day in the confident belief that Zehmer was bound to transfer title to the farm. But did he really, or did counsel simply invent those steps (e.g., borrowing money from his brother) in an effort to show that Lucy was truly serious about the sale? The question would be one

2. The Court apparently assumed that $50,000 was a realistic price for Zehmer's farm, and perhaps it was. But how was it arrived at? Though eager to find that Zehmer's intent to sell was serious, the Court could point to no evidence that the two men actually bargained over price. That is odd, in a way, because evidence of hard bargaining would be the best indication that buyer and seller were both in earnest, while the absence of such evidence suggests the contrary. In the history of the world, no farmer has ever sold a farm without initially asking more than the farm is worth, and no farmer has ever bought a farm without initially offering less. But as far as we know, $50,000 was the only number the parties considered on this occasion, and Lucy's speedy agreement and aggressive follow-up leads one to assume that $50,000 was seen by him as highly favorable. Zehmer's best argument, I think, would have been that $50,000 was an absurd figure, that the farm was actually worth much more, and that he had in fact received better offers from others. The "joke," presumably, must then have been obvious to both.

Whether that argument could have been made or was simply overlooked, I can't say.

of fact, perhaps to be resolved by a court or jury at a much later date, during which time the promisee would be uncertain about what steps he *could* safely take (e.g., to plough or not to plough) in reliance on the promise.

On a slightly different front, suppose the parties clearly and consciously manifest assent, but each has in mind an object or an act that is wholly different from the act or object contemplated by the other. In the famous *Peerless* case,[3] decided by the Court of Exchequer in 1864, the plaintiff agreed to sell to the defendant, and the defendant agreed to buy, 125 bales of Surat cotton at a stated price. The cotton thus sold was to arrive on the ship Peerless sailing from Bombay, but when the Peerless, or at least *a* Peerless, reached port at Liverpool the defendant refused to accept and pay for the merchandise. As it turned out, there were two ships named Peerless sailing from Bombay, and while the plaintiff clearly had in mind the Peerless that sailed from Bombay in December, the defendant just as clearly meant to designate the Peerless that sailed from Bombay in October. The contract contained nothing that clarified the matter because neither party had any idea that there were two ships Peerless in the world. It may be supposed that the December Peerless arrived in Liverpool some weeks or months after the October Peerless and that the market price for cotton had fallen below the original contract price. Apparently conceding that he and the defendant had had different Peerlesses in mind, the plaintiff argued that as 125 bales of Surat cotton had in fact arrived from Bombay aboard a ship called "Peerless", the agreement between the parties was in all respects satisfied and the defendant was bound. In any event, said plaintiff, the time of sailing was not expressly mentioned by the parties in their agreement and, hence, should not be viewed as material to their understanding.

Finding that there had been no "consensus ad idem"—no agreement on the same thing, presumably—the Court held for the defendant. Since the defendant intended to buy one lot of merchandise—the cotton goods carried by Peerless–October—while the plaintiff intended to sell another—the cotton goods carried by Peerless–December—there was no contract or agreement which the Court could enforce. Thus, Pollock, C.B., intending to highlight the weakness of plaintiff's position, observed that "It may as well be said that if there is a contract for the purchase of certain goods in warehouse A., that [contract] is satisfied by the delivery of goods of the same description in warehouse B." Plaintiff's counsel apparently withered in the face of this incisive riposte, but perhaps he

---

3. Raffles v. Wichelhaus, Court of Exchequer, 1864, 159 Eng.Rep. 375.

should have grasped the nettle. Assuming the "goods" stored in Pollack's warehouses were indeed of "the same description", a buyer could hardly reject them on the ground that they had been drawn from one location rather than another, unless place of storage had an effect on quality, physical condition or the like. For the same reason, everything else being equal, the defendant in the *Peerless* case should reasonably have been indifferent to the mere identity of the vessel that was employed to carry his merchandise across the seas.

Quite obviously, however, much more was at stake for both parties than the name of a ship. As with other commodities, the market price of cotton in Liverpool no doubt fluctuated from week to week, perhaps widely, so that in offering to sell December-shipment cotton at a predetermined price the plaintiff was making a bet on the state of the market at the anticipated arrival date. The defendant, by contrast, was betting on the market price for October shipments and thus, in effect, took or thought he was taking a very different gamble. Presumably, neither party knew or had reason to know of the other's intention. Having wagered their money on two different events—the value of October cotton-futures in one case, of December cotton-futures in the other—the only possible conclusion was that there had been no wager to start with[3a]. Although the parties probably did not suffer equally (plaintiff, unlike defendant, may have had unrecovered shipping costs plus the drop in market price to grieve over), the Court was limited to an all-or-nothing result. Either a contract for the sale of cotton had been formed by mutual assent or it had not. Without a consensus ad idem, there was simply no agreement to which the parties could be bound.

The *Peerless* case is mentioned again in Chapter 5 in connection with the problem of contract interpretation, and it has bearing as well on the subject of "mistake," which is taken up in Chapter 7. More generally, the requirement of mutual assent once more becomes an issue—this time with implications for social policy—in connection with so-called contracts of adhesion, discussed in Chapter 4.

A. Offer and Acceptance

1. *Offers.* When is a communication to be regarded as an "offer" and when is it to be taken merely as an invitation to engage

---

3a. But then why didn't the defendants ask for their cotton when the October Peerless hove into port? See Simpson, *Contracts for Cotton to Arrive: The Case of the Two Ships* Peerless, 11 Cardozo L. Rev. 287 (1989). Simpson suggests that some sort of loss splitting, presumably through arbitration, would have been a good way to resolve the dispute.

in bargaining and negotiation? The distinction, obviously, is important to both the offeror and his offeree. A property-owner who is interested in selling his property requires current market information before deciding on an offering price. Such information may be available from brokers or other middlemen, but if the property is more or less unique—say, an operating business—then it may be that prospective buyers themselves will be the only real source of reliable market data. In the latter event, the owner needs to issue some sort of communication that will induce buyers to go to the trouble and expense of valuing the property and submitting bids. The question, I suppose, is how he can do that—what he can legally say to signify the reality of his intentions—without actually offering the property for sale. Buyer-offerees are, of course, equally concerned with the legal significance of the property-owner's utterances. A buyer who accepts what he believes to have been an "offer" will necessarily assume that his economic position has changed materially. He may then be led to take some costly and irreversible step—borrow money, sell property of his own, reject other opportunities—in reliance on what he thinks is a binding agreement. He will of course be disappointed, perhaps seriously disadvantaged, if the communication which he confidently regarded as an offer was really, or at least legally, just a feeler.

The words "I hereby offer to sell you Blackacre for $1,000 cash" could hardly be clearer and plainly constitute a promise to convey Blackacre if the offeree agrees to pay the offering price. But suppose the message waffles slightly: "I am eager to sell Blackacre but would not take less than $1,000 for it. Please let me know promptly if you are interested." Is this an "offer" that will become a binding contract if the addressee says "I accept," or is it merely an invitation to *make* an offer which the owner can then take under advisement? The subject-property is designated and a price is mentioned; hence all the operative terms are present that a true offer would be expected to include. While the phrase "would not take less" lacks the firm promissory smack of "I hereby offer", one cannot entirely fault the addressee for thinking that Blackacre will be his if he agrees to the $1,000 figure.

In the end, as usual, it is the surrounding circumstances that really matter. If the two parties mentioned above have been bargaining over Blackacre for the past six months, steadily trading proposals and counter-proposals in an effort to find a mutually acceptable price, then "would not take less" or "would not pay more" might well be taken as an offer. If there has been no prior bargaining, a different inference seems plausible. Given that a seller's constant aim is to get the highest price he can for his property, the quoted communication probably should be seen as nothing more than the first step in an open auction. The words "would not take less than . . ." fairly imply that Blackacre is up for sale to the highest bidder, with the number "$1,000" intended to be understood as the *minimum* selling price—equivalent to an auctioneer's "upset price"—rather than the figure which the owner is now prepared to accept as final. The decided cases (what few there are) generally support the latter construction. Absent special facts (e.g., a history of party-to-party negotiations), the courts are likely to conclude that a communication which advises interested parties that designated property is for sale at a price not below $X merely establishes the basis of an auction, but does not constitute an "offer".

Dealings between merchants—manufacturers and retailers, for example—can present the same problem of ambiguous intent, although it may be supposed that general familiarity with trade custom and practice reduces the occasions for dispute to a minimum. In *Fairmount Glass Works v. Crunden–Martin Woodenware Co.,*[4] the plaintiff, Crunden–Martin, wrote to the defendant requesting "the lowest price you can make us . . . for ten carloads of Mason green jars, complete, with caps, packed one dozen in a case. . . ." Defendant promptly answered, saying "we quote you Mason fruit jars . . .: Pints $4.50, quarts $5.00, half gallons $6.50 per gross, for immediate acceptance, and shipment not later than May 15. . . ." Plaintiff next day sent a telegram ordering "ten carloads as per your quotation. Specifications mailed." At this point, apparently, defendant became aware that its inventory of Mason jars had already been cleaned out—not a single jar in the warehouse—and at once communicated the bad news to the plaintiff: "Impossible to book your order. Output all sold. . . ." Unable to find another source of supply at the same favorable prices, plaintiff sued for breach.

Holding for the plaintiff, the Court found that the defendant's initial communication constituted an "offer" in legal terms rather than a mere invitation to deal. The price quotations were issued by defendant in response to a specific inquiry, one which, significantly, made clear the particular quantity of Mason jars that plaintiff had in view. Most important, perhaps, defendant's request for "immediate acceptance" implied that the next and *last* step in the transaction was expected to be plaintiff's yes or no. In effect, plaintiff was entitled to assume that inventory sufficient to cover its order had been earmarked by defendant, provided only that plaintiff's reply

4.   106 Ky. 659, 51 S.W. 196 (1899).

should be, as it was, immediate. Finally, the Court was not much troubled by the fact that plaintiff's telegram failed to specify pints, quarts, etc., since the defendant's offer appeared to confirm that merchandise was available in each category.

Although easy to approve on its own facts, the *Fairmount* case does *not* stand for the proposition that the circulation of price quotations by a supplier of goods constitutes an offer, or a set of offers, that can be "accepted" and thus converted into a binding contract by prospective purchasers. To be sure, such circulations are intended to generate business in the form of purchase orders, but as a general rule it is the order itself that constitutes the "offer" and the purchaser who plays the role of offeror. Even when prices are quoted in response to a specific inquiry, the normal understanding, which may or may not be made explicit, is that orders are solicited subject to available stocks or to change of price without notice. In commercial usage, the word "quotation" implies the reservation of a right on the supplier's part to accept or reject customers' orders more or less at will, and in a sense the real question in the *Fairmount* case was whether the language of the defendant's initial communication—"we can quote you ..."— should not have been understood to include that reservation. As suggested, the additional words "for immediate acceptance" presumably convinced the Court that the defendant actually intended to depart from the customary pattern of solicitation and, hence, that "quote" meant "offer" under the circumstances.

Perhaps the last serious issue that comes up under the heading "offer" concerns the effect of retail advertisements. In the silly but never-to-be-forgotten case of *Lefkowitz v. Great Minneapolis Surplus Store,*[5] the defendant put an ad in the local newspaper which said:

"Saturday. Each...$1.00

1 BLACK LAPIN STOLE

BEAUTIFUL

worth $139.50...$1.00

First Come

FIRST SERVED"

Lefkowitz, though a male person, was first in line on Saturday and demanded the beautiful stole for a dollar. The Store refused to sell, asserting that the garment was available to women customers only

5. 251 Minn. 188, 86 N.W.2d 689 (1957).

and reminding Lefkowitz that it had thrown him out when he tried to pull the same stunt on an earlier occasion.

Holding that the advertisement must be construed as an "offer" because it invited a particular performance—getting in line first on Saturday—the Court awarded Lefkowitz damages of $138.50 and thus taught the Store a painful lesson. The Store may have intended to restrict its offer to women, but that restriction did not appear in the advertisement itself and it could not be added after the offer had been accepted.

Sensible decision? Too literal, or not literal enough? The "first come first served" language in the ad was really nothing more than a common retailer's sales pitch—"Hurry! Offer ends soon!", "One-day sale!", "Call now!", etc. But even if treated as a legal "offer," it is obvious that the "offerees" were intended to be shoppers drawn to the Store by the prospect of a bargain and presumably having an interest in looking at other merchandise as well. Lefkowitz was not a "shopper" in the sense intended. Having paid $1 for the rabbit-fur stole, his next step, I assume, would have been to try to sell the thing for $20 to one of the ladies lined up behind him at the door, no doubt generating a lot of ill will for the Store itself. The Store manager was aware of all that—Lefkowitz had been there before. The Court could have, perhaps should have, held for the defendant on the ground that any store is free to reject a customer whose known aim is commercial mischief.

The *Lefkowitz* case aside, it is well understood that public advertisements, like the merchant's price quotations, are not to be regarded as offers in a legal sense. Intentionally misleading advertising may be punishable or enjoinable under local consumer protection statutes—and of course the advertiser's reputation for fair dealing is at stake—but in general advertisements are regarded as nothing more than invitations to deal. This is true even though the advertisement is specific as to price, quantity, time-limit and other details. Shoppers are presumed to understand that advertised goods may or may not be available by the time they get ready to buy. In legal terms, therefore, it is the customer, not the advertiser, who occupies the status of "offeror".

2. *Acceptance.* Assuming an "offer" has been made, the next and final step in the formation of a contract is, obviously, acceptance by the offeree. Once accepted, the offer becomes a contract: both parties are bound and neither can renege without liability to the other. At the same time, as noted, an offeror is free to revoke his offer and terminate the offeree's power to accept, provided only that he acts before the offeree has recorded his acceptance. If the

offeree acts first, and if his action qualifies as an acceptance under relevant legal standards, the deal is done. Inevitably, cases arise in which the offeror, faced with an apparent acceptance by the offeree, seeks to revive or restore his power of revocation by arguing that the effort to accept was ineffective. What constitutes an effective acceptance may thus, in a given case, become a question of considerable importance.

The answer, it turns out, depends upon the requirements of the offer itself. The offeror is master of his offer (in the standard phrase), and just as the offeror can set and insist upon the substantive terms of the deal—price, quantity, time of payment and so on—so the offeror can dictate the form and manner of the offeree's acceptance. In an ordinary commercial setting, the offer (itself a promise by the offeror to do or pay something in exchange for something else) seeks a reciprocal promise from the offeree. This is evident and unambiguous, I suppose, where an offeror seeks to purchase goods or services to be delivered or performed in the future. The offeror presumably plans to make a variety of contractual commitments himself—to lenders, suppliers, customers, etc.—and therefore requires an undertaking from the offeree that can be relied upon today. Whether the offeree does or doesn't perform in the future is of course important, but it is not the question of the moment. What matters for present purposes, and matters critically, is that the offeror be able to commit himself to others on the basis of the offeree's commitment to him. Accordingly, the offeror seeks a promise from the offeree at this stage, nothing else and nothing less.

A promise constituting an acceptance would normally be stated in appropriate language, whether written or oral. On some occasions, however, especially where the offer is a routine or recurring event, the accepting offeree might simply skip the formality of verbal expression and proceed directly to perform the act that the offer calls for. Thus, a purchaser sends a seller an order (i.e., offer, see above): "Please ship promptly 1,000 units of [merchandise] at your quoted price of $10 per unit." The seller-offeree could respond by mailing the purchaser a notice of acceptance—in effect, a promise to deliver—in which event, no doubt, there is a contract to which both parties are bound. Suppose, however, that the seller, a man of action, says nothing but "promptly" loads the merchandise on a truck with appropriate instructions for delivery. Can the purchaser—asserting that his offer sought (but never got) acceptance from the seller in the form of an express promise to deliver the goods—revoke the offer before (maybe even after) the truck arrives? One would hardly think so: the purchase-order could have

46

required written notification of acceptance, but in fact it didn't. Instead, the order appeared to contemplate that performance itself would suffice as an act of acceptance and that a separately stated promise was unwanted or unnecessary.

UCC 2–206 makes it clear, where sales of goods are concerned, that an offer—usually a purchase order—can be accepted by any reasonable "medium", including the commencement of performance. In particular, unless otherwise unambiguously indicated, an offer to buy goods for "prompt shipment" is to be construed as inviting acceptance either by promise or by the act of shipment itself. Restatement Sections 32 and 62 announce a similar principle and establish also that acceptance by performance is a two-way street. Thus, performance by the offeree is regarded as equivalent to an expressly stated promise: in effect, having shipped the goods or otherwise commenced performance, the offeree becomes a promisor in his own right; he is legally bound to the terms of the offer and no more free than the offeror to treat his contractual obligations as terminable short of completion.

What qualifies as the "commencement of performance" for these purposes? In *Ever–Tite Roofing Corp. v. Green,*[6] the defendant-homeowners submitted a written order to the plaintiff-contractor for the re-roofing of defendants' residence. The order form, furnished by the plaintiff's salesman, stated among other things that "This agreement shall become binding only upon written acceptance [by] . . . the Contractor, or upon commencing performance of the work." Since the work itself was to be done entirely on credit, Ever–Tite requested a credit-report on the Greens from a local lending institution, a procedure which apparently took some ten days to complete. A favorable report having been received, Ever–Tite sent a crew of workmen and a truck loaded with supplies to the Greens' house for the purpose of starting the job. On arriving, however, the Ever–Tite people found another crew hard at work on the roof and were told by the Greens that their services were not required. The Greens, it appeared, having waited a week and heard nothing from Ever–Tite, made a deal with another roofing company which was willing to, and did, begin the work at once.

Ever–Tite thereupon sued for breach, claiming damages of $85.37 for the workmen's transportation and wages plus $226 for

---

6. 83 So.2d 449 (La.App.1955). There may at first be something slightly confusing about the Greens being regarded by the Court as "offerors." But so they are. Although the seller, Ever–Tite, prepared and furnished the order form, it is the buyers, the Greens, who are treated as submitting that form as an offer to buy, and the seller who is treated as receiving that offer as "offeree."

lost profits. Resisting, the defendants argued that the plaintiff never actually commenced performance—and, hence, did not "accept"—before being told that the defendants' offer had been withdrawn.

Reversing the trial court, which had held for the defendants, the Supreme Court of Louisiana directed that judgment be entered for the plaintiff-contractor. Under general rules, said the Court, an offer that does not specify a time-limit remains open for a reasonable time (unless revoked). Given the necessity of a credit-check, of which defendants were presumably aware, ten days was plainly reasonable in the circumstances presented. More critically, the Court held that plaintiff's act in loading its truck and transporting men and materials to the Greens' residence must be viewed as "commencing performance"; hence, the plaintiff had accepted before becoming aware (indeed, before it *could* become aware) of the Greens' intention to hire another roofer. In effect, there was a binding contract once the truck got underway, presumably because it was then, and at that point, that Ever–Tite began to incur unrecoverable expenses—$85.37—on the Greens' account. The amount was small, to be sure, but it would have cost the defendants even less—the price of a single phone call—to have notified the plaintiff of their decision to revoke.

Although a bit tough on the Greens (who, in effect, paid more than once for the same roof), the decision in *Ever–Tite* may ultimately have been beneficial both for the home-repair industry and for individual homeowners generally (at least in Louisiana). Thus, why should a company like Ever–Tite insist on being free to accept a repair contract *either* by formal written communication to the customer *or* by "commencing performance of the work"? As indicated, the company really cannot accept the customer's order until a favorable credit report is received (unless the customer is prepared to pay in advance), because repair contracts, like most consumer obligations, are routinely assigned to a lender which provides the funds to finance the work. On the particular day it receives notice that the buyer's credit has been cleared, however, the company may find that all of its work-crews are engaged on other repair jobs. Alternatively, it may find that it has a crew that is not so engaged. In the former event, the company would wish to transmit a written acceptance to the customer in order to lock up the contract; but in the latter event, instead of taking time to write a letter, it would prefer to send out the crew itself at once. The company's larger aim is to maintain a relatively constant workforce and to keep its workers busy at all times. This, in turn, presumably means lower costs and a resulting benefit to consumers. While the Greens' roofing job amounted to little in itself, the company obviously thought that an important practice was at stake both from its own standpoint and that of the industry.

The Court may have thought so as well. In practical terms, the *Ever–Tite* decision means that home-repair customers can avoid commitment only if they act before the necessary credit-check is completed. Thereafter, by one means or the other, they are almost certain to be bound.

The contract held to have been entered into in the *Ever–Tite* case was, of course, a bilateral contract—that is, a contract based on the exchange of one promise for another. The offeree's promise in *Ever–Tite,* as has been seen, was made by commencing performance rather than saying "I promise," but the legal effect was the same. In some situations, by contrast, the offeror seeks nothing *but* a performance—a promise or commitment by the offeree to do something in the future is unwanted or irrelevant. Contracts of this sort—referred to as unilateral—are uncommon and probably not very important, yet they do present an issue that commentators have at times found challenging. Briefly stated, if an offer seeks a performance, and only that, is the offeror free to revoke the offer before the performance has been completed, even though the offeree, acting in reliance, has already begun performance and made a sacrifice of time and effort? Thus (and the illustration may well be representative of the class[7]), suppose X offers to pay Y $5 if, by nightfall, Y will find and return X's cat, which has somehow strayed away. Y says, "Okay, I'll start looking." He spends all day searching through the neighborhood and at last locates the cat at the top of a tree. Not having a ladder, Y climbs the tree with great difficulty and crawls out on a shaky limb to grab the cat. At that moment, X, watching from the sidewalk below, yells up: "Forget it, Y! I've found that life is simpler without a cat. Leave him up there."

Can Y recover against X? Taken literally, X promised to pay only when the cat was found *and* returned; the offer could be accepted only by a completed performance and until accepted could be revoked. But the idea that Y could be induced to put in a long day's work, perhaps relinquishing other income-producing opportunities, and then be denied his reward just when the goal was in sight is shocking and ignominious. Still, there is a certain symmetry in the positions of the parties. Not having been asked for a promise and not having given one, Y can presumably stop searching if he tires of the effort. X has no right to claim performance from Y;

---

7. *But see* Pettit, *Modern Unilateral Contracts,* 63 B.U.L.Rev. 551 (1983).

Y can quit whenever he likes and leave X to find the cat and climb the tree himself. The parties could have protected themselves by placing their agreement on a bilateral footing—X promising to pay Y $5 in return for Y's promise to search diligently—but apparently neither was prepared to make the commitment that an exchange of promises would have entailed.

All this is fairly silly, I concede, but it probably remains true, in general, that unilateral offers of the sort just illustrated are revocable by the offeror at any time prior to completion of performance. To be sure, a court determined to escape the latter conclusion probably can find a way. Possibly (though with difficulty on the "facts" given), X's offer might be treated as seeking a series of completed performances—(1) searching, (2) finding, (3) returning—so that some compensation would be due to Y at the end of each segment rather than only on final recovery of the cat. In the alternative, X's offer, unless entirely unambiguous, might be construed as seeking a promise *through* the commencement of performance. As in *Ever–Tite,* Y's act in beginning the search could then be viewed as the acceptance of an offer to form a bilateral rather than a unilateral contract.

Section 45 of the Restatement moves some distance in the latter direction by treating the commencement of performance in response to a unilateral offer as conferring an "option contract" on the offeree—a right to complete the performance that has been commenced if he chooses to do so. In effect, X is regarded as having made a twofold offer to Y: (a) to pay $5 if Y finds and returns the cat, and (b) to treat the offer as irrevocable if Y begins the search. The Restatement stops short of converting all unilateral contracts into bilateral contracts, however. While barring revocation by the offeror once the offeree has commenced to perform, Section 45 does not bind the offeree to complete the performance. The offeree can abandon the undertaking short of completion without incurring liability to the offeror, although of course in that event the offeror's duty to perform (pay the $5) does not arise. In *Ever–Tite,* by contrast, the commencement of performance by itself constitutes a "promise"; accordingly, the contractor-offeree, now a party to a bilateral contract, has a binding obligation to complete what it began.

3. *At-will Employment.* An interesting convergence of "bilateral," "unilateral," and "no-contract-at-all" has arisen in connection with the enforceability of noncompetition agreements between employers and at-will employees. Most ordinary employment *is* at-will, meaning that the employee can be fired at any time or can quit at any time, perhaps subject to brief notice by the employer in the

case of firing. If at the time he is *initially hired* the employee is required to sign a noncompetition agreement restricting his right, on termination of his employment, to engage in a business or profession similar to his employer's, no question arises—at least with respect to the requirement of consideration—as to the employee's being bound thereby. The employer offers to hire the employee on certain terms and promises to pay a salary. The employee, presumably giving up other employment opportunities, accepts and promises to work under the terms that have been offered, which include the noncompetition agreement. The result is a bilateral contract supported by consideration on both sides even though neither party is legally obligated to continue the employment beyond a single day.

But suppose the at-will employee is asked to sign a noncompetition agreement *during* the course of his employment, that is, while already on the job. At that point the employee depends on his job for a living and may have no other alternatives. If he says no to the noncompetition agreement, he gets fired on the spot and is out of work. Obviously under pressure, he says yes and signs the noncompete. A year later he is fired or quits the job—having by that time learned a great deal about his employer's business—and decides to go into the same business for himself. Can he be enjoined? Has he received consideration for his promise not to compete?

The courts have given two different answers—yes and no—inspired by three different legal rationales. The several opinions in *Lake Land Employment Group of Akron v. Columber*[8] run the gamut. Columber, having then been employed by Lake Land on at at-will basis for several years, in 1991 signed a noncompetition agreement at his employer's insistence. The agreement provided that for a period of 3 years after termination of his employment he would not engage in a competitive business within a 50–mile radius of Akron. Columber continued his employment with Lake Land for ten more years, was then discharged, and at once formed a corporation that engaged in a business similar or identical to Lake Land's. Lake Land, invoking the noncompetition agreement, sought an injunction as well as money damages. Columber defended on the ground that the noncompetition agreement was without consideration.

Reversing the court below, the Supreme Court of Ohio held that the noncompetition agreement was adequately supported by consideration and hence enforceable: "The presentation of a non-

8. 101 Ohio St.3d 242, 804 N.E.2d 27 (2004).

competition agreement by an employer to an at-will employee is, in effect, a proposal to renegotiate the terms of the parties' at-will employment.... The employee's assent to the agreement is given in exchange for forbearance on the part of the employer from terminating the employee." Putting it bluntly, the Court held that an employer who says "sign this or we'll throw you out" is making an offer the employee *can* refuse but (on reflection) decides to accept. There is a deal. Thus, Lake Land and Columber exchanged promises—Lake Land to continue Columber's employment, Columber not to compete—creating a *bilateral* contract within the meaning of Restatement Section 71(2).

Two Justices dissented, although Justice Pfeiffer's dissent could have been a concurrence. Briefly and somewhat cryptically, Pfeiffer argued that there could have been no bilateral contract at the time Columber signed the noncompete because Lake Land, free to fire him the following day, at that point promised nothing. If consideration *was* present, it must have been Lake Land's action in continuing Columber's employment for a reasonable length of time thereafter. By implication, Columber sought and expected a *performance* from Lake Land, of which the practical effect, or consequence, would be to convert his at-will employment into employment for a term. It would follow that if Lake Land had fired Columber shortly after he signed the noncompete, there would have been a failure of performance and hence a failure of consideration on Lake Land's part. But if Lake Land continued Columber's employment for a reasonable period (as in fact it did), then there would be consideration within the meaning of Section 71(3). To quote another court faced with similar facts, the parties would thus have "forged a binding *unilateral* contract out of a former, invalid bilateral contract."[9]

The remaining dissenter, Justice Resnick, utterly denied the presence of consideration and concluded that there was no contract at all. Columber, she asserted, got nothing and, being an at-will employee with his job at stake, obviously faced coercion. Lake Land, by contrast, "winds up with both the noncompetition agreement and the continued right to discharge the employee at will, while the employee is left with the same preexisting 'nonright' to be employed for so long as the employer decides not to fire him." Pretty plainly, Justice Resnick regarded Lake Land's demand on Columber as an abuse of status, of which the proof was that Columber got nothing from Lake Land other than that which he already had, namely, an unprotected right to work until fired.

9. Central Adjustment Bureau v. Ingram, 678 S.W.2d 28 (Tenn. 1984).

Who was right? And further, was the requirement of "consideration" truly and deeply relevant to the outcome? We are not told by the Court just what Lake Land's business was, but I would guess that "Lake Land Employment Group" was in the business of furnishing temporary clerical personnel to banks, insurance companies and other employers whose need for office help might rise and fall from time to time. If that was the case, Lake Land's "assets" would have been largely intangible—customer lists, of course, but also a highly prized file cabinet filled with the names of men and women available for part-time work at an hourly wage—people who were reliable about showing up when they promised to show up, and who were competent to do the clerical work that the banks, etc. required. It takes a lot of time and effort to compile those names and keep them up to date, and Lake Land's business depended heavily on that resource.

But then how could Columber go into the very same "temp" business immediately after leaving Lake Land? The answer is obvious. Having worked in the Lake Land office for more than a decade, Columber knew all the part-timers very well, knew how to reach them, knew what Lake Land paid them, and of course knew the names of Lake Land's customers. Apart from the noncompetition agreement (which he said he only vaguely remembered signing), Columber was evidently prepared to convert Lake Land's valuable contacts to his own profitable use. The Court majority certainly understood the situation, and undoubtedly felt that Lake Land deserved to be protected from what would otherwise be an act of legal piracy. The formal "consideration" requirement—essentially a legal nuisance—had to be overcome to get to the desired result, and the Court majority did just that.

B. Revocation and Counteroffer

1. *Firm Offers.* The discussion just above deals with the question of what action on the part of an offeree is to be regarded as "acceptance" such that the offeror is bound thereby to complete the transaction in accordance with the terms of his offer. Our assumption has been that *until* the offeree accepts—whether by making a return promise or by commencing performance—the offeror is free to revoke. The question to be considered here is whether that assumption is always valid—or, rather, what significant exceptions should be attached to it. At stake from the offeror's standpoint is the ability to regain control of the economic interests that are affected by the offer. The offeror may have changed his mind about selling or buying, he may be dissatisfied with the

offeree for some reason, or he may simply want to return to the auction market in the hope of a better price. In any such event his aim will be to shut down the outstanding offer at once. The offeree presumably sees the matter in opposite terms: from his standpoint there is plainly an advantage, and perhaps some urgency, in keeping the offer alive and available until he, rather than the offeror, has made the final decision to take it or leave it.

In *Dickinson v. Dodds,*[10] the plaintiff received a memorandum from the defendant on Wednesday offering to sell him certain real estate—land and buildings—for £800. The offer was to be "left over until Friday, 9 o'clock A.M." On Thursday the plaintiff learned from his agent that the property had been offered or sold to another investor (one Allan, also named as a defendant), whereupon the plaintiff raced to the house in which defendant was staying and handed to defendant's mother-in-law a written acceptance of defendant's offer—which, however, she somehow afterwards forgot to give him. Early Friday morning, apparently having lain in wait all night, plaintiff and his agent intercepted the defendant at a railway station leaving town and again tried to hand him a copy of the acceptance. "You are too late," cried the defendant, ducking into his compartment, "I have sold the property."

Reversing the trial court, the Court of Appeal held that plaintiff was not entitled to specific performance and likewise not entitled to restrain conveyance of the property or to impress a trust upon the property if it had already been conveyed. Despite his written assurance that the offer to sell would be "left over until Friday, 9 o'clock A.M.", the defendant was free to revoke at any time prior to the plaintiff's acceptance. A promise to hold an offer open, being a mere *nudum pactum,* is not binding—that, said the Court, is "one of the clearest principles of law"—and can always be withdrawn on notice to the offeree. To be sure, defendant never actually notified the plaintiff that the offer had been revoked or that the property had been sold to someone else. In fact, however, plaintiff admitted that he knew about the prior sale, and that knowledge, though circumstantially derived, was equivalent to being told by defendant "in so many words, 'I withdraw the offer' ".

Postponing for a moment our own judgment of the merits, I think it is easy to see why the Court in *Dickinson* would have been most reluctant to affirm the lower court's decree for specific performance. In effect, it couldn't: no matter what the plaintiff's rights might have been, the contract entered into between the two defendants (by which Dodds conveyed the real estate to Allan) was

10. Court of Appeal, Chancery Division, 1876, 2 Ch.Div. 463.

entirely valid and enforceable; even if the plaintiff had been wholly ignorant of the prior sale, no legal basis existed (at least no contract rule) for treating Allan's title to the property as defeasible. For the same reason, Dodds had nothing left to convey once the deal with Allan was done. Accordingly, there was no one to whom a decree for specific performance could have been directed who either could or would have had a duty to obey it.

Money damages, however, remained a possibility, so that the doctrinal issues in the case—(i) whether the offer should have been viewed as irrevocable at all events until Friday at 9 A.M., and (ii) if not, whether indirect knowledge of a prior sale should be regarded as equivalent to a direct communication from the offeror—still need to be sorted out. As to the first issue, I think everyone would agree that the bare language of the defendant's offering memorandum— "This offer to be left over until Friday, 9 o'clock"—was insufficient by itself to establish the defendant's true intent with perfect clarity. One possible reading—that stressed by plaintiff—is that the phrase "left over until" means that the offer is "firm," or irrevocable, up to the date and hour given. The other reading, no less plausible I think, is that the offer, though at all times revocable *with* notice to the offeree, will expire without notice once such date and hour have passed. The Court chose the second construction over the first on the ground that consideration for the defendant's promise was lacking. What the defendant actually intended is not completely apparent. However, if we contemplate term offers generally, the likelihood that consideration *will* be present where an offer is intended to be irrevocable is obviously great. Thus, suppose the term for which Dodds' offer was "left over" had been 90 days instead of only Wednesday-to-Friday. If such offer were irrevocable, then Dickinson would find himself in the enviable position of being able to benefit from any appreciation in the value of the underlying property during the 90-day period, while leaving the risk of any decline with Dodds. Generally, if property subject to an irrevocable option goes up in value during the relevant term, the option-holder will exercise his option and eliminate the offeror's interest. If the property goes down in value, the optionee will allow the option to lapse and the loss will fall on the offeror. Options thus being valuable economic rights in themselves, it is presumptively unlikely that the owner of marketable investment property would actually grant an irrevocable option (otherwise known as a "call") to another investor without demanding and receiving from the latter a premium—that is, a monetary consideration—in return. He might, of course, but since doing so entails a significant economic detriment, the *presumption* is plainly contrary.

The practical issue that confronted the Court of Appeal in *Dickinson v. Dodds* was simply *which* of the two commercial arrangements mentioned above the offeror and offeree had intended to create—a revocable offer subject to a deadline, or an option. Presumably recognizing that property sellers do not customarily grant irrevocable options without getting paid for them, the Court resolved the ambiguity that resides in the words "left over until Friday" by finding the promisor's undertaking to be *nudum pactum*—a promise without consideration—and hence unenforceable as an option contract. What the Court meant, simply, was that offers must be presumed to be revocable unless a fee or premium is paid to the offeror. Adding a deadline for acceptance means that the offer expires automatically on the date named, but nothing more.

Turning to the second issue in *Dickinson v. Dodds*—whether indirect knowledge of the prior sale should be deemed equivalent to direct notice of revocation—perhaps we could begin by wondering why *any* notice of revocation was required on the part of the offeror. Why not imply the term "revocable without notice" or "subject to prior sale or withdrawal by the owner," since in fact Dodds' written offer contained nothing either way on that question. The standard answer, no doubt, is that once there is an "offer," revocation has to be made known to the offeree in order to prevent further wasteful expenditure on his part. Until notified, Dickinson might continue to spend time and money on investigation, appraisal, arrangement of financing, etc., all of which would be halted and the wasteful outlays avoided once notice of revocation was received. On the other hand, the somewhat accidental hearsay through which Dickinson learned of the sale to Allan is hardly an efficient way of implementing the latter policy, and one might suppose that the court would have demanded something less ambiguous than mere rumor if it really meant to take that policy seriously. Having sold the property to Allan, it would have cost Dodds very little to send Dickinson a message notifying him that the offer was withdrawn—assuming he thought such notification was actually called for.

In *Petterson v. Pattberg*,[11] decided by the New York Court of Appeals in 1928, the plaintiff owed the defendant the sum of $5,450, the debt being secured by a mortgage on certain real estate belonging to the plaintiff. The defendant-mortgagee, presumably eager to convert the mortgage-loan into cash, offered to reduce the principal of the debt by $780 if the plaintiff prepaid the entire amount due (less the $780 discount) by May 31. Late in May the plaintiff appeared at the defendant's door, knocked loudly, and in

---

11. 248 N.Y. 86, 161 N.E. 428
(1928).

response to the question "Who's there?" answered simply: "It is Mr. Petterson. I have come to pay off the mortgage." "Too late," cried Pattberg, perhaps throwing his shoulder against the door to keep it shut. "I have sold the mortgage to another investor." In fact, Pattberg did, afterwards, open the door a tiny crack, but he then refused to accept the cash that Petterson tried to thrust upon him, leaving Petterson to fume and mutter on the doorstep. It turns out that Petterson had already sold the real estate to a third person purportedly free and clear of the mortgage, and hence was obligated to pay that person the full amount of the mortgage-debt now held by Pattberg's assignee, namely $5,450. Claiming breach, Petterson sued Pattberg for the $780 discount.

Holding for the defendant, a majority of the Court of Appeals found that Pattberg had effectively withdrawn his offer when he informed Petterson (through the closed door) that he had sold the mortgage to someone else. Since that communication took place before Petterson could actually make "tender" of his money, the offer must be regarded as revoked. Such withdrawal or revocation sufficed to terminate the offer, said the Court, citing Williston's great treatise for the proposition that "If the offeror can say 'I revoke' before the offeree accepts, however brief the interval of time …, there is no escape from the conclusion that the offer is terminated." The dissenting judges, finding the result to be "extraordinary," insisted that the plaintiff had done all that he was asked to do when he declared his intention and ability to pay as soon as the door was opened, and therefore should be deemed to have accepted the defendant's offer.

Apparently not completely comfortable with a bare recital of Williston's "rule," Judge Kellogg, writing for the majority, went on to add—rather strikingly—that in his view the result in *Petterson v. Pattberg* would have been the same even if Petterson had tendered the money *before* the offer was withdrawn and Pattberg had then simply refused to receive it. "This would be so," said Judge Kellogg, "[because] the act requested to be performed was the completed act of payment, a thing incapable of performance unless assented to by the person to be paid." In effect, the Judge appeared to regard the defendant as having retained a legal right to accept or reject the plaintiff's tender, just as if the plaintiff were the offeror and the defendant were the offeree instead of the reverse.

Otherwise slightly puzzling, the "sense" of Judge Kellogg's dictum becomes clearer, perhaps, if we make the very plausible assumption that Pattberg was at all times ready and willing to sell his mortgage investment to anyone who came along (not just Petterson) and, further, that he would have made his interest in selling known to as many people as might possibly have an interest in buying. The same may have been true of Dodds, who, just as a home-seller does today when he "lists" his property, would be likely to have told everybody in sight (not just Dickinson) that his property was up for sale to the first or the highest bidder. If so, Petterson and Dickinson, having finally decided to buy, should not have been entirely surprised to learn that they were indeed too late and that the property had already been disposed of. More generally, where marketable investment property is concerned—securities, real estate—no prospective buyer or investor has a right to assume that he is the sole offeree or indeed that he is an offeree at all in legal contemplation. Put differently, an expression of willingness to sell such property, even for a stated price, is more likely to be a solicitation or an invitation to bid than a legal offer whose acceptance prior to revocation binds the seller. So viewed, the seller's "assent" (as Judge Kellogg put it), rather than the buyer's "tender," would be the final and indispensable step in a concluded bargain. The Courts in *Petterson* (certainly) and *Dickinson* (possibly) would have sensed or understood all this but in the end found it easier and simpler, the somewhat shaky facts permitting, to hold that the defendant had "revoked" than to raise the question of whether there had really been a legal offer in the first place.

The use of a consideration test to distinguish revocable offers (or, indeed, mere solicitation) from irrevocable offers seems natural and apt where transactions in investment property are concerned, but of course it may be that in a given case a property seller actually perceives advantage in making an irrevocable offer *without* consideration. Thus, suppose an individual owns land that is worth either a lot or a little depending on whether it has substantial mineral content. A mining company indicates that it may be willing to undertake the necessary geological testing if the landowner will make an irrevocable offer to sell the property for a price of $1 million. On the assumption that he can't do the geological work as well or as cheaply himself, the landowner might be very glad to grant the mining company an option to buy for a limited period. In these circumstances, as Restatement Section 87 recognizes, the law ought to, and in general presumably does, accept a recital of nominal consideration—"$1 in hand paid, receipt whereof is hereby acknowledged, plus other good and valuable consideration"—as adequate to bind the offeror. More generally, in the case of an offer of goods by a "merchant", UCC 2–205 rejects the rule of *Dickinson v. Dodds* and provides that a firm offer can be made by means of a signed writing, no consideration being required, if the offer is limited to a reasonable time not exceeding three months.

2. *Revocation and Reliance.* As suggested, the rule of *Dickinson v. Dodds* seems plausible despite its formalism where one-shot property transactions are concerned. But in cases involving what might be called cooperative relationships—offeror and offeree being linked in a joint undertaking of some sort—the question of revocability takes on a different color. Here the most familiar context is that of the routine construction bid. Thus, the Lancaster School District invites contractors to submit bids on a school construction job, all bids to be in by July 28 at 8 P.M. Drennan, a licensed general contractor, sits in his office on the afternoon of July 28 preparing a bid for last-minute submission. The telephone rings constantly as various subcontractors call in their own bids for specialty work—plumbing, electrical, etc.—each of which Drennan posts on a master-sheet for use in making his final submission to the School District. Among his callers is Star Paving Co., which offers to do the paving work for $7,131. Star's figure turns out to be the lowest bid for paving received that afternoon, and Drennan therefore includes it in his own bid to the School District. When the bids are opened on July 29, Drennan proves to be low-bidder and is awarded the contract. Happy with this outcome, Drennan drops in next morning to say hello to the good folks at Star only to be greeted with the news that their paving bid was a great mistake—too low by half—and that they have now decided to withdraw it. Apparently unwilling to renegotiate, Drennan later contracted with another paving concern to do the work for $10,900, and then sued Star for the difference.

Finding for the plaintiff, the Supreme Court of California held in *Drennan v. Star Paving Co.*[12] that Star's offer to do the paving work for $7,131 included a "subsidiary promise" not to revoke until "plaintiff should have at least an opportunity to accept [that offer] after the general contract had been awarded to him." It was true, the Court said, that consideration in a conventional sense was lacking—Drennan paid nothing to Star in exchange for the latter's surrender of its ordinary right of revocation. Where, however, the offeror's aim is to induce the offeree to rely on the offer and to make commitments of its own on the basis of such reliance, Restatement Section 90, applicable in California, waives the requirement of consideration and turns the offer into a binding promise. Star, of course, knew that Drennan would rely if its bid for the paving work was the lowest, and "it is only fair," said Justice

12. 51 Cal.2d 409, 333 P.2d 757 (1958). See Becker, Promissory Estoppel Damages, 16 Hofstra L. Rev. 131 (1987).

Traynor, that Drennan should have a reasonable chance to say yes thereafter.

The *Star Paving* decision is inevitably to be contrasted with the Second Circuit's decision in *James Baird Co. v. Gimbel Bros.*,[13] in which, on roughly similar facts, Judge Learned Hand held that the subcontractor's offer could be revoked even after the general contractor had submitted its own bid (the winning bid, as it turned out) using the subcontractor's price-quotation. The subcontractor's offer, said Hand, looked for an acceptance from the offeree in the form of a return promise, not merely "reliance" through the submission of a bid. While the offeree plainly based its bid-submission on the offeror's price-quotation, that was not "the act" by which the offeror expected to be bound. The doctrine of promissory estoppel, in Hand's view, was aimed at cases involving reliance on donative promises; but it had no application to offers that sought consideration in the form of an exchange.

Comparing *Gimbel* with *Star Paving,* the elements of fairness and orderly conduct pretty plainly weigh in favor of the latter. The most compelling feature, quite obviously, is the circumstance that the general contractor—Drennan or Baird—is bound by its own bid once the contract has been awarded, and indeed in most cases it cannot withdraw its bid without a substantial penalty even if the subcontractor's revocation is received before the award is made. If the *Gimbel* rule were followed, general contractors might be obliged to add a premium to their bids in order to reflect the risk that one or another of their subcontractors will revoke before acceptance. The law would then have operated, in effect, to increase the overall cost of ordinary construction projects without adding anything of positive value to the process.

To be sure, both *Star Paving* and *Gimbel* asserted that they had made a mistake in calculating their bids; and if "mistake," here, is taken to mean a serious underestimate of material and labor costs, the assertion in each case was probably true. The next best price that Drennan was able to get for the paving work was more than 50% higher that Star's original bid, which might account for Drennan's very prompt if unsuccessful attempt to accept Star's offer. Presumably, however, as Justice Traynor pointed out, the burden of misjudgment (and the resulting loss) is more suitably imposed on the offeror who originated the price-quotation than on the offeree who relied on it. Put differently, an offeror who has blundered in calculating his costs ought not to be able to salvage his error through revocation once the offeree has included the offer

13. 64 F.2d 344 (2d Cir.1933).

in a bid of his own. That, in any event, is the effect of the court's decision and may also be its major consequence.

While it seems easy, thus, to come down on the side of *Star Paving,* the somewhat troubling fact remains that promissory estoppel is a one-way street in this context. Having been awarded the Lancaster school contract, Drennan was free, if he wished, to make a new round of phone calls in order to determine whether any of Star's competitors would care to go a little lower than $7,131 for the paving work. Neither Drennan nor Baird was bound, even conditionally, to award the subcontract to the defendant; use of a subcontractor's figure in submitting its own bid—often, as in *Baird,* on a lump-sum basis—does not constitute acceptance on the general contractor's part of any particular subcontractor's offer; and the subcontractor cannot claim to have "relied" since it would have incurred the cost of working up its bid even if the general contractor had finally used the figure submitted by a different subcontractor. Worried about this problem but unable to escape it, Justice Traynor asserted that the general contractor was simply *not* at liberty to delay acceptance in the hope of getting a better price— meaning, presumably, that Drennan's claim to promissory estoppel would be forfeited if it were shown that he had gone on to make inquiries of other paving companies after the main contract was awarded. But even so, Drennan might well think it worthwhile to shop around a bit before communicating his acceptance—and might even think it quite legitimate to do so given the last-minute pressure under which general contractors are obliged to act in preparing their final bids. *Star Paving* thus tilts the balance of advantage to the general contractor, though even in this rough-and-tumble context considerations of business standing and reputation are likely to count more than legal rules in promoting fair dealing on both sides.

In *Star Paving* the doctrine of promissory estoppel was applied to convert a revocable offer into an option contract, ultimately allowing the offeree to trump the offeror's hasty effort at withdrawal. Enforcement meant compensating the plaintiff's expectation interest, which was measured by the difference between Star's bid and the greater amount Drennan was finally obliged to pay to another paving contractor for the same work. Restatement Section 90 provides, however, that the remedy for breach "may be limited as justice requires", and in some instances—*Hoffman v. Red Owl Stores, Inc.*[14] is among the best known—the courts have concluded

14. 26 Wis.2d 683, 133 N.W.2d 267 (1965).

that "justice" required compensating the plaintiff's reliance inter-est instead.

In *Red Owl,* the plaintiff was an ambitious small-town bakery owner who, in 1959, contacted a representative of the Red Owl chain with a view to getting a Red Owl supermarket franchise. In the course of discussions plaintiff stated that all the capital he had available for investment was $18,000, to which the Red Owl people replied that that sum would be quite sufficient to set up in business as a Red Owl store. Subsequently, at the urging or at least with the active encouragement of Red Owl, plaintiff (a) sold his bakery building at a loss of $2,000, (b) bought a small grocery store in order to gain experience as a grocer, (c) shortly afterwards sold the grocery store for an amount roughly equal to his cost, (d) put $1,000 down on land in a neighboring town where the new Red Owl would be constructed, and (e) incurred $265 in personal moving and rental expenses. All this preparatory activity took place over a period of about three years, during which Red Owl steadily main-tained its promise that a franchise would be offered once all conditions had been met. Not much, however, was ever said by either party about the specific terms of the expected franchise and no final plans to build the new store were actually made. Finally, in 1962 Red Owl indicated that the plaintiff's capital investment requirement had been raised to $34,000 and that a proposed equity investment by plaintiff's father-in-law would have to be made in the form of a gift or subordinated loan, a condition Hoffman couldn't meet or wouldn't. At that point, Hoffman abandoned his efforts to meet Red Owl's demands and sued Red Owl for breach.

Why did Red Owl keep raising its capital investment require-ment—from $18,000, as originally proposed, to $24,000, then to $26,000, finally to $34,000? My guess: Having observed him in action for three years, Red Owl decided that Hoffman lacked the skill and experience needed to manage a large supermarket—too big a job for him, too much responsibility—and privately hoped that he would simply go away. In effect, Red Owl put Hoffman through a three-year try-out period *at his own expense.* He flunked. In the end, Red Owl concluded that giving Hoffman a franchise could wind up costing the company money—if, for example, they had to bail him out at some point—and might even damage the great name Red Owl in the eyes of shoppers.[15]

The case was tried to a jury, which found that Red Owl had represented to the plaintiff that he would be offered a franchise if

---

15. For a different account, see Scott, Hoffman v. Red Owl Stores, *and* the *Myth of Precontractual Reliance,* 68 Ohio State L.J. 71 (2007).

he met certain conditions and that plaintiff had relied on those representations and fulfilled all the conditions required. The jury then awarded damages of $3,265 for items (a), (d) and (e), above, plus an additional $16,735 to reflect an alleged loss on the sale of the grocery store mentioned in (b) and (c). On appeal, the Supreme Court of Wisconsin ordered a new trial with respect to the last-named item on the ground that so large an award of damages from the sale of the grocery store was not supported by the evidence. As to the three smaller items, however, the Court upheld the jury award solely on the basis of promissory estoppel. The "promissory representations" made by Red Owl in the course of their negotiations induced the plaintiff to take the steps described above, and the consequence, when such representations failed, was to leave the plaintiff with fairly heavy reliance losses. Since promissory estoppel contemplates a "remedy ... limited as justice requires," the jury's action in compensating him for those losses was (except as noted) sustained.

It should be stressed that Hoffman made no claim against Red Owl for expectation damages based on anticipated profits from the proposed franchise. If he had, he almost certainly would have failed, because Red Owl never actually offered him a franchise in terms that were definite or clear enough to be accepted, even under an induced reliance or estoppel theory. Indeed, no offer of a franchise was made in any form—Red Owl merely indicated that it *would* make such an offer if the stated conditions were satisfied. In affirming the jury's damage award, the Court did not and presumably could not find a conventional breach of contract on Red Owl's part. Instead, it identified an actionable course of conduct—leading Hoffman on, obviously—for which Restatement Section 90 and the doctrine of promissory estoppel were held to provide independent grounds for relief. As applied in *Red Owl,* promissory estoppel was not merely a substitute for consideration or a device for converting a revocable offer into an option contract. Rather, Section 90 was made to "serve as a distinct basis of liability, without regard to theories of bargain, contract, or consideration",[16] and with its own special damage standard. So viewed, the doctrine would appear to have come a long way from its origins: having begun as a rationale for the enforcement of future-gift promises, it then developed into a rule equally applicable in a commercial setting, and now operates (at least it did in *Red Owl*) to impose fair-dealing requirements on

---

16. Henderson, *Promissory Estoppel and Traditional Contract Doctrine,* 78 Yale L.J. 343 (1969). And see, Katz, *When Should an Offer Stick? The Eco-nomics of Promissory Estoppel in Preliminary Negotiations,* 105 Yale L.J. 1248 (1996).

parties engaged in *pre-contractual* negotiations, with no enforceable promise having yet been made by either.

How far is it proper to go with Section 90? In the fairly recent *Bacardi*[17] case, the plaintiff, Stout, was a liquor distributor operating in Northern Indiana under the name General Liquors, Inc. General had a long-standing agreement with Bacardi under which General was appointed as the exclusive regional distributor of Bacardi products. The agreement was "at will," meaning that either party could terminate the distributorship without notice. Bacardi, one supposes, was General's largest account.

A mighty wave of consolidation among liquor distributors suddenly rolled through Northern Indiana, and General, feeling slightly imperilled, entered into negotiations for the sale of its business to another distributor, National Wine & Spirits Co., which no doubt wished to eliminate General as a competitor. National was aware that General was not under immediate pressure to sell and in fact had an attractive alternative, namely, to continue its own profitable business, of which the exclusive right to distribute Bacardi products was the most important feature. Accordingly, National offered a sweet price, one that General was tempted to accept.

As it happened, National was the regional distributor for Ronrico, also in the rum-making business. As a business practice, a distributor can only represent one rum distiller at a time, so that if General did sell out to National, Bacardi would have to look for a new distributor and do it in a hurry. From Bacardi's standpoint, therefore, a decision by General to sell to National was (for the moment, at least) highly undesirable.

While negotiating with National, General repeatedly sought Bacardi's assurance about the future status of its distributorship. If, in the end, General decided to stay in business for itself, could it depend on Bacardi as it had in the past? Such assurance was vital to General because it preserved General's alternative course of action, which in turn enabled General to maintain its bargaining strength in dealing with National. General very carefully kept Bacardi up to date on the negotiations with National, including National's final offer. In return, General received from Bacardi an "emphatic avowal" that it had no intention of taking its business elsewhere.

On July 23rd, a fateful day, General finally came to a decision. It would reject National's offer, however tempting, and continue in

17. D & G Stout, Inc. v. Bacardi Imports, Inc., 923 F.2d 566 (7th Cir. 1991).

business for itself. Accordingly (in the Court's words), "Stout [president of General] again sought assurances from Bacardi. The supplier unequivocally reconfirmed its commitment . . ., and Stout replied that, as a result, he was going to turn down National's offer and would continue operating. Later on the 23rd, Stout rejected National's offer. *That same afternoon*, Bacardi decided to withdraw its line from General."[18] Bacardi, one assumes, had by this time made a better deal with another distributor, rendering General superfluous and expendable.

Shocked but still breathing, General returned to National and attempted to revive National's rejected offer. Too late. National had learned of Bacardi's switch and shrewdly judged that General, its operating business now rendered virtually defunct, no longer had any bargaining leverage with respect to the sale price. In the end, National did buy General's assets—inventory, delivery trucks, etc.—but the price paid was much lower than National's previous offer.

Urging promissory estoppel under Section 90, Stout sued Bacardi to recover the difference between National's rejected offer and the fire-sale price that General finally had to accept. The trial court, reasoning that the contract between General and Bacardi was and would remain terminable at will, concluded that Bacardi's promise was not legally enforceable and hence was not one on which General might reasonably rely. The court entered summary judgment for Bacardi, and Stout appealed.

In an opinion by Judge Cudahy, the Seventh Circuit reversed and remanded for a determination of General's loss, which, it indicated, would be the difference between the rejected offer and the final sale price. Citing Indiana cases awarding damages under Section 90 for a broken promise of at-will employment, the Court held that Bacardi's last-second repudiation in effect destroyed General's "negotiating position" and left General with no alternative but to sell the business to National at its much lower liquidation value. General (said the Court in effect) had an economic interest in National's original offer. and hence deserved to be compensated for its "forbearance" in rejecting that offer and relying on Bacardi's apparent commitment. The Court noted that Indiana law allowed no more than reliance damages (presumably, out-of-pocket losses and expenditures) under Section 90; State law would not permit a recovery of expectation damages or damages for "lost opportunities" in a promissory estoppel case. Here, however, General and National had concluded all of their negotiations and agreed on a

18. Id., at 570 (emph. supp.).

final sale price. It was as if the sum named had already been received by General, was already in hand, but then relinquished on the basis of Bacardi's assurances.

In evaluating the decision, I think it may be important to observe that General and Bacardi were *both* engaged in the same strategy. Each was anxious to keep their relationship alive in the mind of the other unless and until something better was decided upon, General not less than Bacardi. The difference between the two was strictly tactical. General, needing Bacardi's continued assurances in order to have a viable alternative, was pretty much compelled to inform Bacardi about the progress of its negotiations with National. By contrast, Bacardi, wanting to discourage General from selling to National, kept secret the discussions it was carrying on with competing distributors. Viewed in a cold-blooded way, I suppose we could criticize General (or Stout) for failing to perceive its own tactical disadvantage and failing to assess the risk. Had it been a bit more acute, General might have demanded a term contract from Bacardi, in that way either securing its position as Bacardi's distributor or else forcing Bacardi to come out of hiding and admit that it was looking for a better distribution deal from others.

So, was the Court's decision to bail out General a sound one? Extending Section 90 to dealings between tough-minded businessmen is surprising—one tends to assume that businessmen know, or should know, how to protect themselves and when to "reasonably" rely. Plainly, however, the Court considered Bacardi's conduct to be egregious, and it decided to punish Bacardi (ultimately, to the tune of nearly $400,000) for what it regarded as gross deception.

But business is business, and I think the outcome can be debated.

Section 90 and the doctrine of promissory estoppel have long engaged, sometimes inflamed, the imagination of contract theorists. Going back a number of years, at least one influential commentator predicted that the traditional idea of contract based on bargained-for consideration and mutual assent was on its way to extinction and would be replaced by the less restrictive and more dynamic concept of reliance.[19] In effect, a promise by one party that induced reliance on the part of the other would be enforceable despite the

---

19. Gilmore, *The Death of Contract* (1974). Going further, some writers have suggested that the courts, acting under Section 90, will now generally enforce a "serious" promise even without a showing of significant reliance by the promis-ee. Yorio and Thel, *The Promissory Basis of Section 90,* 101 Yale L.J.111 (1991). Other writers think otherwise; Hillman, *Questioning the "New Consensus" on Promissory Estoppel,* 98 Col. L.Rev. 980 (1998).

absence of contract "formalities," including, in particular, agreement between the parties on the elements of an exchange. Enforcement, in this view, would be based on the rectification of a harm— once again, induced reliance—rather than the existence of a bargain. It followed, or seemed to follow, that if contract enforcement was seen to be the righting of a wrong and essentially compensatory, then what once had been regarded as a distinct field of law called "Contracts" would blur and fade and then reappear in a new guise as a branch of the law of Torts.

As it happens, it didn't happen.[20] Traditional bargained-for consideration continues to be the fundamental basis for contract enforcement (in the view of the courts and of most writers), with promissory estoppel remaining a separate, subordinate and "dichotomous" category. To be sure, the latter has grown in importance and was bound to do so given the influence of the Restatement, but there is no real indication that it has succeeded in swallowing, smothering or strangling the former.

Finally (and in order to keep perspective), I should add that the factor of "induced reliance"—indeed, the whole doctrinal panoply of "offer," "acceptance," "counteroffer," "revocation" and "assent"—really has no practical relevance to the complex transactions with which law firms are often involved today. An obvious example would be the acquisition of a corporate business, a transaction that would have been negotiated by controlling stockholders or professional managers (eagerly assisted by accountants, investment bankers and numerous counsel) dealing with each other face-to-face over a lengthy period of time. In that context, neither the buyer nor the seller can be identified as the "offeror" or the "offeree," and it is well understood that there is no enforceable obligation on either side until the parties actually and simultaneously exchange signed copies of the final agreement. Buyer and seller have a duty to be honest in their fact-disclosures, but both parties are aware from the beginning that the deal is not done until the documents have been executed, and rarely could either party claim damages or reimbursement by asserting that an "offer" had been "accepted" or by invoking "promissory estoppel."

3. *Binding Preliminary Agreements.* As stated earlier, a mere "agreement to agree" does not, without more, create an enforceable contract. The classical rules of offer-and-acceptance contemplate that the parties will have bargained out and agreed upon the terms of their exchange, with terms not specifically covered to be filled in

20. *See*, Barnett, *The Death of Reliance*, 46 J.Legal Ed. 518 (1996); Feinman, *The Last Promissory Estoppel Article*, 61 Fordham L.Rev. 303 (1992).

by resort to the standard gap-filling provisions of the UCC or the common law (to which the parties are assumed to have agreed as well). It is also true that the courts will sometimes interpolate vital terms, even price, when the parties' prior dealings make their intentions unmistakably plain.

But suppose the parties wish to launch an enterprise that can only move forward in stages necessarily separated in time, and suppose that the costs to be incurred at each successive stage, and by whom, are not fully foreseeable. Which of the two parties will perform the tasks that will have to be performed when performance is required, and at what cost, cannot be determined today but have to be left open for the time being. Very commonly, in these circumstances, the parties will enter into a preliminary agreement, referred to variously as a "memorandum of understanding" or "letter of intent". The preliminary agreement contains a description of the enterprise and affirms that the parties intend to cooperate. As to questions not yet resolved or resolvable, the parties evidently intend that those matters will be worked out when the needs of the enterprise become clearer.

Following Judge Leval's well-known classification in the *Tribune* case[21], preliminary agreements can be divided into two groups. Type I preliminary agreements fully reflect the terms of the parties' deal and simply await the drafting of a contract in standard legal form. Type II preliminary agreements contain *some* important features of the parties' understanding, but, as above, leave other issues open and still to be negotiated. What distinguishes Type I from Type II, obviously, is that the parties to a Type I preliminary agreement have nothing further to negotiate and clearly intend to be bound. " '[D]espite the anticipation of further formalities, a contract has been reached. . . .' ". By contrast, Type II preliminary agreements are partial and incomplete. They include open terms and call for future approvals. The parties evidently intend to be bound to *something*, but no one knows exactly what.

In *Brown v. Cara*,[22] JMB (Brown's corporation) and Tracto (Cara's corporation) signed a two-page Memorandum of Understanding expressing their intention to "work together to develop, build, market and manage a new real estate venture planned for an existing site at 100 Jay Street in Brooklyn, NY." The Jay Street property was owned by Tracto, which agreed to "provide the property at no cost" to the coventure, while JMB agreed to "lead

---

21. Teachers Ins. & Annuity Ass'n v. Tribune Co., 670 F.Supp. 491 (S.D.N.Y. 1987). And see Kostritsky, *Uncertainty, Reliance, Preliminary Negotiations and* *the Holdup Problem*, 61 SMU L. Rev. 1377 (2008).

22. 420 F.3d 148 (2d Cir. 2005).

the development effort," including rezoning, conceptual design, marketing, etc. A division of proceeds was also provided for. Still to be negotiated, among a number of matters relating to financing and operations, were the terms of a "construction management agreement," which would presumably establish JMB's fee for serving as general contractor and overall supervisor of the project.

JMB evidently spent time and money getting the property rezoned and completing other necessary preparations as required. It then submitted a construction management agreement to Tracto at Tracto's request. Just what that proposed management agreement contained we are not told, but whatever it was, it caused Mr. Cara such deep "displeasure and offense" that he refused to continue with negotiations, ceased all collaboration, and never spoke another word to the astonished Mr. Brown. Was Mr. Cara just very thin-skinned, or had Tracto received a better offer? We don't know, but in any case JMB sued, seeking enforcement of the Memorandum of Understanding through specific performance or other injunctive relief.

The District Court apparently granted JMB a limited *quantum meruit* recovery but otherwise dismissed the cause of action, presumably on the ground that no enforceable contract had been formed. On appeal, the Second Circuit reversed and remanded, holding that the Memorandum was a Type II preliminary agreement that bound the parties to "negotiate in good faith [the] terms necessary to pursue development of the Jay Street Property." The general working framework of the Memorandum was clear, the Court found; the parties agreed to "work together" to carry out their program. A number of open matters remained to be negotiated, but unless approval for rezoning of the property was forthcoming, time spent on such negotiations would be wasted. It was logical, therefore, for the parties to leave those matters for later negotiation and to retain a certain flexibility until the rezoning contingency was resolved. But that did not mean that either party could abandon the undertaking on the asserted ground that there was no contract at all. An exchange of promises to negotiate in good faith was implied by the Memorandum and was enforceable as a contract obligation, an obligation that Tracto breached when it ceased to communicate with JMB.

What happened on remand is not reported, but I would guess that a cash settlement fully compensating JMB's reliance and well in excess of the lower court's *quantum meruit* award was the final outcome. Imposing the Type II "rule" on Tracto makes sense in context. The parties expected JMB to make substantial expenditures as a first step in their development project. Unless reasonably assured that Tracto had committed itself to carrying the project forward, JMB would obviously be unwilling to make those expenditures, and presumably the rezoning and other necessary initial steps would never take place. JMB's reliance outlays were vital in determining whether the project really had any value or whether it lacked feasibility and should be dropped.

So the outcome in *Brown v. Cara* seems altogether reasonable. What can be criticized, I think, is the parties' failure (or that of their lawyers, if any) to include a "further negotiation" requirement in the Memorandum itself. If well-advised, the parties to a Type II memorandum of understanding or letter of intent would include a final paragraph affirming (i) that the parties' regard this agreement as a firm commitment and specifically intend to be bound thereby, and (ii) that the parties mutually accept an obligation to resolve all open terms and conditions through good-faith negotiation. A question of good faith versus bad faith might still arise if the parties cannot finally agree, and there could be litigation. But one supposes that if the circumstances, as in *Brown v. Cara*, involve an initial investment by one party in the clear expectation of further steps towards a common goal, then, if the other party refuses to negotiate in a reasonable manner, a court is likely to award the investing party compensation for its reliance. The predicate for such an award is, of course, the legal duty, express or implied, to negotiate in good faith.

4. *The Mirror–Image Rule: Counteroffers and Qualified Acceptance.* If an offeree purports to accept an offer but in doing so adds various conditions and qualifications of his own, is the acceptance binding on the offeror, at least in part? Generally speaking, the answer is no: the common law rule, reflected in Restatement Section 59, is that a statement of acceptance is effective only if it is a mirror image of the offer and expresses unconditional assent to all of the terms and conditions imposed by the offeror. A purported acceptance which alters those terms or adds qualifications does not bind the offeror, even if the changes or additions are minor. As indicated below, the mirror-image rule has been specially adapted by the UCC for routine merchandise transactions, but in situations not affected by the Code its application as an all-or-nothing principle is largely unquestioned. The rational basis of the rule, I think, is evident: in making an offer to exchange one thing for another, the offeror empowers the offeree, by accepting, to terminate or constrain the offeror's interest in the subject-matter of the offer. It would obviously be impermissible to allow the offeree to bind the offeror to pay a higher price or accept a lower price in the proposed exchange than the offeror has promised to pay or accept, and for

the same reason we cannot permit the offeree to add or eliminate conditions. This is so because the elements of an offer must be assumed to be interconnected: the price, quantity and character of the property or services to be exchanged are primary, but the terms of payment, the security arrangements required of the offeree, the indemnities, warranties and representations to which the offeree is asked to commit himself—each of these features has a positive dollar-value in the mind of the offeror. The rejection or dilution of any one of them by the offeree, or the addition of other features, presumably increases the offeror's cost or adds to his risk, so that the offeror would then be prompted, in his own interest, to recalculate the value of the transaction as a whole. The added or rejected feature may or may not be a deal-breaker—the offeror may be willing to agree to it—but that decision is obviously up to the offeror. In effect, there *is* no deal, and nothing to which the offeror is bound, until all of the dependent conditions on which the offeror insists have been accepted by the offeree.

The mirror-image rule yields a further implication. If an offeree responds to an offer by making a counteroffer—in effect, proposes terms *other* than those contained in the original offer—the common law treats that response as the legal equivalent of an outright rejection. The consequence is that a subsequent effort by the offeree to accept the original offer is ineffective. The offeror can simply disregard the counteroffer and go on to make a deal with someone else on whatever terms he likes. While the rule, so stated, is well settled and is echoed by Restatement Section 39, I think one's first reaction is to feel slightly troubled at the notion of treating counteroffer and rejection as legal equivalents. Faced with an express rejection, an offeror would naturally conclude that he was at liberty to make a deal with another buyer and would consider it unnecessary to direct any further communication to the offeree. But a counteroffer—essentially, a bid below the offering price—is rather different psychologically and might well be thought to shift the burden of response to the offeror. To be sure, offerees have no affirmative duty to respond to offers and are generally free to disregard them; but a counterofferee—who, after all, initiated negotiations by making the original offer—would seem to have a further obligation to the process itself; indeed, silence on the counterofferee's part is more likely to suggest that the counteroffer is being studied than that the original offer has been dropped or withdrawn.

Reduced to an isolated problem of communication, the issue—whether a counteroffer should be viewed as a rejection or as a kind of inquiry on the part of the original offeree—seems pretty close.

But perhaps the common law rule can be understood and supported if one envisions an offeror and offeree dealing with each other at a distance and by correspondence rather than face to face or by telephone. Thus, suppose a seller writes to a prospective buyer offering to sell Blackacre for $1,000. The buyer writes back offering $800. Evidently, offeror and offeree appraise Blackacre differently. Seller's highest priority is, of course, to locate somebody who more nearly agrees with *his* appraisal, and if a second buyer promptly appears and is willing to pay $1,000, seller may be compelled to make the deal at once or risk losing his price by taking time to notify the first offeree. If, next day, seller receives a purported acceptance from the first offeree, that communication has simply got to be treated as ineffective: as in *Dickinson,* no legal basis exists for discharging seller's obligation to convey Blackacre to the second buyer, yet there is only one Blackacre. Moreover, in view of the second buyer's willingness to pay $1,000 without haggling, we can assume that Blackacre had a higher value to him than to the first offeree, so that any legal rule that conferred a superior claim on the latter would presumably be inefficient.

As noted, Restatement Section 39 adopts the common law rule on counteroffers. The same section adds, however, that a counteroffer shall not be treated as a rejection if the offeree "manifests a contrary intent"—if, for example, the offeree's aim was merely to "inquire" about the possibility of different terms. But how can we tell? Again, suppose Seller offers to sell Blackacre to Buyer for $1,000. Buyer's response: "I'm willing to buy for $800—would you take that much?" Seller's reply: "No." The meaning and legal effect of the original offer is plain, but the same cannot be said of Buyer's response—or, indeed, of Seller's one-syllable reply. Is "I'm willing ... would you take ...?" a counteroffer or a mere inquiry? The differences in consequence are obviously great. If it is a mere inquiry, then (a) Seller cannot bind Buyer to the $800 figure by simply saying "Yes" at that point, and (b) Buyer's power to accept the original offer of $1,000 is not terminated. If it is a counteroffer, the contrary is true as to both elements. But in any case Seller said "No," which seems clear enough. But is it? On one reading, "No" could mean, "No, and I withdraw my original offer." But on another: "No, but my offer to sell at $1,000 still stands." Apart from a resort to the surrounding circumstances for clues to the parties' intent, the quoted words, few and simple as they are, raise problems of interpretation that are fairly difficult to handle with confidence.[23]

---

23. *See* Restatement Section 39, Illustration 1.

The problem of ambiguous expression in this context is illustrated by the Supreme Court's decision in *Minneapolis & St. Louis Railway Co. v. Columbus Rolling–Mill Co.*[24] The plaintiff, Railway, on December 5th wrote a letter to the defendant, Rolling–Mill, requesting a price-quotation "for 2000 to 5000 tons 50 lb. iron rails, March . . . delivery."

On December 8th, Rolling–Mill wrote back advising that it would "sell 2000 to 5000 tons of 50 lb. rails for fifty-four . . . dollars per gross ton . . . If our offer is accepted, shall expect to be notified of same prior to Dec. 20th . . ."

On December 16, Railway directed Rolling–Mill by telegram to "enter our order for twelve hundred tons rails . . . as per your favor of the eighth", and on that day also sent a letter to the same effect.

On December 18th, Rolling–Mill wired back, saying, "We cannot book your order at present at that price."

On December 19th, Railway fired off another telegram instructing Rolling–Mill to "enter our order for two thousand tons rails, as per your letter of the [eighth]." This, apparently, was followed by a long, dead silence, until, on January 19th, Rolling–Mill informed Railway that it denied the existence of any contract between the parties.

Insisting that its second telegram—that of December 19th—constituted an acceptance of Rolling–Mill's offer of December 8 to supply "2000 . . . tons", Railway sued for breach. The market price for iron rails (it is almost needless to say) took a sharp and unexpected jump in the latter part of December, moving from $54 a ton to the high $60's.

The Supreme Court, affirming a jury verdict, held for the defendant. The applicable rule of law, said the Court, is that a purported acceptance which varies the terms contained in the offer to which it responds is equivalent to a rejection by the offeree. In consequence, negotiations are at an end. The offeror (Rolling–Mill) can renew the original offer if he cares to, but if he doesn't, it cannot be revived thereafter through a tender of acceptance by the offeree (Railway). Rolling–Mill having offered to sell not less than 2,000 tons, Railway's telegram of December 16th, in which it proposed to purchase only 1,200 tons, must be viewed as a counter-offer and hence a rejection, and this entitled Rolling–Mill to treat the original offer as withdrawn. In effect, Rolling–Mill need not have responded at all to the December 16th wire. Once that telegram had been sent, the original offer was dead.

24. 119 U.S. 149, 7 S.Ct. 168, 30 L.Ed. 376 (1886).

Battle of the Forms. The mirror-image rule presumably ...es to reflect the common law generally, but in one signifi- ...ntext—routine merchandise transactions—the rule has been supplanted and substantially modified by UCC 2–207. The setting is one in which a buyer—say a retailer—orders a quantity of goods from a seller at a stated price for delivery by a certain date. The purchase order may have been submitted to the seller on a printed order form and then accepted or acknowledged by the supplier on a printed acknowledgment form of its own. The two forms agree as to the main elements of the transaction—price, quantity, description of goods—but each form also includes (presumably on the back and in small print) a dozen or more paragraphs drafted by counsel and specifically designed to protect and favor the sender in the event of a dispute between the parties. Alternatively, the buyer's order might be communicated orally to the seller's sales representative, face-to-face or over the phone, and similarly accepted, with a printed confirmation from the seller to follow. Once again, the seller's confirmation reflects the main elements of the transaction but, as above, includes fine-print provisions that were never thought of or mentioned by the buyer when the order was placed.

We can assume with near perfect certainty that no one on either side of the transaction actually takes time to read and study the fine-print material—it is the front of the forms that carries all the operative data. Yet the fine-print provisions are undeniably there; at least formally, they are part of the bargained-for exchange.

One consequence, if the common law mirror image rule applies, is that there is no contract at all, which creates an opportunity for one party or the other to legally evade its obligations. The buyer, for example, having apparently placed a firm order for certain merchandise but finding that the market price dropped soon after, could then refuse to accept delivery on the ground that the seller's acknowledgment or confirmation was really a "counteroffer" and rejection. That, presumably, constitutes an act of legal "opportunism" and as such unwelcome.

More often, no doubt, a dispute between the parties would arise *after* the transaction has been completed, that is, after the merchandise has been delivered and paid for. Performance by both parties makes it clear that there was a "contract," but the question then is *whose* boiler-plate provisions govern the transaction where the two forms apply differently to the issue in dispute. The answer—again at common law—is furnished by the so-called "last shot" rule. Under that rule, the last form that passed between the parties must be regarded as a counteroffer and rejection of any

prior offer. The transaction having been performed, th
sumption is that the party receiving the counteroffer
accepted all of its terms without objection. Since the
knowledgment or confirmation of the buyer's order is lil
been the "last shot" fired in the exchange of forms—first the
buyer's order, *then* the seller's acknowledgment or confirmation—
the common law rule favors the seller-counteroffer. It is therefore
likely to be the seller's boiler-plate that governs.

Pretty plainly, however, these legally generated uncertainties
have no place in the field of day-to-day sales of merchandise. Buyer
and seller never really intended or expected that the fine-print
provisions in their respective forms would be taken into account in
determining the acceptability of the deal on either side; nor would
the substance of those provisions have been consciously "priced"
into the transaction.

UCC 2–207(1) largely overthrows the mirror-image rule in this
context by treating the supplier's acknowledgment (or confirmation) as an "acceptance" of the purchaser's offer rather than a
counteroffer, even though it includes terms that are "additional to
or different from" those that appear in the purchaser's order-form
(or that were orally agreed to). Unless the supplier expressly
conditions its acceptance on the purchaser's assent to the supplier's
terms, there is a "contract" of which the terms are those contained
in the purchaser's offer. As a consequence, neither purchaser nor
supplier can afterwards refuse performance by seizing upon boiler-
plate discrepancies that had no economic significance to either
party at the time they made their deal.

Although the battle of the forms is thus generally resolved in
favor of the purchaser-offeror, 2–207(2) does confer one limited
benefit on the supplier-offeree. If the supplier's form contains
"additional" terms (as distinguished from "different" or conflicting
terms), such terms are not simply thrown out but, instead, are
treated as "proposals" for addition to the contract. Such "proposals" are considered to be adopted by the purchaser unless (a) the
offer limits acceptance to its own terms, (b) the additional terms
are objected to by the offeror, or (c) the additional terms "materially alter" the contract. If "material," the additional terms are
deemed rejected unless the purchaser expressly agrees to be bound
thereby, no doubt a rare event. Whether a particular additional
term—for example, a requirement that disputes be submitted to
arbitration—is or is not "material" has been fought over on occasion and presumably depends on trade practice and other circumstances.

Finally, in many cases—especially where the parties have dealt with each other over a long period—goods will have been ordered, shipped and paid for before any dispute arises. Even if their respective "writings" do not otherwise establish a contract under 2–207(1)—if, for example, the offeree expressly made its acceptance conditional on the offeror's assent to the offeree's terms, which assent was never given—the conduct of the parties shows that both proceeded on the assumption that an enforceable agreement existed between them. Under these circumstances, 2–207(3) provides that "the contract" shall consist of those terms on which the parties' writings do agree—neither form gaining primacy over the other—plus supplemental terms supplied by the UCC.

Criticized as confusing and clumsily drafted, 2–207 has generated more than its share of interpretative issues over the years.[25] Put very briefly, the problem with 2–207 is that it tries to do too much by running together, in a single section, both the rules governing offer-and-acceptance (2–207(1)) and the rules governing the content of the contract itself (2–207(2) and (3)). In addition, there appears to be no particular reason in policy why, in effect, the buyer's form should now generally dominate the seller's, neither party having been aware that the two forms differed on boiler-plate details at the time the deal was done. Proposed revisions (long standing but never adopted) would separate the two elements by putting the offer-and-acceptance rules in one section and the contract-content rules in a separate section. The latter provision would eliminate the uncertainties of present 2–207(2) by treating all "contracts," whether formed by performance *or* by offer and acceptance, as containing the terms on which both parties' forms agree—with neither form dominating the other—plus supplemental terms supplied by the UCC.

Shall we linger a moment and observe 2–207 in action (or in inaction)? In *Roto–Lith, Ltd. v. F.P. Bartlett & Co.*[25a]—a decision relished by the casebooks as an example of how *not* to apply 2–207—the plaintiff was a manufacturer of cellophane bags used for wrapping vegetables, the defendant a supplier of emulsion with which the bags would be sealed. Plaintiff's order for a drum of N–132–C emulsion was acknowledged by defendant on a form that

---

25. To mention just one such issue, 207-2 deals only with "additional" terms. But suppose the seller's acknowledgment contains a "different" term, one that directly conflicts with a term in the buyer's offer. Some commentators interpret 2–207(2) to mean that the conflict is to be resolved in favor of the buyer-offeror. Others, perhaps a majority, support a "knock-out" rule under which conflicting terms are both eliminated, with the missing term then being supplied by the UCC. *Northrop Corp. v. Lictronic Ind.* 29 F.3d 1173 (7th Cir. 1994).

25a. 297 F.2d 497 (1st Cir.1962).

disclaimed "all warranties ... whatsoever" owing to the "variable conditions under which these goods may be ... used" and further stated that "If these terms are not acceptable, Buyer must so notify Seller at once." No such notice being received, the emulsion was shipped and paid for. The stuff didn't work, needless to say, and the buyer sued.

Holding for the defendant-seller, the court found that the notification requirement just quoted made the seller's acceptance expressly conditional on the buyer's assent to the disclaimer of warranties. The seller's acknowledgment, therefore, was a counteroffer rather than an acceptance of the buyer's order. The buyer, then, having failed to protest the disclaimer, and having received and paid for the goods, was deemed to have accepted the seller's counteroffer and as a result "became bound." It would be an absurdity, the court thought, to regard the defendant's disclaimer as a mere "proposal" under 2–207(2)—one that the buyer could simply ignore—since no buyer would willingly adopt such an unfavorable term unless compelled to do so as a condition of the sale.

The *Roto–Lith* decision has generally been rejected by courts and commentators on the ground that it runs counter to the apparent aim of 2–207, which is to impart controlling status to the form submitted by the buyer/offeror. Treating the seller/offeree's acknowledgment as a counteroffer rather than a "proposal" gives the seller a last shot at imposing its own terms on the deal. That, however, is precisely opposite to the statute's evident intent. Going further, even if the court was right in treating the seller's acknowledgment and warranty disclaimer as a counteroffer, there was surely no express assent thereto on the buyer's part, merely silence. Lacking such assent, the proper conclusion, it seems, should have been that the writings of the parties failed to create a contract under 2–207(1), in which event, the goods having been delivered and accepted, 2–207(3) would be applicable. Under that subsection, the conduct of the parties would be deemed to have established a "contract," one that would include those terms on which the two forms did agree, plus the supplemental provisions of the UCC, of which 2–315, the warranty of fitness, would apparently have favored Roto–Lith, the buyer.

Just why the plaintiff in *Roto–Lith* didn't pre-test the N–132–C emulsion before it placed its order is a puzzle. Roto–Lith the packager was in a far better position than Bartlett the glue-maker to determine whether the emulsion would actually stick to the surface of a cellophane bag or would slip and slide and drip all over the frozen vegetables inside. In any case, Bartlett made clear its own lack of information on this fascinating question when it expressly disclaimed "all warranties ... whatsoever" and gave a good practical reason for such disclaimer. Had Roto–Lith responded by insisting on a warranty of fitness, Bartlett would evidently have refused to sell. The outcome in *Roto–Lith* thus seems more or less fair and reasonable, even if, as noted, the court erred in disregarding or misapplying 2–207. But since subsequent decisions appear to be unanimous in rejecting *Roto–Lith*, it follows that warranty disclaimers—which are almost invariably "material"—can be safely relied upon by a supplier only when the disclaimer calls for, and gets, the express assent of the buyer, thereby escaping the status of a "proposal" under 2–207(2). This, in turn, has the presumed virtue of requiring the buyer to give real attention to the disclaimer and to test or otherwise satisfy itself about the product before making a commitment.

Rolling Contracts

A more contentious and disputed role for Section 2–207 arises in connection with what are generally called "rolling contracts"—so called because the goods in question are received and paid for before the "contract" has been furnished to the buyer. The fact-pattern is simple and familiar. A buyer (whether a business or an individual consumer) orders computer software from a producer, either by telephone or over the internet, and pays by credit card. In due course, a box containing the product arrives. When opened, the box is found to contain (along with the product itself) a lengthy set of documents setting forth various conditions and limitations, among which might be warranty disclaimers, limitations on remedy and, commonly, a provision stating that any dispute between the parties shall be referred to arbitration. A Notice is included (in large red type) which states that the conditions and limitations just described shall be deemed to be accepted by the buyer unless the product is returned to the seller within a stated period, say 30 days. The buyer usually doesn't bother to read all this printed stuff and probably throws it away along with the box itself.

Finding after two or three months that the software has major defects, the buyer ultimately brings suit against the seller seeking a refund of the purchase price but also claiming substantial damages by reason of the product's failure to perform as advertised. Pointing to the warranty disclaimer, the remedy limitations and the arbitration provision, the seller moves to dismiss.

Does this everyday transaction "fall into the abyss of Section 2–207,"[26] as one writer puts it? Assuming for the moment that it

---

26. Gillette, *Rolling Contracts as an Agency Problem,* 2004 Wisc. L. Rev. 679.

does, the question that remains is whether the seller's contract terms are or aren't binding on the buyer.

In the *Step–Saver* case,[27] the plaintiff, Step–Saver, sent the defendant, TSL, written purchase orders for 142 copies of the defendant's Multilink Advanced program (whatever that may be) for incorporation into the plaintiff's "multiuser electronic system," which plaintiff sold to its customers. The purchase orders specified product, price, shipping instructions and payment terms, but nothing more. The defendant shipped the product promptly, together with an invoice that precisely reflected the terms of plaintiff's orders. On each package shipped, however, was stamped a so-called box-top license. The box-top license disclaimed all warranties, and stated further that—

> "Opening this package indicates your acceptance of these terms and conditions. If you do not agree with them, you should promptly return the package unopened ... within fifteen days ... and your money will be refunded."

The Multilink Advanced program didn't work, apparently, and the plaintiff was obliged to make refunds and pay other compensation to its own complaining customers. A suit for damages followed.

Holding for the plaintiff, the Third Circuit found that the box-top license was equivalent to a written acceptance that contained "additional terms," of which the warranty disclaimer was obviously one. Such additional terms must be regarded as "proposals" under 2–207(2), and as the warranty disclaimer would "substantially [*i.e.,* 'materially'] alter the distribution of risk between the parties," it could not become a part of the agreement. Opening the packages, said the Court, did not constitute "assent" to the warranty disclaimer by Step–Saver.

The *Step–Saver* case involved a transaction between "merchants"—buyer and seller were both operating businesses. Would or should the outcome be the same if the buyer is an individual consumer? It is plain that 2–207 applies to buyers who are ordinary consumers just as well as to merchant buyers, so that the answer appears to be yes. Indeed, in the case of a consumer, under the first sentence of 2–207(2) "additional terms" are to be construed as "proposals" and excluded (unless accepted) without regard to whether they are "material."

In *ProCD, Inc. v. Zeidenberg*,[28] involving a purchase by a consumer rather than a "merchant," the Seventh Circuit held,

27. Step–Saver Data Sys., Inc. v. Wyse, 939 F.2d 91 (3d Cir. 1991). To the same effect, *Klocek v. Gateway, Inc.*, 104 F.Supp.2d 1332 (D. Kan. 2000).

28. *ProCD, Inc. v. Zeidenberg*, 86 F.3d 1447 (7th Cir. 1996). To the same effect, *Hill v. Gateway 2000*, 105 F.3d 1147 (7th Cir. 1997). Topic discussed in

nevertheless, that 2–207 was inapplicable. The buyer-defendant—posing, at least, as an ordinary consumer—bought the plaintiff's software product at a retail store, and thereafter attempted to exploit the product commercially. The Court held that the buyer was bound by the terms of a license enclosed in the box containing the product, which license specifically prohibited commercial use of the software. 2–207 did not apply, according to Judge Easterbrook, for the reason that only one form, the license, was involved in the transaction. That being so (in the Court's view), the prohibition against commercial use was binding on the buyer and would not be treated as a mere "proposal."

Apparently, Judge Easterbrook assumed that "the battle of the forms" implies a conflict between the buyer's *written* order form and the seller's *written* acceptance. That, of course, is incorrect—2–207 plainly covers transactions in which the buyer's order is communicated orally, face to face or by phone, and is followed by a written "confirmation" from the seller. The Official Comment to 2–207 makes that perfectly clear, and it is very hard to believe that Judge Easterbrook was unaware of it. His aim, quite obviously, was to avoid the "abyss" of 2–207 altogether. But some would say he did that by ignoring the commands of the statute.

Even so, the outcome in *ProCD* seems entirely sensible. The Court, stressing "common sense" and practicality, pointed out that all sorts of consumer goods (an airline ticket, for example, or an insurance policy, even a concert ticket) are bought and paid for before the detailed terms of the agreement are made known to the buyer. But all would agree, I think, that those terms are contractually binding and cannot be treated by the buyer as mere proposals. One way to reach that result is to treat the seller (*e.g.* the airline) as the offeror (or, perhaps, the counterofferor) and the customer as the offeree whose "acceptance" consists of his taking and using the product without objection. Yet another would be to treat the customer as the offeror and the seller as the offeree, but with the "offer" consisting of the form furnished by the seller along with the product. Pretty awkward semantically either way you look at it. At all events, Easterbrook's position in *ProCD* is that the "rolling contract" is essentially indistinguishable from an over-the-counter retail purchase, to which 2–207 obviously has no application.

Taken together,[29] *Step–Saver* and *ProCD* suggest that there is a difference between merchant-buyers and consumer-buyers

Craswell, *The Sound of One Form Battling*, 98 Mich. L. Rev. 2727 (2000).

29. A forced cohabitation, I admit. The *ProCD* decision has not everywhere been accepted; see, *e.g.*, *Klocek v. Gateway*, supra, n. 27.

(though of course 2–207 makes no such distinction, other than by treating all additional terms as "proposals" in the case of consumers). Merchant buyers, who engage in repeat transactions, presumably know how to cope with the battle of the forms and with the operation of 2–207. Accordingly, the seller's "additional terms" are treated as "proposals," and assuming they "materially alter the contract," are excluded unless expressly assented to by the buyer. Where the buyer is an individual consumer, on the other hand, the truly important question is not whether a contract has been formed, but whether the unread conditions imposed on the consumer are fair. Are those conditions within the consumer's reasonable expectation, or are they so burdensome and inequitable as to be "unconscionable"? If the *ProCD* decision is followed, and if 2–207(2) provides no protection to consumers by eliminating unread terms, the question of fairness or "unconscionability" becomes more urgent and would apparently have to be dealt with directly, if at all, under a separate set of standards or criteria.

So the question is: Do we need a doctrine of "unconscionability" as protection for consumers, and if we do, what should those standards or criteria be? That question, much debated, is discussed in some detail in Chapter 4, below.

Chapter 4

UNFAIRNESS AND UNCONSCIONABILITY

A. Traditional Elements: Duress, Incapacity and Misrepresentation

Contracts, as noted, are voluntary, self-inspired arrangements by which private individuals seek to enhance their personal interests through the familiar process of arms-length exchange. In general, we can assume that each of the contracting parties acts without coercion (no gun to her head), that each is reasonably clear about her own preferences (knows what she likes), and that each has sufficient information about the world to distinguish intelligently among alternative goods and services (can tell a hawk from a handsaw). Possessing these common attributes—free will, self-knowledge and a modicum of practical information—an individual who makes promises on which others place reliance is normally bound by contract even if the commitments she has made seem improvident or idiosyncratic. The legal system obviously cannot undertake to assess the comparative wisdom or sagacity of the parties as a general precondition to the enforcement of contract obligations.

If, on the other hand, either party lacks or can be presumed to lack the attributes of informed volition, then the customary basis of contract is in doubt. Recognizing this, the law has traditionally regarded contracts as void or voidable if made by persons lacking legal capacity, including "infants" (generally, persons under 18), drunks and the mentally ill, or if entered into under conditions of duress, or if induced by fraud or misrepresentation. The intuitive basis for treating a promise as non-binding under such circumstances is clear, I think, but inevitably there are borderline definitional issues—particularly in the areas of "duress" and "misrepresentation"—that test the limits or the application of the concept. Some of these are sorted out briefly in the discussion that follows. The much larger and infinitely more contentious question of consumer safeguards and so-called contracts of adhesion is reserved for Section B.

1. *Duress.* Promises extorted by violence or threat of violence are obviously not enforceable. Formation of a contract requires "assent" on the part of each of the contracting parties, and while a

gun to the head will almost always compel an affirm
from the victim, the law, for reasons too plain to req
treats the resulting "agreement" as void. Economic
threat to discharge an employee, for example, unless the emplˇˇ
agrees to release a valid claim she has against the employer—may
likewise vitiate a contract, though in these circumstances the
contract is likely to be regarded as voidable at the victim's option
rather than void at inception.

Perhaps the most interesting question in the duress field—one
that may actually require us to articulate our rationale more
carefully—concerns the enforceability of an agreement to modify an
existing contract, where the modification is assented to by one
party as a consequence of the other party's threat to breach.[1] Thus,
A promises a performance to B. Before the performance has been
completed, A demands that B agree to a change of terms, say an
increase in A's compensation. Eager, perhaps desperate, for A's
performance, B agrees, but later reneges. The rule at common
law—referred to as the "preexisting duty rule"—is that the performance of an act which the promisee (of the modification, A) is
already bound by contract to perform is not "valid consideration"
for the change that the promisor (B) has apparently agreed to. The
enforcement of B's subsequent promise would accordingly be
barred on the ground that a fresh consideration for that promise
was lacking. Though sometimes criticized as formal and "scholas-
tic",[2] on one view the preexisting duty rule can be commended for
protecting B from what may have been an effort at coercion or at
least undue pressure on A's part. As in *Alaska Packers*, noted
below, A's threat to breach might have been made after B had
spent substantial amounts in reliance on the expected performance
and at a time when A knew that it was simply too late for B to find
a substitute in the market. Under these circumstances, as suggested, the rule, if applicable, serves to block A's attempt at a hold-up

1. For discussion, see Narasimhan, *Of Expectations, Incomplete Contracting, and the Bargain Principle,* 74 Cal.L.Rev. 1123 (1986); Muris, *Opportunistic Behavior and the Law of Contracts,* 65 Minn.L.Rev. 521 (1981); Hillman, *Policing Contract Modifications under the U.C.C.: Good Faith and the Doctrine of Duress,* 64 Iowa L.Rev. 849 (1979).

2. *See, e.g.,* Schwartzreich v. Bauman–Basch, Inc., 231 N.Y. 196, 131 N.E. 887 (1921). The plaintiff, having entered into a 1–year employment contract with the defendant at a stated salary, later prevailed on the defendant to make a new contract increasing the salary to meet a competitor's offer. Having been discharged, Plaintiff sued for damages based on the new salary rate. *Held,* judgment for the plaintiff affirmed. The parties effectively rescinded the first contract by mutual consent. They then went on to form a second contract in which their exchange of promises constituted valid consideration. The fact that the rescission of the old contract and the creation of the new contract took place simultaneously was "unimportant".

or, rather, may discourage A from attempting a hold-up in the first place.

On the other hand, applying the rule in an automatic fashion, and without some sense of why they actually did propose and agree to the modification, might result in the frustration of the parties' real interests by making it difficult or impossible to carry on cooperative relations in the future. Especially in the case of long-term contracts—the construction of a building would be an obvious example—circumstances affecting performance could change, as time passed, in ways that were not anticipated when the agreement was entered into, and the parties might very well think it better now to modify the terms of the agreement than to allow their relationship to sink into conflict and litigation. Where the modification of a contract entails something of value for each of the parties—a creditor, for example, agrees to extend the maturity date of a loan, while the debtor, in turn, consents to a higher rate of interest—then, as a technical matter, there is consideration on both sides and the new promises are mutually enforceable. But if the modification runs in favor of one party only, a strict application of the consideration requirement would prevent enforcement even though the change is reasonable and acceptable to the promisor.

Recognizing a certain tension in policy goals, the Restatement first affirms the preexisting duty rule, stating in Section 73 that the "performance of a legal duty owed to a promisor ... is not consideration", but then in Section 89 (under the topic-heading Contracts Without Consideration) provides that a promise modifying a contractual duty will be binding on the promisor "if the modification is fair and equitable in view of circumstances not anticipated by the parties when the contract was made". Going somewhat further, but essentially reflecting the same tension, UCC 2–209 simply eliminates the need for consideration in this context, requiring only that the modification be made in "good faith" and for a "legitimate commercial reason". Where there is "extortion" or "coercion", on the other hand, or "the use of bad faith to escape performance", both the Code and the courts regard the modification as ineffective and will permit the promisor to treat her consent to it as voidable.

While the distinction between "legitimate" commercial conduct and "extortion" looks like a garden-variety line-drawing problem, the issue may actually be a bit more subtle than that. Thus, we could imagine a case—perhaps *Austin Instrument,* discussed below, is one—in which the threat to breach exhibits both elements at once: it is legitimate from the standpoint of the party doing the threatening, but coercive in its impact on the party under threat. In deciding whether or not to apply the doctrine of duress, we would then have to determine which of the two parties' interests to treat as paramount. No equivalent dilemma is presented in the case of a physical threat, obviously, because the outcome is the same whether our focus is on the threatening party or the party threatened.

In the well-known *Alaska Packers* case,[3] the defendant, owner of a salmon cannery, had a contract with the plaintiffs, a group of hearty sailors, to operate its fishing boats in certain remote northern waters. The sailors signed "articles" under which each was to be paid $50 for the "season" (the season, apparently, being short) plus 2 cents a fish. At the very last moment, however, and when it was plainly too late for the defendant to hire replacement personnel, the sailors threatened to stop work and jump ship unless the defendant agreed to sign new articles doubling their pay to $100. The defendant did agree, but then later, the catch being in, refused to pay more than the $50 originally promised. Finding that the plaintiffs' conduct was willful, arbitrary and "without any valid cause", the court held that the defendant's promise to come through with an extra $50 had been given for no consideration and, hence, need not be performed. While the defendant might, theoretically, have chosen to sue the sailors for breach instead of consenting to the modification, as a practical matter it had no choice since the sailors would obviously be unable to respond in damages.

As in the gun-to-the-head case, the result in *Alaska Packers'* probably can be accepted without pausing to distinguish between the parties' respective interests. Plainly, the defendant's consent to the pay raise was a forced consent, the alternative being the loss of much of its investment in the cannery itself. The plaintiffs apparently timed their threat so as to maximize the defendant's vulnerability—plaintiffs had received no competing offer and no change had occurred in the market for their services or the conditions of their work that would explain or legitimate an effort to get an increase in compensation. As suggested, therefore, the outcome is the same whether we emphasize the absence of a "legitimate reason" on the plaintiffs' part or the defendant's lack of choice; under either test, there appears to have been considerable justification for applying the doctrine of duress.

By contrast, *Austin Instrument Inc. v. Loral Corporation*,[4] a four-to-three decision of the New York Court of Appeals, is a case in

---

3. Alaska Packers' Ass'n v. Domenico, 117 Fed. 99 (9th Cir.1902), discussed in Threedy, *A Fish Story: Alaska Packers; Association v. Domenico*, 2000 Utah L. Rev. 185.

4. 29 N.Y.2d 124, 324 N.Y.S.2d 22, 272 N.E.2d 533 (1971).

which choice of rationale may finally become impossible to avoid. In *Austin,* the defendant, Loral, having been awarded a $6 million contract by the Navy for the production of radar equipment, entered into a subcontract with the plaintiff for the manufacture of various precision gear components. The Navy contract contained a strict delivery schedule—the radar equipment was for use in Viet Nam—and imposed liquidated damages for late deliveries or cancellation. After shipping some of the gear parts but not all, Austin apparently realized that it was going to lose money on the subcontract, and it thereupon notified Loral that it would cease further shipments—would, in effect, breach the contract—unless Loral agreed to a retroactive price increase. Equally important, Loral had meanwhile been awarded a second Navy contract for radar equipment and announced that it proposed to subcontract with another component manufacturer. Having presumably tooled up for the first Navy contract, Austin demanded that Loral give it the right to make all the gear components to be furnished under the second as well. Unable to reach a settlement after three or four weeks of discussion, Loral finally agreed to both demands because (as it told Austin in a letter written by counsel) "We have feverishly surveyed other sources of supply and . . . they could not even remotely begin to deliver on time. . . . Accordingly, we are left with no choice or alternative but to meet your conditions." Subsequently, Loral refused to complete payments under the second contract. When Austin sued for the amount still due, Loral in effect counterclaimed to recover the increase in price that it had agreed to pay and did pay under the first contract.

Finding that money damages would have been inadequate and that Loral could not have obtained the gear parts from other sources in time to meet its obligations to the Navy, a majority of the Court of Appeals, reversing the court below, held for Loral. Austin's threat to stop deliveries confronted Loral with the danger of liquidated damage claims or cancellation by the Navy as well as loss of standing as a defense contractor, all of which "deprived Loral of its free will". Hence, the contract modification was voidable on grounds of duress. The dissenting judges would have affirmed the decision of the lower court, which found that Austin's demand for renegotiation during a "time of continual rising of material and manufacturing costs"[5] was by no means uncommon or improper. Doubting whether Loral had been truly diligent in canvassing alternative suppliers, the dissenters evidently felt that

---

5. Quoted from the majority opinion of the Appellate Division; 316 N.Y.S.2d 534.

Austin's request for a price increase was "a commercially understandable renegotiation" rather than "an exercise of duress."

Just how to weigh the disputed facts in *Austin Instrument* is, of course, a matter of debate. On the whole, however, the approach taken by the dissenters—emphasizing Austin's motives in demanding a price increase rather than the impact of that demand on Loral's "free will"—seems the more plausible and consistent of the two. The critical issue, I think, should not have been Loral's state of mind, which would always have been fiercely hostile to any proposal for a price increase, but whether Austin's insistence on renegotiating was the sort of hold-up move that the contract law should refuse to encourage. The question, really, is whether or not Austin's behavior should be seen as strictly "opportunistic"— whether, like the sailors in *Alaska Packers'*, Austin consciously and deliberately chose to threaten breach at a time when it knew that true renegotiation was impossible. On this score, however, and no matter how the facts are viewed, it seems pretty clear that Austin's threat to breach was triggered *not* by Loral's vulnerability but by its own loss experience under the first subcontract and its disappointment over the second.

Where market changes—sharply rising labor and material costs in *Austin*—confront one of the contracting parties with the prospect of substantial losses, the other contracting party ought not to be greatly surprised by demands for modification and by threats of breach, express or implied. The "Official Comment" to UCC 2–209 (nowhere mentioned in the *Austin* opinion, incidentally) states that "such matters as a market shift which makes performance come to involve a loss may provide [a good faith] reason" for the original promisor (Austin) to seek modification, even though failure to perform will constitute an actionable breach. In effect, the promisor regards it as less costly to pay damages than to meet its contract obligations unless the contract terms are modified. The original promisee (Loral), faced with a demand for modification, is then obliged to choose between (i) claiming damages and (ii) renegotiating and making financial concessions in order to induce the promisor to perform. If expected damages are "adequate" in the sense that they fully compensate the promisee for the value of the contract, then, presumably, the promisee will choose alternative (i) and decline to renegotiate. But if expected damages are inadequate, renegotiation may be preferable and it may be in the promisee's interest to accede to the promisor's demands. As the Court majority stressed, Loral's *economic* loss would have included the Navy's substantial liquidated damage claim and the impairment of Loral's reputation for reliability and its chances for future defense con-

tracts. Quite possibly, neither of these elements of loss—almost
certainly not loss of business reputation and future contract opportunities—would have been recoverable against Austin under existing contract damage rules (in particular, the "certainty" and "foreseeability" limitations described in Chapter 8). Accordingly, while
Loral was compelled to accept a price increase in order to get timely
delivery of the gear components, the increase might still have been
smaller in amount than the difference between the value of the
contract to Loral, taking everything into account, and the damages
Loral would receive in an action against Austin. Put differently,
Loral might actually have expected to lose less by paying Austin
more than by collecting damages for breach. In these and like
circumstances, *both* parties may be better off if the contract terms
are modified and performance ensues. The promisee no doubt feels
bitter and distressed ("feverish," according to Loral) at being asked
to renegotiate, but the process referred to would not usually merit
application of the doctrine of duress, because it is precisely what
the Code provision mentioned above appears to contemplate. And
this is so, I think, even when defense contracts are involved, and
even in war-time.

2. *Misrepresentation and Concealment.* The requirement of
"assent", which is fundamental to the formation of a binding
contract, implies in a general way that both parties to an exchange
shall have a reasonably clear conception of what they are getting
and what they are giving up. If the identity or the character of the
property or service being bought or sold is overtly misrepresented
by one of the contracting parties, then the other party's assent is
obviously less than meaningful and any agreement that results will
be regarded as voidable. This follows as a matter of law even
though there is no specific intent to defraud—that is, even if the
misrepresenting party is unaware that her statement or representation is false. Representations of fact, at least if material and if
relied upon in good faith, constitute an "inducement" to the
receiving party for which the representing party is deemed responsible. If the inducement is worthless, then, whether she acted
fraudulently or innocently, the party responsible for having offered
it will, in effect, be obliged to restore the offeree to status quo.

All this is standard fare. What is less clear under the decided
cases is whether, or in what circumstances, *non-disclosure* of a
material fact—mere silence—should be treated as the legal equivalent of misrepresentation. Thus, A offers to sell her house to B for
$100,000. There are termites in the basement and it will cost
$5,000 to get rid of them. Having lived in the house for years, A
knows about the termites. B doesn't. Does A have a legal duty to

bring the matter to B's attention? If she says nothing, can B afterwards rescind? Or can A simply leave it up to B to check out the condition of the house for herself before she buys?

In *Swinton v. Whitinsville Sav. Bank*,[6] the Supreme Court of Massachusetts held that the seller of a home "infested with termites" had no legal obligation to disclose this circumstance to the buyer, even though the seller knew about the termites and knew the buyer didn't. A property-seller cannot, of course, make false representations about the property—can't tell lies and get away with it—but "bare nondisclosure" is a different matter and creates no liability. Were the rule otherwise, the Court reasoned, "every seller [would be] liable who fails to disclose any nonapparent defect known to him in the subject of the sale which materially reduces its value and ... [s]imilarly ... every buyer would be liable who fails to disclose any nonapparent virtue known to him ... which materially enhances its value...." Given the frailties of human nature, a standard "so idealistic", if imposed as a strict requirement of law, would be unworkable. Accordingly, buyers and sellers dealing at arms-length must each look out for themselves—caveat emptor, caveat venditor—at least in Massachusetts.

The *Swinton* decision has been followed by some courts but rejected by others on the ground that it no longer reflects "American mores". And it is specifically disapproved by Section 161 of the Restatement, about which a further comment is made below. In making our own evaluation, we should of course bear in mind that the effect of the *Swinton* decision—that is, its consequence for *future* home-buyers and sellers—is simply to require the buyer to conduct her own investigation of the house, hiring a plumber to inspect the water-pipes, an electrician to examine the wiring, and an exterminator to look for bugs, rather than relying for such information on the seller. All this costs money, however, so that if, as in *Swinton*, the seller *already* knows about a defect in the premises, it will be cheaper for the seller to disclose it than for the buyer to have to discover it for herself. From the standpoint of efficiency, therefore, a rule that requires disclosure may be superior to caveat emptor.

But does it really matter? Not much, I think, in the generality of cases. Even if the law required the home-seller to disclose everything she knew, the buyer could never be sure in advance that the seller actually *had* accurate knowledge about the state of the water pipes and the wiring, and it seems virtually certain that she would want to undertake her own investigation before making a

6. 311 Mass. 677, 42 N.E.2d 808 (1942).

commitment to buy, whatever the expense. Where a casual transaction between nonprofessionals is in view—the sale of a residence, a used car, a diamond ring—the buyer would almost never be satisfied to act on the basis of the seller's disclosures, since the buyer would have no reason to assume that the seller actually knew all there was to be known about the property. In this context, therefore, the disclosure rule, whether contrary to *Swinton* or in accord, probably has little significance in practice.

At all events, as noted, the *Swinton* decision is rejected by Section 161 of the Restatement, which treats non-disclosure as equivalent to misrepresentation where the undisclosed fact concerns a "basic assumption" made by the other party to the contract and where the non-disclosure "amounts to a failure to act in good faith". The good-faith condition, otherwise rather mysterious, is evidently intended by the Restatement to distinguish between cases that involve a seller's knowledge of hidden defects—the *Swinton* case itself—and cases involving so-called market information which is typically the product of research and special expertise on the part of a potential buyer. In general (and as observed at greater length in Chapter 7 in connection with the related subject of "mistake"), an individual who spends time and money developing information about the intrinsic value of certain property does not and should not have a legal duty to disclose her findings to the property's present owner. Just as an inventor is rewarded with a patent or an author with a copyright, so, in effect, the developer of market data is rewarded with the right to keep the information to herself until she can acquire the property for her own account. Thus, fancifully, if the buyer in the *Swinton* case had been a geologist whose research convinced her that there was a gold-mine under the seller's residence, she would surely have had no obligation to tell the seller that the property was actually worth a thousand times the asking price. While the seller could be said to have made a "basic assumption" that the property was intended for residential use only, there would be no "failure to act in good faith" on the geologist's part if she bought it without disclosing, i.e., surrendering, the fruits of her research.[7] Hence, the Court in *Swinton* was pretty clearly wrong in supposing that a decision that required a seller to reveal a "nonapparent defect" would similarly require a buyer to reveal a "nonapparent virtue". The two cases may be alike in respect to the element of concealment. In respect to the obligation of disclosure, however, they can be, and presumably would

---

7. Kronman, *Mistake, Disclosure, Information, and the Law of Contracts,* 7 J. of Legal Studies 1 (1978).

be, treated differently even if the Court, succumbing to its "moral sense", had required the home-seller to come clean about the termites.

Nearly thirty years after the *Swinton* decision, the same Massachusetts Court came back to the nondisclosure issue and found a factual and legal distinction that enabled it to hold for the victim without deserting the rule of caveat emptor. The legal distinction is between "half truths" and "bare nondisclosure." In *Kannavos v. Annino*,[8] the plaintiff, responding to a newspaper ad, entered into negotiations with the defendant for the purchase of defendant's residential rental properties, of which one, No.11 Ingersoll Grove, became the subject of the present lawsuit. The defendant made complete disclosure of the rent rolls and operating expenses, but failed to inform the plaintiff that the building was being operated as a multi-family dwelling in violation of a zoning ordinance and without the necessary permit. Kannavos agreed to Annino's price and closed the transaction at the office of a local bank from which the purchase money was borrowed. The bank-mortgagee was represented by an in-house lawyer. Kannavos had no legal representation of his own and may have thought he could depend on the bank's lawyer to see that title transfer and other legal details were properly handled.

Soon thereafter, the city began proceedings to abate the illegal use of the building, which obviously reduced the value of No.11 substantially. Kannavos promptly brought an action against Annino for rescission. Holding for the plaintiff, the Supreme Court found that the defendant-seller, by word and conduct, had induced the plaintiff to believe that No.11 was, in the words of the newspaper ad, "housing suitable for investment and that the housing could continue to be used for that purpose." The ad itself, and the discussion that followed, implied that multi-family use was legally permissible, although Annino knew that such use was in fact illegal. Having asserted that No.11 was "suitable for investment," the seller in effect uttered a "half-truth," which misled the buyer. This, said the Court, amounted to active misrepresentation and was "much more than 'bare nondisclosure' as in the *Swinton* case." The fact that Kannavos acted without hiring counsel to conduct due diligence, though notably incautious, did not alter the seller's duty to tell Kannavos the whole truth and disclose the zoning violation.

The decision in *Kannavos* is undoubtedly correct, but the distinction between half-truth and bare nondisclosure is troublesome. In *Swinton*, after all, the house was offered for residential

---

8. 356 Mass. 42, 247 N.E.2d 708 (1969).

occupancy despite the seller's knowledge that "predatory insects" threatened the structure itself and made long-term residential use impossible without additional expenditure. Termite infestation may be less serious than illegal operation, but I suppose the *Swinton* court would have reached the same conclusion even if the undisclosed defect had been more dramatic—a gaping hole in the roof, for example. The element of half-truth, one would think, is present in any case in which a seller offers property for a specific use with knowledge of a hidden defect that renders such use impossible or impracticable. Yet the Court in *Kannavos* was careful to say that its decision was consistent with Swinton by reason of the alleged distinction between half-truth and bare nondisclosure.

Any other plausible basis for distinction? One dimension on which *Swinton* and *Kannavos* differ factually is with respect to the character of the property sold, and perhaps that difference helps to explain why or how the two decisions can comfortably coexist. Neither opinion gives us a look at the contract involved, but I think we can assume that neither contract contained any representation by the seller regarding the omitted subject-matter—nothing about pests in *Swinton*, nothing about zoning in *Kannavos*. In that they were alike. The question, then, is whether (and if so, what) contractual representations should be *imputed* to the sellers and supplied by default. In *Swinton*, personal-use property was being sold by a nonprofessional previous owner. Under Massachusetts law, personal-use property (home, used car) was evidently deemed to be sold on an "As Is" basis, meaning, in effect, that the buyer was expected to do his own investigating rather than relying on the seller to disclose any defects. Accordingly, no representation with respect to the condition of the house would be imputed to the seller by default.

As to the sale of an operating business, however, the contract of sale would routinely include, among other boiler-plate representations (*e.g.*, that no taxes were due for prior years, that no material litigation was pending or anticipated), an express representation that "the Seller has conducted the business in full compliance with all applicable laws, federal, state and local." Any form book one cares to look at will confirm that observation; and no doubt Kannavos' lawyer, if he'd had one, would have included or insisted upon a "full compliance" representation simply by following a form used in similar transactions. The default established by standard usage is thus consistent with the outcome in *Kannavos*, and as a matter of law should be assumed to have been intended by the seller in the absence of anything to the contrary.

Arguably, then, the Court's distinction between half-truth and bare nondisclosure, otherwise kind of wobbly, was merely a short-hand way of saying that the default rule is one thing when applied to the sale of personal-use property but another when applied to the sale of an operating business. In effect, the Court supplied poor Mr. Kannavos with what he sadly lacked; *viz*; the advice of competent counsel.

B.   Standardized Forms and Unconscionability

Consumer transactions of all kinds—purchasing a car, renting an apartment, applying for an insurance policy—are regularly carried out on the basis of printed, standard-form contracts prepared by the seller or by the industry-group to which the seller belongs. In addition to price and merchandise description, the contract form includes various technical provisions that purport to define the rights and duties of the parties in some detail. Drafted from the seller's perspective, these standardized clauses are generally intended to minimize the seller's risks and responsibilities—for example, by narrowing the scope of the seller's warranties or by expanding its legal remedies in the event the buyer fails to make installment payments when due—and, by the same token, to impose burdens or other limitations on the buyer.

The buyer, we can safely assume, is unaware of the detailed content of the standard-form agreement at the time she signs it. She is given no real opportunity to read the document, and as the technical provisions are written in legal language, she couldn't fully understand them if she studied the agreement all day. In any case, even if read, understood and loudly objected to, the standard-form contract terms are simply not negotiable. The buyer may in some instances (say a used car purchase) bargain with the seller over price, but the remaining contract terms are offered on a take-it-or-leave-it basis. Indeed, the seller's representative—salesman, rental agent—would usually have no authority to alter the document. To be sure, the buyer can always shop elsewhere; but she is likely to assume, often correctly, that the same or a similar standard-form contract is employed by other sellers in the field, so that dragging herself from one office or showroom to another in search of better terms would be a wasted effort.

In this familiar setting, are there, and should there be, any limits on the seller's legal ability to enforce the contract against the buyer? Before answering, I suppose we ought to acknowledge that where ordinary consumer transactions are concerned there is really no practical alternative to the use of standard-form purchase agreements, whatever their shortcomings. Sellers of mass-merchandise products (cars, apartment space, insurance policies) obviously cannot take time to negotiate a detailed contract for each individual transaction, and the buyer herself would not wish to incur the heavy expense (e.g., legal fees) that such negotiations would entail. The rights and obligations of seller and buyer do need to be spelled out in writing, but both parties have a real interest in minimizing the cost of contracting. Standard-form agreements are the best and probably the only way of avoiding transaction costs that might otherwise overwhelm the transaction itself, and since it is the seller, not the buyer, for whom such transactions are a constant and repeated event, the drafting of the contract form quite naturally becomes the seller's responsibility. The result, however, as stated, is a document which thoroughly favors the seller's interest—one, moreover, to which the buyer is compelled to "adhere" if she wants the merchandise, because the seller will not make the goods available on any other basis.

But suppose the factor of market dominance is lacking; suppose the seller operates in a strictly competitive economic environment and has plenty of business rivals eager for the buyer's trade. While a seller—say a department store—would usually have greater resources and possess more commercial sophistication than its customers, even the simplest consumer knows that there are many places to shop and that close substitutes for the brand she wants are readily available. Is "unconscionability" confined to the relatively rare monopoly situation or should it apply to consumer transactions generally, even though in most circumstances the ordinary consumer is not without a "meaningful choice" both among competing sellers and among alternative goods?

In *Williams v. Walker–Thomas Furniture Co.*,[9] decided by the D.C. Court of Appeals in 1965, the Company, a retail store, sought to repossess various household items that it had sold to Williams, a welfare recipient, over a period of some five years. Each sale (including the last, a stereo set sold for $514.95) was on credit, Williams being obligated to make monthly installment payments, called "rent", until the full purchase price was satisfied. The printed form purchase agreement contained a so-called cross-collateral or "dragnet" provision of which the purpose was to secure the customer's indebtedness by empowering the Company, in the event of a default, to repossess not only the particular item (say the stereo set) to which the indebtedness related, but every other

9.   350 F.2d 445 (D.C.Cir.1965).

article purchased from the Company on which any balance remained due at the time the latest purchase was made. In mechanical terms, this purpose was accomplished under the contract by assuring that a balance would be due on each previous installment sale until the customer had paid off her indebtedness to the Company for *all* purchased articles, current and past. The cross-collateral clause read as follows:

"[T]he amount of each periodical installment payment to be made by (purchaser) to the Company under this present lease shall be inclusive of and not in addition to the amount of each installment payment to be made by (purchaser) under such prior leases, bills or accounts; and all payments now and hereafter made by (purchaser) shall be credited pro rata on all outstanding leases, bills and accounts due the Company by (purchaser) at the time each such payment is made."

Williams having defaulted on the stereo installments, the Company, pointing out that under the above provision she still owed 3 cents on one item and 25 cents on another, sought to "scoop up" all the merchandise it had ever sold her,[10] presumably leaving behind nothing but a couple of orange crates and the empty stereo carton. Represented by the legal assistance office of the bar association, Williams resisted on the ground that the cross-collateral provision was unconscionable and therefore not enforceable. Finding no legislative authority for the defense of unconscionability—the UCC, and with it Section 2–302, had not yet been made applicable in the District of Columbia—the District Court reluctantly held for the Company. In so holding, however, it did not hesitate to express its opinion of the Company's aims and methods:

". . . at the time of this and the preceding purchases, appellee was aware of appellant's financial position. The reverse side of the stereo contract listed the name of appellant's social worker and her $218 monthly stipend from the government. Nevertheless, with full knowledge that appellant had to feed, clothe and support both herself and seven children on this amount, appellee sold her a $514 stereo set. . . . We cannot condemn too strongly appellee's conduct."

On appeal, the Circuit Court held that the defense of unconscionability was available in the District of Columbia as a matter of common law and required no specific statutory authorization. Accordingly, the District Court's decision was reversed and the case remanded for a finding on the "possible unconscionability" of the

---

10.   Skilton & Helstad, *Protection of the Installment Buyer of Goods under the UCC,* 65 Mich.L.Rev. 1465 (1967).

rovision at issue. By way of guidance to the court below, ght indicated that "unconscionability" meant or included t factors: an absence of meaningful choice on the buyer's part (in effect) and the presence of contract terms "unreasonably favorable" to the seller. Meaningfulness of choice might be negated by the "manner" in which the contract was entered into, and with respect to "manner" the question was: "Did each party to the contract, considering his obvious education or lack of it, have a reasonable opportunity to understand the terms of the contract, or were the important terms hidden in a maze of fine print and minimized by deceptive sales practices?" If the latter were the case, then, where the contract terms were also found to be "commercially unreasonable" and "so unfair", enforcement should be refused.

The "unconscionability" principle, now reflected in UCC 2–302 and represented by a fairly substantial body of recent case law, has been discussed at greater length and with more intensity, I think, than any recent issue in the contracts field.[11] Legal scholars tend to divide across quite a broad spectrum in their evaluation of that principle, with ethical premises playing an unmistakable part in the debate. One difficulty, as the *Walker–Thomas* court candidly acknowledged, is how both to apply and to contain the concept of unconscionability—how to protect people from being dealt with by car-dealers and furniture companies in ways that violate their expectations as consumers, while at the same time continuing to honor "freedom of contract" as a fundamental tenet of the legal system. The answer furnished by the cases, and presumably accepted by the UCC, is that a contract entered into by competent adults is binding without regard to anyone's opinion of its fairness; but where the circumstances indicate that one party did not, or could not, fully comprehend the meaning of the contract, then the court is free to use its own judgment to determine whether the contract terms are fair. Thus, the threshold issue in *Walker–Thomas* is whether the Company made the cross-collateral provision clear to Ms. Williams at the time she signed the form contract. If so, there can be no "unconscionability". If not—if, in effect, the bargaining process was tainted by non-disclosure and incapacity—then, and presumably only then, the reviewing court can deny enforcement to those contract terms which it finds to be unfair.

11. *See, e.g.,* Rakoff, *Contracts of Adhesion: An Essay in Reconstruction,* 96 Harv.L.Rev. 1173 (1983); Leff, *Unconscionability and the Code—The Emperor's New Clause,* 115 U.Pa.L.Rev. 485 (1967); Eisenberg, *The Bargain Principle and its Limits,* 95 Harv.L.Rev. 741 (1982); Epstein, *Unconscionability: A Critical Appraisal,* 18 J. Law & Econ. 293 (1975); Slawson, *Standard Form Contracts and Democratic Control of Lawmaking Power,* 84 Harv.L.Rev. 529 (1971).

But while plausible in theory, in fact and a
unconscionability defense usually reduces itself to th.
tion of "substantive fairness". It is, after all, basic to the p-
of unconscionability that form language is seldom understood o.
even read. The shopper in a store or a showroom does not take time
to pore over the contract, and the salesman (who probably couldn't
make one if he tried) would rarely attempt an explanation of its
terms. The law could respond by insisting on the classic principle
that "one who does not choose to read a contract before signing it
cannot later relieve himself of its burdens...." But that "rule"
having been discarded in the present context, consumers are almost
always free to seek relief from contract terms which they regard as
oppressive and unreasonable by asserting that they did not "know-
ingly assent" to those terms when the contract was entered into. In
the end, therefore, it is likely to be substantive fairness, rather
than defects in the bargaining process, with which the reviewing
court will be concerned.

Shifting our attention to the fairness issue itself, I suppose the
first point we would agree upon is that the challenged contract
term—say the cross-collateral provision in *Walker–Thomas*—must
be considered and appraised as of the time the contract was entered
into by the parties—before the fact, so to speak—rather than
afterwards and in hindsight. The question to be asked is not
whether Ms. Williams *now* feels oppressed by the repossession of
her household goods—she obviously does—but whether it was unconscionable to include that term in the purchase agreement at the
time she bought the stereo set. Would she have agreed to the cross-
collateral provision if she had fully understood it, or would she have
attempted to negotiate different terms with Walker–Thomas? If the
latter, what *are* the terms to which she would finally have given her
full, conscious assent?

The answer cannot simply be that Ms. Williams would have
preferred a purchase agreement that omitted the cross-collateral
clause. No doubt she would, but I think we have to assume that if
cross-collateralization were eliminated, the store would then insist
(and in future *will* insist) on some adjustment to the credit terms
that it offers to its low-income customers. Thus, Ms. Williams
"borrows" $514—the price of the stereo set—from Walker–Thomas.
The cost to Ms. Williams, i.e., the interest rate she pays on the loan,
obviously reflects her credit-worthiness as a borrower. The more
property she puts up (or is led to put up) by way of security, the
lower the cost of credit to her and to others at the same modest
income-level. If the cross-collateral provision is held to be unenforceable, so that the lender's only security in the event of a default

is (as I guess it would be) the stereo set itself, then, no doubt, the interest rate demanded by the lender will increase correspondingly and Ms. Williams' monthly installment payments will be that much higher. In finding, or at least strongly suggesting, that the cross-collateral provision should be regarded as unconscionable, the Court in *Walker–Thomas* also in effect decreed that Ms. Williams and other low-income people who want to buy home-appliances on time must in the future pay more for credit.

We can now restate the question asked just above—whether Ms. Williams would have agreed to the cross-collateral clause had she understood its meaning—in the following way. Assuming full awareness on Ms. Williams' part, which of the two alternative credit arrangements should we suppose that she would actually have preferred—easier security terms and higher interest charges, or harsh security terms and lower interest charges? The Court (wittingly or unwittingly) decided that Ms. Williams would choose the former combination—easier terms and higher interest—if she, and presumably other low-income consumers, were able to make a conscious choice. By contrast, Walker–Thomas (and probably most of the other retailers in that neighborhood) evidently believed that customers would react more favorably to the opposite pattern—strict security requirements and lower interest—because monthly payments would be smaller. As to who was "right"—the Court or Walker–Thomas—we will of course never know. The strict-security component was in no real sense "chosen" by Ms. Williams; rather, it was slipped into the transaction and hidden from view.

Decisions like *Walker–Thomas* are sometimes criticized on the ground that they represent an unwanted and improper intervention in the lives of poor people (who, it is said, ought to be as free as the rest of us to throw their money away), but I think that this may somewhat overstate the issue. While everyone agrees that the use of standard form contracts is a necessary incident of mass-merchandising, it is also undeniably true that consumers (not just poor consumers) do not and cannot know all that the contract contains at the time they make their purchases. Where there is reason to doubt that the consumer would actually prefer the terms contained in the form contract (if she understood them) over an alternative set of terms, there may be some sense in the notion that a court (agency or legislature) should act to supply the missing element of conscious volition, rather than leaving that decision to producers and sellers who draft the contract forms.[12] The question, ultimate-

---

12. Goldberg, *Institutional Change and the Quasi–Invisible Hand,* 17 J. of Law & Econ. 461 (1974). And see, Cras-well, *Property Rules and Liability Rules in Unconscionability and Related Doctrines,* 60 U. Chi. L. Rev. 1 (1993).

ly, is whether Judge Wright or the Walker–Thomas Furniture Company is in a better position to make a "meaningful choice" on behalf of Ms. Williams and other consumers. The choice *will* be made, in effect, by one or the other. Hence, arguably, the unconscionability doctrine operates not as a means of controlling or intervening in people's lives, but as a device by which the choice-function is allocated to a court, rather than to the other contracting party, where the circumstances show that the consumer cannot choose for herself.

As a final comment on the *Walker–Thomas* case, and looking at the facts a bit more narrowly, we might feel some doubt about how much additional financial security cross-collateralization actually provided for the lender-seller, perhaps even whether it provided any. Apart from the stereo, the items that the Company sought to repossess presumably consisted of a few inexpensive pieces of furniture, no doubt hard-used, whose second-hand resale value (net of selling expenses) would have been small indeed. One might even question whether the resale value of such "collateral" would be likely to have exceeded the cost of bringing up a moving van to haul it all away. On the other hand, the Company's legal *right* to seize and carry off the bulk of Ms. Williams' household furnishings, not just the stereo, would surely operate as a grave threat to the family's morale and modest sense of well-being. Faced with the prospect of an apartment stripped of every comfort, Ms. Williams might be driven to do almost anything, make almost any sacrifice, in order to keep her payments up to date. There is, thus, more than a hint of coercion about the cross-collateral arrangement—not physical coercion, to be sure, but something rather similar in its impact on Ms. Williams. Viewed from this standpoint—and, of course, depending on the circumstances—the word "unconscionable" seems particularly apt.

C. Public Policy

Restatement section 178 provides that a promise or other contractual term may be held unenforceable on grounds of "public policy" if it appears to conflict with clear legislative intent or is contrary to principles of equity and fairness that are well recognized and of long standing. As distinguished from contracts void on grounds of "unconscionability," "public policy" operates as a defense against enforcement even where the disadvantaged party was fully aware of the term in question and apparently assented to it with full knowledge of the intended consequences. The question is whether the contract term itself meets the standard of "legality."

General statements not being very useful in this area, I can really do no better than to illustrate the scope and limit of the public policy "doctrine" by describing two familiar casebook decisions that focus on much the same public policy issue, namely, whether a seller or lessor of property can immunize itself, by contract, from tort claims for personal injury caused by its own act of negligence. The first case, *Henningsen*, was regarded as "path breaking" in its day; the second, *O'Callaghan*, also beat a path of its own but in the opposite direction.

In *Henningsen v. Bloomfield Motors, Inc.*[13], the plaintiff bought a new Plymouth from the defendant-dealer. The steering mechanism failed ten days after the car was delivered and the plaintiff's wife was injured. Plaintiff and his wife brought suit against the defendant and against Chrysler, the manufacturer, for breach of the warranty of merchantability, that is, a warranty against defective manufacture. Absent any contractual disclaimer, an implied warranty of merchantability would, under the law, entitle a car buyer to damages for personal injury even if (in the Court's words) "due care were used in the manufacturing process." Seeking to avoid such liability, the defendants pointed out that the purchase agreement did, in fact, specifically disclaim all warranties, express or implied, other than liability to replace defective parts for a period of 90 days following purchase. While the defendants presumably stood ready to replace the defective steering mechanism, they contended that the contract effectively eliminated any further liability, including liability for personal injuries. The contract was, of course, a standardized purchase agreement, with the warranty disclaimer (really, an implied disclaimer) printed in small type on the back of the form.

The Supreme Court of New Jersey held for the plaintiffs— meaning, in the circumstance, that the contractual disclaimer, insofar as it sought to defend the car-maker against personal injury claims, would be regarded as void. It was true, said the Court, that competent parties are free, in general, to make any lawful agreement (of which this was surely one), and that anyone who signs a contract without reading it carefully does so at his peril. Here, however, overriding considerations of public policy–in effect, the need "to protect the ordinary man against the loss of important rights"—made it appropriate to disregard the conventional premises of laissez-faire and to treat the warranty disclaimer as a nullity.

13.   32 N.J. 358, 161 A.2d 69 (1960).

Need for protection of "ordinary" men arose for several reasons, in the Court's view, but among the most important appears to have been the quasi-monopoly position occupied by the Big Three auto manufacturers (GM, Ford and Chrysler), which together produced 93.5% of the passenger cars sold in this country (in 1958). The same standard form warranty disclaimer was used by all three, or by their dealers, so that a car buyer could neither negotiate nor shop elsewhere for better terms. A car buyer "must take or leave the automobile on the warranty terms dictated by the maker. He cannot turn to a competitor for better security." There was, in effect, a kind of "duress" in the sense that the desired goods would simply be withheld by the auto cartel had the plaintiffs been unwilling to swallow the boiler-plate contract terms as well.

In *O'Callaghan v. Waller & Beckwith Realty Co.*[14], the plaintiff, presumably an older lady, was a tenant in defendant's apartment building. Crossing the courtyard she tripped over a patch of broken pavement, was injured, and subsequently sued the defendant for negligence in failing to maintain the property in safe condition. This sad event took place during a period of acute housing shortage in Chicago following World War II, and at a time when the State rent-control law set a strict maximum on apartment rents, including the apartment leased to the plaintiff. There appears to have been no question about the defendant's negligence in failing to meet its safe maintenance obligation; indeed the jury awarded the plaintiff damages of $14,000. On appeal, the defendant showed that the plaintiff's lease contained a specific exculpation clause, which (in the Court's words) "clearly purports to relieve the lessor and its agents from any liability to the lessee for personal injury or property damage caused by any act or neglect of the lessor or its agents." Conceding that the quoted term, if valid, would bar her recovery, the plaintiff argued "vigorously" that such a clause was contrary to public policy, and hence invalid, in a lease of residential property.

The Illinois Court held for the defendant (with two dissents). Treating a negligence-exculpation clause as contrary to public policy would be appropriate in a setting in which one party has a dominant position relative to the other–employer-employee, for example–but the relationship between landlord and tenant does not have that characteristic, even during a period of acute housing shortage. Landlords compete with one another–there are, literally, thousands of them–as do competing housing accommodations of all kinds. And shortages do not last forever. The legislature apparently

14.   15 Ill.2d 436, 155 N.E.2d 545 (1959).

did what it thought essential to cope with the housing shortage when it adopted rent control; it was not the Court's business to extend that legislation by prohibiting exculpatory clauses when the legislature evidently deemed such a prohibition unnecessary. Finally, nothing was presented at the trial to show that Mrs. O'Callaghan was concerned about the exculpation clause in the lease or that she ever attempted to negotiate with the defendant about modifying or eliminating it.

The *Henningsen* and *O'Callaghan* decisions make an obvious contrast both as to legal analysis and as to what constitutes compelling "public policy." From the standpoint of legal analysis, the New Jersey Court in *Henningsen* began by finding that the implicit warranty disclaimer was so well hidden that the car-buyer could not have understood and "assented" to it no matter how carefully he read the contract. But even if the plaintiff had understood the disclaimer or were somehow deemed to have assented, there would apparently have remained the larger public policy question of whether a car-maker *could* properly disclaim liability for personal injury resulting from defective manufacture. The context, as the Court stressed, was one in which the big three car companies held a quasi-monopoly position in the auto business, leaving the car-buyer with no choice among products and no bargaining power apart from simply going without a car. The Court did not and, I suppose, could not foresee that foreign auto imports, especially Japanese imports but others as well, would within a very few years virtually revolutionize the industry and eliminate the quasi-monopoly of the big three. Whether that development, if foreseen, would have altered the Court's view of public policy one doesn't know, but probably not. The Court made it plain that manufacturers of cars and presumably other "dangerous instruments" cannot free themselves from liability for personal injury by warranty disclaimer, apparently without concern about how or whether current market conditions might change in the future.

In *O'Callaghan*, the exculpation provision in the plaintiff's apartment lease was clear and explicit. And hence binding on the plaintiff. "Freedom of contract," the Court declared, "is basic to our law." Whether Mrs. O'Callaghan was likely to have read and understood the meaning of the exculpatory clause was apparently irrelevant. More important was the fact that—at least in normal times—a tenant's rent would be lower by reason of that provision than if the landlord accepted liability for negligence. The tenant thus benefitted from the exculpatory provision, whether aware of it or not. To be sure, a thoughtful tenant, once aware, would presumably feel it necessary to buy personal accident insurance, the cost of which would be a set-off against the lower rent. The landlord (again in normal times) would have made the very same calculation, *i.e.*, whether the saving of premiums for liability insurance exceeded the loss in rental income. If the two parties reached different results as to net benefit, they would proceed to bargain with each other to the usual point of price efficiency. That familiar, textbook paradigm would surely apply to a *commercial* lessee–and if so, why not to Mrs. O'Callaghan? As to public policy, the Illinois Court evidently viewed the immediate post-war housing shortage as a short-term condition that would in time be relieved by new home construction. Hence it was not an appropriate context for the creation of an enduring legal rule that would continue to govern landlord-tenant relations long after the housing shortage ceased to exist. A legislature that enacts a rent-control law can terminate rent control when the housing shortage ends; but a court that prohibits exculpatory provisions on grounds of public policy would thereby establish a precedent difficult to reverse when conditions altered–as, in time, they did.

Chapter 5

CONTRACT INTERPRETATION: PAROL EVIDENCE; TRADE USAGE; GAP FILLERS

A good deal has been said already—more or less by the way—about contract interpretation, and I somewhat doubt whether a bare recital of general principles, apart from the particular contexts in which they might apply, is really very useful. Restatement Section 201(1) quite sensibly provides that where the parties attach the same meaning to the terms used in their agreement, the interpretation of the agreement should be in accordance with that meaning even if a third party, presumably viewing the matter from an objective standpoint, might interpret the contract language differently. The converse is also true: whatever an objective observer might think, if the contracting parties attach different meanings to the same term, then neither is bound by the understanding of the other unless one of them knew or had reason to know what the other understood the disputed term to mean. Apart from these "rules"—which properly emphasize a subjective, party-oriented approach to contract interpretation—neither the Restatement nor the decisional law or commentary offers much that goes beyond the invocation of ordinary good sense in dealing with the vagaries of language. In any case, as is often pointed out, problems of contract interpretation are far more likely to arise because of clumsiness and ineptitude on the part of the draftsmen or the contracting parties themselves than because of philosophic differences about the meaning of meaning. A further comment on this topic appears at page 117.

In *Frigaliment Importing Company v. B.N.S. International Sales Corp.,*[1] the issue (the Court said) "is, what is chicken?" The plaintiff, a Swiss importer, sent an order to the defendant, an American exporter, for 75,000 pounds of "Grade A Chicken" at $33 per 100 pounds. The defendant, allegedly a newcomer to the poultry trade, accepted the order and promptly shipped. When the merchandise arrived in Switzerland, however, instead of the tender young "broilers and fryers" which plaintiff intended to resell to its

---

1. 190 F.Supp. 116 (S.D.N.Y.1960). And see Perillo, *The Origins of the Objective Theory of Contract Formation and Interpretation*, 69 Fordham L.Rev. 427 (2000); Young, *Equivocation in the Making of Agreements*, 64 Columbia L.Rev. 619 (1964).

customers—presumably retailers and restaurants—and which plaintiff clearly had in mind when it forwarded its purchase order, the shipment was found to consist of stringy old stewing chicken— good for boiling up in a soup with noodles and a chunk of carrot, but entirely unsuitable for the grill or the lightly buttered frying pan. A second shipment, also of stewing chicken, was apparently aborted by the defendant when it realized that plaintiff would not accept the merchandise. Plaintiff sued for breach of warranty under the equivalent of UCC 2–313(1)(b), which provides that "Any description of the goods which is made part of the basis of the bargain creates an express warranty that the goods shall conform to the description."

Holding for the defendant, Judge Friendly found that the term "chicken", not otherwise specified, could properly be taken to refer to "stewing chicken or fowl," and that the defendant, in accepting the original order, actually believed that stewing chicken was the product it was asked to deliver. Defendant's subjective belief would not be significant, said the Court, if it did not coincide with an objective meaning of the disputed term, but in fact the regulations issued by the Department of Agriculture included six classes of poultry under the heading "Chicken"; to-wit, Broiler or fryer, Roaster, Capon, Stag, Hen or stewing chicken, and Cock or old rooster. Since defendant's subjective intent thus agreed with the relevant definition—or at least with one such definition—there was no breach of warranty. To be sure, the plaintiff wanted and expected broilers or fryers (not Hen, Stag or anything else). However, the burden was on the plaintiff to show that it had used and communicated the term "chicken" in the narrower rather than the broader sense; and that burden it failed to carry.

Accepting (since we must) that the defendant did not know and had no reason to know what sort of merchandise the plaintiff customarily imported, the reasoning (if not the outcome) in *Frigaliment* still seems rather doubtful. The Court did not really answer the question, "what is 'chicken'?" Rather, it answered the question, "is stewing chicken 'chicken'?", which is a somewhat different question. Thus, stewing chicken *is* "chicken" under the Department regulations, but so are broilers and fryers, and no real explanation is given in Judge Friendly's opinion for preferring the defendant's subjective/objective understanding to the plaintiff's. Plaintiff was no more or less accurate and precise than defendant in its understanding of the critical term, and its own subjective intent was just as firmly fixed. The Court may have meant to imply that offerors generally bear a heavier obligation to be clear and specific about contract language than offerees, but the respective roles of offeror and offeree in a fast-moving commodities market are difficult to separate and the opinion does not suggest any particular reason why a greater "burden" should be imposed on one market operator than the other.

Probably (as Judge Friendly indicated in a later decision), *Frigaliment* should have been regarded as another instance of "lack of mutual assent" and decided by reference to the doctrine of the *Peerless* case.[2] Importer and exporter obviously attached different meanings to the term "chicken," neither (apparently) having reason to know about the particular meaning intended by the other. The legal result, then, is simply a failure of "consensus" and neither party has a claim based on "contract". Under these circumstances, if the *Peerless* doctrine applies, the consequence should be to nullify all outstanding obligations: there is no breach of warranty on defendant's part, but plaintiff has no duty to accept and pay for any undelivered merchandise. The actual outcome in *Frigaliment* is thus, probably, unobjectionable. Since the first shipment of stewing chicken was apparently accepted, paid for and resold to customers, that transaction as a practical matter was irreversible and any resulting loss (e.g., refunds to customers) had to be borne by the plaintiff. With respect to shipping costs, spoilage, etc. incurred in connection with the second shipment, the dollar loss no doubt fell on the defendant. Both parties thus suffered some financial damage, and that is sad, but as neither had a contract claim against the other—there being no contract—the law itself provides no remedy.[3]

Rightly or wrongly reasoned, *Frigaliment,* like *Peerless,* highlights the fallibility or variability of language itself and the possibility that the parties to a contract may use the same words to express quite different aims and expectations. At some point, it appears, the element of misunderstanding or ambiguity is simply overwhelming and there is nothing sufficiently common or mutual to make a contract out of.

---

2. Discussed in Chapter 3, above.

3. Question: How did the two parties in *Frigaliment* manage to misunderstand each other so completely? It's worth noting that communications between plaintiff and defendant were largely carried on through an intermediary—one Stovicek, a minor Czech official who was in New York to attend a trade fair—rather than directly by the parties themselves. Just how Stovicek got involved we don't know. But since he brought them together in the first place, presumably receiving a commission from one or both, you would think that Stovicek's testimony as to each party's probable understanding would be highly relevant. Is it possible that Stovicek, eager to get the deal done, told the Swiss importer one thing and the American exporter something else? A wild surmise, perhaps, but who knows. Having quickly and quietly returned to Bratislava (or wherever), Stovicek was apparently out of reach when the case came to trial.

That said, I should emphasize that the latter outcome
and unusual. Generally speaking, contract law dislikes bre__
and frustration and prefers instead, where reasonable, to construct
an enforceable contract out of whatever raw materials of intention
the parties have made available. Where, for example, the parties
have failed or omitted to specify a "term" in what would otherwise
be a binding agreement—even so vital a term as price—the courts
may supply the missing element by resorting to trade usage or to
any prior course of dealing between the parties "which is fairly to
be regarded as establishing a common basis of understanding. . . ."[4]
While the courts will not enforce a mere "agreement to agree",
there is a tendency—supported by both the UCC and the Restatement—to find an understanding by reasonable reference to custom
or to the parties' previous conduct. In *Frigaliment,* by contrast,
there had been no prior course of dealing between plaintiff and
defendant, and evidently trade usage was too various to be relied
upon.

The discussion that follows takes up three further problems of
contract interpretation (out of many that could be chosen) which
likewise involve ambiguity of expression and intent. The first—the
parol evidence rule—concerns the relationship between spoken
agreements and written contracts. The issue, briefly stated, is
whether written documents clear on their face should be subject to
expansion or contraction by reference to prior oral agreements
which are, of course, invisible. The second concerns trade usage.
The third—exclusive dealing arrangements and other flexible commitments—returns to the question of how to enforce agreements
that are indefinite or that fail to make provision for a critical
change in circumstances.

A.   The Parol Evidence Rule

When applicable, the parol evidence rule renders unenforceable
oral agreements entered into prior to the adoption of a written
contract. Restatement Section 213 expresses the substantive concept in terms of "discharge": a written agreement that is found to
be "completely integrated"—that represents a full and final embod-
iment of the parties' understanding—effectively discharges any
prior agreement that falls within its scope. The consequence in
evidentiary terms is that proof of the alleged prior agreement is
inadmissible and cannot be placed before the trier of fact, which
might of course be a jury otherwise inclined to sympathy for the

4. Restatement Section 223; and see
UCC 1–205, 2–208.

alleged promisee. The judge himself makes the first and critical determination as to whether the written contract is in fact an integrated agreement. If it is, then, as stated, the prior oral agreement is discharged and evidence thereof is excluded for lack of relevance.

The purpose of the rule is apparent. Since the completion and execution of a written contract is typically the concluding point in the bargaining process, one's ordinary expectation is that the document itself will contain all the conscious and important elements of the deal. All sorts of things might have been said in the course of negotiations; tentative understandings might have been reached on particular issues but then later dropped or traded away or even forgotten. Once reduced to writing, however, the terms of agreement can be reviewed and revised more or less at leisure and finally articulated to everyone's satisfaction. The parol evidence rule assumes that the formal writing reflects the parties' minds at a point of maximum resolution and, hence, that duties and restrictions that do not appear in the written document, even though apparently accepted at an earlier stage, were not intended by the parties to survive. In addition, and quite apart from the survival of matters discarded in the course of negotiations, there is the obvious danger of outright fraud. If the contracting parties are entirely free to introduce evidence of prior oral agreements, what is there to stop an unscrupulous party from offering, or threatening to offer, evidence of a prior agreement that is altogether specious?

But suppose that none of these illicit factors is present. Suppose the parties used the written contract to express the central elements of their agreement—price, delivery date, identity of the property to be transferred—but assumed that various other obligations, mutually agreed upon and very much part of the deal, would be met in good faith and without a need for lengthy written elaboration. Even more simply, suppose they have a written agreement covering one transaction and a prior oral agreement on another. If applicable in these circumstances, the parol evidence rule would operate not as a safeguard against false or erroneous claims but as a rule of forfeiture, which would clearly be unfair and undesirable. While it might be simplest to adopt a very strict exclusionary rule where prior oral agreements are concerned, the consequences in a given case—one in which there really is no doubt about the parties' intent—could be harsh. It is not obvious, moreover, what a very strict rule would actually consist of, unless it took the form of a universal statute of frauds which permitted enforcement *only* with respect to written contracts. Short of doing that, the need is for an exclusionary principle that leaves room for

judgment, good sense, sound discretion and similar sterli
attributes. As the cases next discussed should illustrate,
evidence rule, in requiring that the pivotal question
gration" be resolved initially and as a matter of law, pro
courts, including the appellate courts, with a very con......aole
measure of flexibility. This, however, may also explain why the rule
is commonly characterized as "murky".

In *Mitchill v. Lath*,[5] the plaintiff entered into a written contract to buy the defendants' farm for $8,400, intending to use the
property as a summer vacation home. The contract, which contained "various provisions usual in such papers", appeared complete on its face, but plaintiff asserted and apparently could prove
beyond a doubt that defendants had orally promised, as part of the
transaction, to remove an "ice house"—an unsightly ramshackle
structure—which belonged to defendants and stood in plain view on
a neighbor's land across the road. Having received their money and
delivered a deed to the farm, however, defendants refused to keep
their promise as to the ice house, and plaintiff sued for specific
performance.

Holding for the defendants, the Court (with two dissents)
found that the oral agreement was inadmissible—really, unenforceable—under the parol evidence rule. The rule, said the Court in
effect, permits admission in evidence of an oral agreement made
prior to the adoption of a written contract only if (a) such oral
agreement is collateral in form (i.e., capable of being expressed in a
separate agreement) and does not contradict the terms of the
written contract, and (b) the written contract fails to fully integrate
and embody the parties' understanding. A prior oral agreement to
sell separate property for an independent consideration is obviously
admissible; a prior agreement to pay more or less than the price
named in the written contract for the very thing conveyed thereby
is obviously not. The hard case, of course, is one in which the prior
oral agreement *adds* to the obligations of one of the parties rather
than contradicting a written term, but at the same time plainly
falls within the scope of the written contract because it relates to
the same subject-matter. Such was the case at hand: defendants'
promise to remove the ice house could have been expressed in a
separate agreement and it did not directly contradict anything in
the written contract; yet it would have added materially to the
defendants' costs by depriving them of the value of the ice house,

---

5. 247 N.Y. 377, 160 N.E. 646
(1928), discussed in Weiskopf, *Supple-
menting Written Agreements: Restating
the Parol Evidence Rule in Terms of*   *Credibility and Relative Fault*, 34 Emory
L.J. 93 (1985). And see, Kniffin, *A New
Trend in Contract Interpretation*, 74
Ore. L. Rev. 643 (1995).

which they apparently operated as a business, plus the expense of removing the structure itself. Ultimately, the issue depended on whether the detailed written contract would naturally appear to an "inquirer" to be complete and final with respect to the conditions governing the sale of the farm. At least to one inquirer—the Court majority—the contract did indeed appear to be complete and final; hence, the oral agreement could not be admitted in evidence. Pretty clearly, the majority felt that an outcome favorable to the plaintiff would signal a substantial relaxation of the parol evidence rule. That rule was "a wise one," however, and it should not be abandoned, "[n]otwithstanding an injustice here and there...."

Wise or otherwise, the words last quoted describe the result in *Mitchill* all too aptly, since it is (i) certain that the Laths did in fact promise to remove the ice house and (ii) very unlikely that the written contract was intended to eliminate that undertaking. The majority really questioned neither proposition. Rather, its concern was to support the safeguard-function of the parol evidence rule by emphasizing the preeminence of written over oral contracts even though the result might well be unjust. Read strictly, *Mitchill* holds that prior oral agreements are enforceable only if they entail separate consideration on the part of the promisee; that is, a promise to pay additionally for some further service. If not, the written contract is nearly always decisive of the parties' obligations.

The *Mitchill* case can be compared with an equally well-known California decision, *Masterson v. Sine,*[6] which appears to treat the parol evidence rule more as an opportunity than a limitation. The Mastersons in 1958 sold their ranch to the Sines—Mr. Masterson's sister and brother-in-law—for $50,000. Under the terms of the deed by which the property was conveyed, the Mastersons reserved an option to repurchase the property at any time within the next 10 years for an amount equal to the original purchase price, $50,000, plus the cost of any ranch improvements made by the Sines. Mr. Masterson having subsequently been adjudged a bankrupt, the present action was brought by his trustee in bankruptcy to establish the trustee's right to exercise the option and obtain title to the ranch, now undoubtedly worth much more than $50,000. The Sines, with loyal support from Masterson himself, asserted that the parties had orally agreed that the repurchase option was nonassignable. It could be exercised by the Mastersons personally, according to the alleged oral agreement, but it could not be transferred to or exercised by Masterson's creditors (or by the trustee on their behalf) or indeed by any other third party.

6. 68 Cal.2d 222, 65 Cal.Rptr. 545, 436 P.2d 561 (1968).

Speaking through Justice Traynor, the Court held that evidence of the non-assignability restriction was admissible under (or despite) the parol evidence rule. The Court conceded that when a written contract is completely integrated, parol evidence cannot be admitted to vary its terms. However, it explicitly rejected the idea that admissibility depends on whether the written contract appears complete on its face. Even if it does, evidence of a collateral oral agreement should be excluded only when the fact finder is likely to be misled. The credibility of the proffered evidence, therefore, not the appearance of the written document, is the basis for decision. If under the circumstances the oral agreement could, or might naturally, have been entered into separately from the written agreement, then proof of such oral agreement should be permitted so as to avoid frustrating the parties' real intent. To be sure, the deed which the Mastersons delivered to the Sines specifically set forth the terms of Masterson's repurchase option. Hence an inquirer might well suppose that any additional terms, such as non-assignability, would naturally appear in the same place. Here, however, the writing was in a standardized form which did not readily lend itself to the insertion of additional terms, and this made it less likely that the special conditions agreed to would necessarily be included in that document. Moreover, the parties to the sale were family members who would presumably feel confident that they could rely on the spoken promises; they were, as well, inexperienced in land transactions and unaware of the disadvantages of failing to put their whole agreement in the deed. Given these circumstances, it could reasonably be said that a collateral understanding such as that alleged might naturally have been added through the medium of a separate oral agreement.

The decision in *Masterson* reflects an understandable solicitude for the Sines. A contrary outcome would have meant that the ranch—which may have been the Sine family's principal source of livelihood—would have been swallowed up in large part by Masterson's business creditors, persons with whom the Sines had had no dealings and to whom they owed nothing whatever. The Court viewed Masterson's repurchase option as a clumsy device for keeping the property in the family, and it does not appear that Masterson ever represented to his creditors that the value of the option could be regarded as part of his personal net worth. On the other hand, if you really believe that brother and sister overtly and consciously agreed that the option was non-assignable, you will, I think, believe anything. Actually (or at least most likely), they never mentioned or thought about the question of assignability at all. If that question *had* been brought to their attention no doubt they would have so agreed, but then, surely, they would have taken the trouble to add the necessary few words—"The option reserved to the Sellers herein shall not be assignable without the express consent of the Purchasers."—to the written contract itself. Of course, neither I nor Masterson's trustee was present when the sale of the ranch was negotiated, so nobody will ever know for certain. The plaintiff-trustee presumably gave up his attempt to draw the option into the bankrupt's estate once the Court had decided that evidence of the oral agreement should be admitted and made no subsequent effort to contest the factual issue at trial. Such a contest would have been useless in any case, since all of the active parties to the negotiations were on the defendants' side of the lawsuit.[7]

The Court in *Masterson* evidently didn't (or wouldn't) share my doubts about the credibility of the prior oral agreement. Instead, having determined as a first step that the evidence of such prior agreement was credible, it then went on to conclude that the written contract could not be regarded as an integrated document. As suggested, the approach thus adopted is essentially contrary to that taken in *Mitchill*, where the question to be decided *first* was whether the written contract appeared to be completely integrated: since it did so appear, proof of the prior oral agreement, although entirely credible, was held inadmissible as a matter of law.

In evaluating the two cases, I think many would feel that the *Masterson* decision, however desirable in outcome, renders the parol evidence rule somewhat circular in application. A prior oral agreement must be excluded if the written contract is found to be a complete integration; whether the written contract *is* completely integrated, however, depends on whether there is credible evidence of a prior oral agreement. Complete integration thus becomes a function not of the written contract but of the quality of the parol evidence—evidence which the written contract, if completely integrated, would effectively exclude. The *Mitchill* decision avoids the same element of circularity by assuming that the written contract is normally complete with respect to obligations falling within its

---

7. Why was *Mrs.* Masterson a plaintiff in the case (students sometimes ask)? Likely answer: to protect her half-interest in the ranch. The opinion states that Mr. and Mrs. M owned the ranch as tenants-in-common; hence Mrs. M had a half-interest in the repurchase option as well. If the Court had held the option to be assignable and the ranch were finally sold by the trustee, Mrs. M. (who apparently had not filed for bankruptcy) would want to be in the position of having exercised her own half-share of the option. She would then be entitled as half-owner of the ranch to half of any sale proceeds above the $50,000 exercise price.

The Court's decision, of course, left the whole matter in *status quo*, which was probably the outcome that Mrs. M, no less than Mr. M, preferred.

scope (i.e., not supported by a separate consider
evidence of a prior oral agreement must be excluded
credible. As the case itself well illustrates, however
to be paid for whatever certainty and clarity is th
Laths plainly did agree to remove that miserable ic
hard to respect an exclusionary rule which, in effect, allowed them
to break their promise.

Choosing between *Masterson* (which admitted a prior agreement that was probably never made) and *Mitchill* (which excluded
a prior agreement that was almost certainly made) is not a comfortable task. In making that choice, however, I suppose we should
remind ourselves that the larger aim of contract law is to support
and implement the common process of exchange by which private
persons seek to generate welfare gains. The enforcement of contracts is the principal contribution that the law makes in this
connection and nothing could be further from the purpose than a
discharge rule that operates to withhold enforcement when the
parties really have agreed. It is also true that the existence of an
agreement needs to be verified before it can be enforced. Agreement
by spoken rather than written word often makes the task of
verification troublesome and costly—especially so when the oral
contract appears to compete with a written contract—and it is fair
enough to impose a heavy burden of proof on the proponent. But a
rule of automatic exclusion—which, as in *Mitchill,* minimizes enforcement costs at the cost of enforcement itself—elevates the less
important value of the two and hence, on balance, seems undesirable. Accordingly, one opts for *Masterson* in the end, though not
without misgivings.

Written contracts frequently contain an explicit merger or
integration clause stating, for example, that "this contract embodies the entire understanding between the parties, and there are no
verbal agreements or representations in connection therewith".
Despite such language, courts following the *Masterson* concept have
been willing to admit evidence of a prior oral condition on the
ground that the "true intent" of the parties is always the ultimate
touchstone. In determining intent, "it is necessary to look not only
to the written instrument, but to the circumstances surrounding its
execution", which may of course show that a prior oral understanding was intended to survive. Justice Traynor himself indicated that
if a merger clause had been included in Masterson's deed, this
might have helped to resolve the assignability issue in the trustee's
favor. Perhaps; yet one's intuition is that nothing short of an
express contractual provision stating that the option was freely
assignable would have won the day for the trustee.

The parol evidence rule has no application to oral agreements made *subsequent* to the execution of a written contract, although the problem of proof and verification seems no less acute. As a consequence, written contracts (especially in the construction field) often contain a safeguard in the form of a specific clause denying effect to any later oral modification. Does that take care of the problem? Or can the clause itself be waived or orally modified? The question, one of some difficulty, is discussed at p. 142, below.

B. Trade Usage

On a slightly different but related topic, the UCC[8] (and likewise the Restatement) makes it clear that the parol evidence rule shall not be applied so as to exclude evidence of "usage of trade" or prior "course of dealing", either or both of which may be drawn upon to "explain or supplement" the written contract. The notion, as suggested earlier, is that trade usage and course of dealing are interpretive elements that help the court to understand the contracting parties' true intent, rather than being additional terms whose admission as such would offend the parol evidence restriction. But where trade usage and course of dealing are inconsistent with the *express* terms of the contract, then, to be sure, the express terms "control."

All this sounds quite reasonable. It does, however, raise a question that appears to be logically prior to the interpretive exercise itself. Thus, how do we decide whether a term in the contract is one that *needs* to be explained or supplemented by resort to trade usage and course of dealing—or whether, on the other hand, that term is complete and sufficient as it stands and fully reflects the parties' intentions, with trade usage and other extra-contractual sources being irrelevant?

In the *Columbia Nitrogen*[9] case, the plaintiff, Royster Co., agreed to sell, and the defendant agreed to buy, 31,000 tons of phosphate every year for three years at an average price of about $50 a ton. The market price of phosphate "plunged precipitously" almost at once. The plaintiff made voluntary price concessions to the defendant for the first few monthly shipments but then insisted on being paid for the rest at the $50 price agreed to by the parties and required by the contract. When the defendant refused to accept delivery, the plaintiff sued.

---

8. UCC 2–202, 2–208; Restatement Section 203.

9. *Columbia Nitrogen Corp. v. Royster Co.*, 451 F.2d 3 (4th Cir. 1971).

Just a garden-variety breach, one would suppose, entitling the plaintiff to damages equal to the difference between $50 and the much lower spot-market price at which the plaintiff was finally compelled to sell its product. Not that simple as it turned out. On appeal from a decision for the plaintiff, the Fourth Circuit reversed and remanded on the ground that the defendant should have been allowed to introduce evidence of trade usage and course of dealing to show that price and quantity adjustments in the face of declining markets were customary and usual among buyers and sellers in the fertilizer business. Such evidence, said the Court, could be used to "supplement" and "explain" the written contract and would therefore be "consistent" with its express terms, including the specific price and quantity terms mentioned above.

But as those terms were entirely plain and unambiguous—31,000 tons at $50 a ton—the decision in *Columbia Nitrogen* is a bit difficult to accept. The difficulty (in the view of some) is that admitting evidence of "trade usage" had the effect (or could have the effect, depending on the remand) of entirely *eliminating* the price and quantity terms of the phosphate contract. Once trade usage was admitted in evidence as a source of "interpretation," the express terms of the contract could be wholly displaced and a "new" agreement substituted for the old—different price, different quantity—which, it is argued, goes too far when the justification for admitting trade usage is merely a change in market price, a risk to which every contract that involves a forward exchange is subject.[10]

Presumably, however, the decision reflects a feeling on the Court's part that a "precipitous plunge" was really not within the contemplation of the parties at the time they made their bargain, and in a sense fell outside the normal range of enforcement despite the general law of contract damages. The Court did not, of course, say how much of a price or quantity adjustment, if any at all, might be appropriate. It did insist, however, that trade usage and course of dealing must be taken into account in determining whether the parties, acting within the conventions of the industry, would have expected an adjustment to be made in the event of a material change in market conditions.

There is no report of a decision on remand, I believe, and in the end the parties probably settled their dispute by splitting the market loss on some basis rather than risking a new trial and an

10. Goldberg, *Framing Contract Law: An Economic Perspective* 183 (2007). And see, Kostritsky, *Judicial Incorporation of Trade Usages: A Functional Solution to the Opportunism Problem,* 39 U. Conn. L. Rev. 451 (2006); Snyder, *Language and Formalities in Commercial Contracts: A Defense of Custom and Conduct,* 54 SMU L. Rev. 617 (2001).

all-or-nothing outcome. It is at least possible that the Fourth Circuit, having in mind a rough idea of fairness and compromise, hoped to promote exactly that result; namely, that the plaintiff would be willing to share the pain and accept a reasonable settlement once the defendant was given some legal means of getting out from under the express terms of the contract.

Southern Concrete Services v. Mableton Contractors, Inc.[11], a case somewhat resembling *Columbia Nitrogen*, takes a very different approach to UCC 2–202. Southern, a supplier of construction materials, agreed to sell approximately 70,000 cubic yards of concrete to Mableton for use in the construction of the building foundation of a local power plant. The contract stipulated that "No conditions which are not incorporated in this contract will be recognized", though it made no specific reference to trade usage or to UCC 2–202. Mableton accepted and paid for some 12,000 cubic yards, but it refused to accept more for the rather compelling reason that it actually *needed* no more to complete its work for the power plant. Whereupon Southern sued for breach, claiming costs incurred plus lost profits. Relying on UCC 2–202, Mableton offered to introduce evidence that, as a matter of custom and trade usage, the quantity stipulated in a concrete-supply contract was subject to renegotiation, presumably in the light of the contractor's actual requirements, which might be over-or under-estimated depending on circumstances.

The Court held for the plaintiff-seller. Trade usage, it agreed, "should be considered in determining what variations in specifications is considered acceptable ... but this court does not believe that section 2–202 was meant to invite a frontal assault on the essential terms of a clear and explicit contract." The parties to a sale of construction materials would often prefer to work out minor disagreements relating to quantity and the like through compromise and settlement—presumably that is the practice in the trade. Yet each party knows that it may resort to strict enforcement of its contract rights in the event of a "major departure" from its contract obligations by the other party. Attempting to cancel more than 80% of the quantity agreed to could not, in the Court's view, be regarded as anything less than a "major departure" and went well beyond the minor quantity variations that are contemplated by trade usage.

A stern and forceful decision, approved by many. As usual, however, we are left with a puzzle: How could the defendant, an experienced contractor, have overestimated its concrete require-

---

11. 407 F.Supp. 581 (N.D. Ga. 1975).

ments by *more than 80%*? Far too much, obviously, to
of a mistake or an error of judgment on the part of th
project estimators. My guess: the defendant's clien
plant—decided for some reason (loss of funding, probably) ᴄᴄ
back its building plans very sharply. But it made that decision *after*
the defendant placed its 70,000–unit order with the plaintiff. The
defendant, then, was left with a need for only 12,000 units of
concrete, and apparently had no contractual recourse against the
power plant. If that guess is right or nearly so, the trade usage
argument might gain a bit more force than the Court allowed it. If
supported by custom and practice, the argument would be that a
significant and *unexpected* cut-back by the builder's client justifies a
corresponding cut-back by the builder in the quantity of materials
ordered from his suppliers. Large-scale changes of plan do occur
from time to time–perhaps especially when the client is a public
utility or a government agency–and all parties, suppliers as well as
contractors, are then expected to cooperate, and usually do cooperate, by modifying their contractual claims accordingly. That (it
would at least be argued) is the well-recognized practice in the
industry.

The Court in *Southern Concrete* never tells us just exactly what
the defendant's excluded evidence consisted of, which makes it
difficult to judge whether the exclusion was justified under 2–202.
If the "story" told in the preceding paragraph is roughly true—and
what other story could there be?—then evidence of trade usage to
"supplement" the written contract would seem defensible.

The apparent conflict between *Columbia Nitrogen* and *Southern Concrete* suggests that "trade usage" gets a lot more respect in
the former decision than in the latter, which, as it happens, largely
echoes a spirited debate among Contracts specialists on how best to
approach the interpretation of contract terms when a dispute arises
between the parties.[11a] Briefly stated, some writers assert that the
better way to interpret contract terms is to read them literally and
without resort to surrounding context, including trade usage, especially where the parties to the contract are relatively sophisticated
and experienced. Other writers insist that "context," not only trade
usage but perhaps other background elements, should be liberally
taken into account in order to discover the parties' real intent. New
York courts (it is said) prefer to interpret contract terms "textual-
ly," that is, just as written, while California courts frequently make
use of "context" in resolving interpretative issues.

11a. Rehearsed in Schwartz & Scott,
Contracts Interpretation Redux, 119 Yale
L. J. 926 (2010).

Columbia Nitrogen and *Southern Concrete* pretty well represent the opposing sides in the "textual" versus "contextual" debate. The litigation in both cases obviously focused on the admissibility of trade usage evidence, that is, "context." *CN* let it in (but probably should have kept it out); *SC* kept it out (but maybe should have let it in). Actually, neither opinion is especially convincing (to the present writer), and neither is more convincing than the other.

C. Filling the Gaps: "Best Efforts" and Other Flexible Commitments

Contracts for the sale of goods are usually specific as to vital terms—price, quantity, date of delivery—so that the question of whether the parties have "performed" can be answered in a straightforward way. Under certain circumstances, however, it may be preferable, even necessary, to avoid specificity and to leave one or more terms at large. Exclusive dealing agreements, and likewise requirements and output contracts, are major examples. Such contracts typically obligate the parties to buy or sell certain goods or perform certain services at a stated price, but intentionally omit to specify the *quantity* of the goods to be purchased or delivered or the extent of the services to be performed. There may be good reasons for the omission—it is not merely an oversight—but the problem which then arises is how, indeed whether, the courts can enforce an undertaking or commitment that is indefinite on its face.

Best efforts. Exclusive dealing contracts, including distributorships and licensing agreements, are common commercial arrangements. A manufacturer, for example, enters into an agreement with a distributor (say a wholesaler) for the sale of a particular product. The distributor is to pay the manufacturer a flat price or perhaps a percentage of the sale price for each item sold. The distributor's right to sell the product is exclusive—the manufacturer cannot sell through any other distributor within a defined geographical area— and in turn the distributor agrees to use its "best efforts" or "reasonable efforts" to generate a high volume of activity. The agreement might be for a specific period or it might be left open as to duration with either party having a right to terminate on giving timely notice.

The business motives that lie behind an exclusive dealing agreement of this sort are easily inferred. From the manufacturer's standpoint the agreement has the advantage of providing instant distribution facilities, including a sales organization, advertising and other promotional know-how, without an out-of-pocket investment on the manufacturer's part. Sharing profits with the distributor, all things considered, is seen as less expensive than creating a sales division internally. From the distributor's standpoint the exclusivity feature makes it worthwhile to allocate funds for advertising and sales promotion without having to worry about the possibility that other sellers of the same product will enjoy the benefit of those outlays, in effect getting a free ride at the distributor's expense. For the same reason the distributor would want to be sure that the manufacturer's termination right was exercisable only after enough time had passed to allow the distributor to earn back its initial expenditures. The larger those expenditures, therefore, the longer the notice period demanded.

The unquantified element in an exclusive dealing agreement of this sort is, obviously, the distributor's promise to use best efforts in selling the product. Just how much the distributor will spend on advertising and precisely what proportion of its sales force will be employed in pushing this (as opposed to some other) manufacturer's product is nowhere specified, and it is conceivable that the distributor might determine that "best efforts" really means very little effort or at least much less than the manufacturer anticipated. Taken at face, the arrangement appears to be somewhat one-sided, which raises the threshold question whether the *fully* committed party—the manufacturer—has received a return promise that properly qualifies as "consideration."

In *Wood v. Lucy, Lady Duff-Gordon,*[10] the parties entered into a contract under which the plaintiff was given the exclusive right to license the use of the defendant's name in connection with the manufacture of dresses, hats, fabrics and the like. Defendant's opinions on women's fashions were then much in vogue, and it was expected that manufacturers and designers would pay handsome fees for her endorsements. The parties agreed to share all revenues equally. At some point, despite the grant of exclusive marketing rights to plaintiff, defendant began placing endorsements independently—in effect, went into the licensing business on her own—and plaintiff sued. The defense was that the contract lacked mutuality. Although the document said a great deal about how endorsements would be handled once they were placed and how revenues would be divided once they were received, it did not actually obligate the plaintiff to take any positive action whatever. Nowhere in the agreement, defendant argued, did plaintiff bind himself to do anything of an affirmative nature—his promise, if any, was illusory—and hence the grant of exclusive rights was without consideration.

10. 222 N.Y. 88, 118 N.E. 214 (1917).

Holding for the plaintiff, the New York Court of Appeals found that a promise on plaintiff's part to use "reasonable efforts" to generate license revenues was properly to be implied. While it did not appear in the contract in so many words, the promise and resulting obligation were unmistakably implicated by the document and by all the surrounding circumstances. That being so, there was a contract. "The law," said Judge Cardozo, "has outgrown its primitive stage of formalism when the precise word was the sovereign talisman, and every slip was fatal. . . . A promise may be lacking, and yet the whole writing may be 'instinct with an obligation,' imperfectly expressed. . . ."

Having thus concluded that a promise to use reasonable efforts could be inferred, the Court apparently also agreed that such a promise succeeds in supplying the needed element of mutuality. It follows that a *failure* on the part of a promisor to use reasonable efforts would be an actionable breach from the promisee's standpoint, which necessarily entails the further conclusion that "reasonable efforts" represents an enforceable standard of conduct. The latter, in a sense, is the boldest element in *Wood v. Lucy*. Having rather easily condemned the defendant for "primitive formalism," the Court might still have hesitated to accept as legally sufficient an implied duty that lacked quantification or other specific character. But it did not, and it appears that the courts now generally agree that a promise, express or implied, to use "reasonable efforts" or "best efforts" to merchandise products or pursue some other business objective creates an obligation that is substantial and legally enforceable against the promisor.

The holding in *Wood v. Lucy* is adopted by UCC 2–306(2) and presumably reflects the perception that the parties to an exclusive dealing arrangement—especially one that stretches out over an extended period—often wisely prefer to deal with future uncertainties through a process of flexible rather than fixed obligation. The distributor wishes to avoid being tied to a specific sales quota, because demand for the product—possibly a new product—is difficult to estimate. Accepting this, the manufacturer is prepared to allow the distributor to adapt to market conditions as they develop, but then counts on the distributor to perform in "good faith" by exerting its "best efforts" to promote sales. All of this seems sensible as far as it goes. It does, however, leave unanswered the question of how to measure or quantify the distributor's obligation when an actual dispute arises. As suggested above, the probable occasion for dispute is easy to imagine: the product sells poorly or, at least, not as well as expected, and the distributor, facing losses, decides to halt or reduce its sales and promotion activities. The manufacturer sues, and the issue is whether the distributor's good faith promise to use "best efforts" has been breached.

In *Bloor v. Falstaff Brewing Corp.,*[11] the Ballantine Beer Company sold its operating business—trademarks as well as various tangible assets—to Falstaff for $4 million plus a royalty of 50 cents for each barrel of Ballantine beer sold over the next six years. Falstaff promised to "use its best efforts to promote and maintain a high volume of sales" of Ballantine products and agreed also that if it should discontinue the sale of beer under the brand name "Ballantine" it would pay Ballantine liquidated damages of $1.1 million a year for the balance of the six-year period. Three years later, however, having sustained heavy operating losses, Falstaff came under new management which proceeded to slash its advertising outlays in an effort to return the company to profitability. That effort proved highly successful, but in the process of converting to a sort of generic beer operation Falstaff allowed the sale of Ballantine products to shrink very drastically in volume, though not to the point of triggering the liquidated damage clause.

Speaking through Judge Friendly, the Second Circuit affirmed the trial court's finding that Falstaff had breached its best efforts covenant. The 50–cent royalty, it said, was an essential part of the original purchase price and could not be slighted even if the defendant showed that there had been no discrimination in its treatment of the Ballantine label and that advertising outlays for the Falstaff label had been curtailed in the same fashion. Falstaff was not required "to spend itself into bankruptcy to promote the sales of Ballantine products," but it could not excuse or justify its failure to use best efforts to maintain a high volume of sales merely by asserting that it could *make* money by operating in a different way. As to the difficult but critical question of damages, the Court approved the trial court's finding that a reasonable estimate of lost sales could be made by comparing the sales of other actively advertised local beers, and then computing what Ballantine sales would have been if its brand had suffered no more than the same relative decline in volume.

The emphasis in Judge Friendly's opinion, as noted, is on the circumstance, or at least the supposition, that Falstaff's management had ruthlessly sacrificed Ballantine's interest to its own lust for profits. "Falstaff," the Court said, "simply didn't care about Ballantine's volume and was content to allow this to plummet so long as that course was best for Falstaff's overall profit pic-

11. 601 F.2d 609 (2d Cir.1979), discussed in Goldberg, *In Search of Best*   *Efforts: Reinterpreting Bloor v. Falstaff,* 44 St. Louis U.L.J. 1465 (2001).

ture. . . ." The Court did not dispute the fact that Falstaff would have suffered further operating losses if it had continued to spend money on television advertising for Ballantine, and we are left to wonder just how far in the direction of financial disaster—how far short of bankruptcy—Falstaff would have been required to go before the Court would concede that its "best efforts" obligation had been satisfied. Putting it differently, while the *Falstaff* opinion is plausible and even slightly ingenious, it really offers nothing more than an *ad hoc* solution to the particular dispute at hand. Best-efforts promisors are warned, in effect, that they cannot simply abandon their obligations when a better opportunity offers itself, but neither they nor their promisees get much in the way of guidance or instruction about how to identify the relevant limits.

Is there or can there be a determinate measure of "best efforts"? Suppose we assume that the parties actually sat down and bargained over the issue in advance. If they did, perhaps they would agree that the wisest course is for the best-efforts promisor to continue to promote and sell the product as long as the promisee's profits exceed the promisor's losses.[12] The promisee can then reimburse or compensate the promisor and still have something positive left over for itself. If, for example, Ballantine beer can be sold for $5.00 a barrel, and if the cost of manufacture and distribution is only $4.90, Falstaff ought to be willing to continue its efforts even though it will also have to pay Ballantine a 50–cent royalty— *provided* that Ballantine is prepared to reimburse Falstaff for the resulting 40–cent loss. Since Ballantine would then be left with a 10–cent profit, it would presumably accept the reimbursement obligation pretty gladly. Ballantine would be better off as long as the royalty it received exceeded the reimbursement that it had to pay. Falstaff would be no worse off, and the customary test of economic efficiency would be met. Using the same criterion, once Falstaff's production and selling costs increased to $5.00, its best-efforts obligation would be deemed exhausted. At that point its reimbursable loss—50 cents a barrel—would exactly equal the royalty, and there would be no benefit to either party in selling more Ballantine beer. Presumably, these results could be achieved even without a specific reimbursement requirement by providing for an appropriate scale-down of the royalty as production costs approached market price.

The contracting parties in *Falstaff* did not of course include any such carefully calibrated measure of "best efforts" in their

---

12. Goetz & Scott, *Principles of Relational Contracts,* 67 Va.L.Rev. 1089, 1149 (1981). And see, Gergen, *The Use* of Open Terms in Contracts, 92 Columbia L. Rev. 997 (1992).

contract. It is just possible, however, though if so only accidentally, that the Court's reliance on comparable brand activity produced a roughly equivalent result.

In a somewhat similar vein, and given the Court's emphasis on "profits", I think it is also possible to treat the *Falstaff* case as one that is concerned less with the meaning of "best efforts" than with the mutual obligations of partners. Thus, the contract between Ballantine and Falstaff can be regarded as an agreement to pool certain resources in a joint enterprise, with Ballantine contributing a (then) valuable brand-name and Falstaff contributing production and distribution facilities. Falstaff was to be responsible for management, with all the judgment and discretion such responsibility entails. The understanding between the two co-venturers was that they would share the revenues of the enterprise. Ballantine's share was to be measured by gross sales at the rate of 50 cents per unit, Falstaff was to receive the remainder. Unanticipated changes in the market led Falstaff to determine that the original business plan—to sell brand-name beer—should be discarded and a substitute plan— to sell generic beer—adopted in its place. In itself this decision seems to have been entirely sensible and realistic and not at all an act of bad faith. It did, however, reveal a painful "gap" in the partnership agreement, because that agreement simply failed to provide a rule or mechanism by which the parties' shares would be redetermined if the manager decided that the brand-name plan should be abandoned. Plainly, however, the act of substituting one business plan for another ought not to have the consequence of terminating the sharing arrangement between the parties or of eliminating or reducing one party's interest to the advantage of the other. But the question then would be how to adapt the partners' original understanding to an altered business setting in which the sale of Ballantine-brand products was largely irrelevant. Resorting to comparable brands as a measure of Ballantine's continuing participation arguably represents the Court's solution to that difficult problem. In effect, Ballantine's claim on the revenues of the "old" enterprise was recast and expressed in the form of an equivalent claim to the revenues of the "new" enterprise, using a phantom version of the old enterprise as a basis for measuring that claim.

Looked at this way, the *Falstaff* decision is really a somewhat heroic effort to fill out the terms of the co-venture agreement, with the "best efforts" provision serving as a handy contractual peg.

Falstaff is a tough case—we deserve an easier one: In *Dickey v. Philadelphia Minit–Man Corp.,*[13] the plaintiff, Dickey, leased property to Minit–Man for the purpose of operating a car-wash service. The lease was for 10 years, with the lessee having an option to renew for a further 10–year term—hence, a possible 20 years in total. The lease provided that the premises were to be used "in the business of washing and cleaning automobiles . . . and for no other purpose." Minit–Man was to pay Dickey 12 ½% of its annual "gross sales" but not less than $1,800 a year. The lease obligated Minit–Man to erect necessary buildings and fixtures—presumably including built-in car-wash machinery—at its own expense, and provided finally that such leasehold improvements were to become the property of the lessor as and when the lease expired for any reason, including the lessee's default.

Unfortunately, the car-wash business turned out to be a loser, at least at this location, and Minit–Man shut the business down after only five years of operation. It still did a bit of polishing and simonizing (waxing), but customers were few. Although gross sales had apparently fallen to nearly nothing, Minit–Man continued to meet the minimum rent requirement, which, as noted, came to $150 on a monthly basis. Dissatisfied with the shut-down and with the prospect of a very modest return on his property for an extended period—as long as 15 years if Minit–Man renewed—Dickey brought an action in ejectment, claiming that Minit–Man had breached by discontinuing the car-wash business in violation of its obligation under the lease. In reply, Minit–Man argued that while the lease restricted use of the premises to cleaning cars, it imposed no obligation to continue the car-wash business if the lessee found it unprofitable to do so. In any event (said Minit–Man), the minimum rental provision gave the lessor all the financial protection from adverse business developments that he had asked for and was entitled to.

The Pennsylvania Court largely accepted Minit–Man's legal arguments—particularly, that a "covenant against a noncomplying use" was not a "covenant to use"—and denied the lessor's right to terminate the lease. The lease agreement did not obligate the lessee to continue the car-wash business; it merely barred use of the premises for any other purpose.

No doubt technically correct, the decision nevertheless left the parties in a kind of economic limbo—the lessor with little to show for his property investment, and the lessee with nothing but an obligation to pay $1,800 a year for the right to do an occasional wax-job. With 5 more years to run on the initial term, 15 if

---

13. 377 Pa. 549, 105 A.2d 580 (1954).

renewed, the lease was burdensome for both parties, not just for one. Quite obviously, then, the Court's decision *must* have led Dickey and Minit–Man, each in its own interest, to seek a settlement that would bring their relationship to an end. The stumbling block, one would think, was the lessor's right to take title to all leasehold improvements on termination of the lease. After only 5 years of use, the building and equipment presumably still had considerable economic value; the lessee probably had not yet even recovered its original cost. Termination would thus impose a forfeiture on Minit–Man and give Dickey something of a windfall. And of course rising land values may also have been a factor.

We don't know how the matter was finally worked out, but one would guess that Dickey either agreed to pay Minit–Man a price for terminating the lease, or, more likely, consented to the removal of the building and equipment by M–M to another car-wash location. Just that, I imagine, is what the Court foresaw—and very probably intended—when it decided the *Minit–Man* case as it did.

Section 2–306(1). Requirements and output contracts raise issues that bear a resemblance to those presented by exclusive dealing arrangements, but on the whole such contracts appear to be less problematic for at least two reasons. The first is that the element of indeterminacy—how much the requirements-buyer will actually demand, how much the output-seller will actually tender— is more readily controllable by agreement than is the promise of a distributor or licensee to use "best efforts." Thus, requirements and output contracts frequently provide for maximum and minimum limitations on the quantity of goods entitled to be required or produced, either in specific terms or by reference to stated estimates based on prior experience. As a result, the risk to either party of being inundated or starved by the other is largely eliminated. Even where contractual limitations are not expressed, the UCC itself operates to fill in the blanks. Thus, UCC 2–306(1) provides that an agreement "which measures ... quantity by the output of the seller or the requirements of the buyer means such actual output or requirements as may occur in good faith, except that no quantity unreasonably disproportionate to ... any normal or otherwise comparable prior output or requirements may be tendered or demanded." By contrast, UCC 2–306(2), while it codifies the rule of *Wood v. Lucy,* says nothing about how *much* effort "best efforts" might consist of.

In *Feld v. Henry S. Levy & Sons, Inc.,*[14] the plaintiff, doing business as the Crushed Toast Company, entered into an agree-

---

14. 37 N.Y.2d 466, 373 N.Y.S.2d 102, 335 N.E.2d 320 (1975).

ment to purchase "all bread crumbs produced" by defendant at 6 cents a bag. Bread crumbs, it appears, were not merely a by-product of defendant's much larger bakery operations, but were produced in quantity by running stale or imperfect loaves through a pair of grinders and then toasting the crumbs in an oven specially adapted for the purpose. The contract, which was for one year, provided for automatic annual renewal but allowed either party to cancel on six-months notice. Defendant made substantial shipments for some months, but then determined that the 6–cent contract price was "very uneconomical" from its standpoint. Accordingly, it quite abruptly and without formal notice of cancellation dismantled its oven, stopped producing bread crumbs in any quantity, and began selling the stale loaves otherwise used for that purpose to animal feed manufacturers. Defendant apparently indicated that it would put the equipment back in place and resume shipments if plaintiff would agree to a rise in price per bag, but plaintiff refused and sued, claiming breach. Defendant responded by arguing that "all bread crumbs produced" meant all bread crumbs produced, and that as bread crumb production had been terminated it had no further obligation under the contract.

While affirming the lower court's denial of summary judgment to either party, the New York Court of Appeals plainly concluded that the defendant's conduct was lacking in good faith within the meaning of UCC 2–306(1). Bread crumbs were obviously a minor part of the defendant's much larger baking business, which continued to generate rye-bread, onion rolls and other good things just as before. Bread crumb losses, if there really were any, could hardly have been great enough to threaten the whole enterprise. Presumably dog-food packagers were offering more for stale loaves than the equivalent of 6 cents a bag, but the realization of less profit than expected, even the absence of profit, would not be sufficient to justify cessation under the good faith standard. Lacking good faith, defendant would have to rely for protection on its right of cancellation, which had been included in the contract for the very purpose of giving either party an opportunity to terminate its obligations in an orderly manner. Although the Court somewhat confusingly intermixed the two subsections of UCC 2–306, its view of the merits was quite clear and one assumes that the defendant settled in the end instead of going on to trial.

The implication of the *Feld* decision, and likewise of the UCC provision, is that requirements and output contracts are essentially subject to the same enforcement standards as conventional contracts in which quantity is a fixed rather than a flexible term. In a fixed-quantity deal, the seller and buyer are obligated to deliver and accept goods in the amount agreed upon even if market changes or raw material costs have made the commitment "very uneconomical" to one or the other. Flexible-quantity deals differ chiefly in the respect that contract obligations are deemed satisfied if the quantity tendered or demanded falls within an expectable range, with upper and lower limits being determined on the basis of what was reasonably anticipated at the time the agreement was entered into. In addition, while the requirements-buyer or output-seller can reduce or even discontinue its participation as part of a general withdrawal from the business itself, it cannot escape the contract by diverting the same materials or facilities to a more profitable use, e.g., dog-food instead of bread crumbs. Elasticity exists, therefore, but the degree of stretch is limited by the overall obligation of good faith.

Chapter 6

PERFORMANCE AND BREACH

The legal problems discussed in preceding chapters—consideration, offer-and-acceptance, capacity and unconscionability—have largely been concerned with the formation of a binding contract. In the main, the question that has been asked is whether promises have been made that are enforceable by legal process. The present Chapter can be regarded as commencing a new or at least a subsequent phase of our subject, in which the issue, generally stated, is whether the contracting parties have *kept* the promises they made. Thus, a contract has been formed—there are undertakings on both sides that are reasonably well specified—but one party claims that the other has breached by failing to deliver the performance required of her under the agreement. The consequences, if the claim of breach is valid, would be twofold: (a) the injured party may be entitled to regard her own performance obligations (if not yet completed) as discharged or suspended, and (b) the injured party would have a right to money damages based on the value of her contractual expectations now impaired or destroyed. Whether there *has* been a breach (and, not infrequently, by whom) is of course the question for decision.

The general topic of performance and breach is usually taken up under two large subheadings, of which the first, "Conditions," is perhaps the less problematic. Thus, a nonperforming promisor can justify her nonperformance if her obligations are conditioned upon the occurrence of an event or a contingency and the event or contingency has simply failed to occur. Example: A agrees to buy B's house for a stated price if a mortgage loan can be obtained at an interest-rate not exceeding 10%; in fact, no such loan is available to A at less than 12%. The interest-rate condition not having been met, A's contractual obligation is excused and B cannot claim breach when A declines to complete the purchase. Of course, 12% is a lot more than 10% over the life of a 30–year mortgage. Would A similarly be excused if a mortgage loan could be had at 10.25%— and if B (having taken his house off the market and missed out on other sales opportunities) offered to reimburse A for the added quarter of a point? Probably she would be excused (see below),[1] though one can at least debate it.

---

1. *Luttinger v. Rosen*, 164 Conn. 45, 316 A.2d 757 (1972).

The second subheading—"Problems of Perform
sumes questions often not dissimilar to the one just ill
arising in the context of a performance already com....
completed. The issue, generally, is whether such performance meets
or falls short of the contractual standard. Example: J, a contractor,
agrees to build a grand mansion for K at a stated price using Brand
X water-pipes. The mansion is built. K moves in but discovers that
J has actually installed Brand Y water-pipes. Brand Y water-pipes
are equivalent in all respects to Brand X water-pipes, but Brand Y
is not Brand X. Can K—asserting that J has failed in this one
respect to fulfil its contract obligations—claim breach and withhold
payment, at least until J has torn the mansion down and rebuilt it
with Brand X pipes? *Surely* debatable, though no doubt a fairly
common problem in one form or another.

Speaking more generally, it is foreseeable (people being what
they are) that the parties to a contract may sometimes be inclined
to behave in an opportunistic manner—may be inclined, that is, to
go out and *look* for reasons to avoid their contract obligations and
claim damages from the other party. Unless our justification rules
are fairly carefully calibrated, for example, we might expect a
promisor who finds her contract duties burdensome to seize on any
minor circumstance, or on any shortcoming in the promisee's
performance, as a ground for suspending or terminating her performance. Behavior of that sort, or the threat of it, obviously adds
to the risks of contracting and ought not to be encouraged or
rewarded. As a practical matter, therefore, we need to distinguish
between significant or "material" grounds for non-performance and
grounds that are trivial or merely formalistic.

The point can be taken further. Even if we rule out opportunistic behavior, I think we would agree that there is both a social and
a private interest in discouraging the precipitous collapse of existing contract relationships, particularly in the case of agreements
that call for continuous and varied performances by one or both
parties over a lengthy period of time. Thus, A agrees for a stated
price to do extensive renovation work on B's house—first the roof,
then the porch, then the basement. In turn, B agrees to make
monthly percentage payments as the work progresses. While the
common sense of the agreement is evident—house-repairs are to
proceed and be paid for on a step-by-step basis—it is not unlikely
that there will be disputes from time to time about the quality of
A's work or about the amount that is due from B. If such disputes
occur frequently and become rancorous, then at some stage, patience and goodwill exhausted, one or the other of the parties may
be tempted to repudiate the entire undertaking—A by walking off

the job or B by declaring that she won't pay A another dime. We might feel sympathy for either decision, but it is pretty clear that no one will benefit if a total break-down of relations occurs. There will obviously be litigation costs if a lawsuit follows, including a cost to the public which supports the legal system. And whatever the outcome of the suit, neither A nor B is likely to obtain what she regards as full compensation for the default of the other. Even if the plaintiff succeeds in establishing that a breach has occurred, the damage award may well fall short of making her whole when account is taken of delays and lost opportunities, the latter being especially difficult to prove. Finally, there may be other persons— workers and suppliers, for example—who will have incurred non-compensable expenses in reliance on or in anticipation of the contract.

For these and related reasons, contract law reflects a preference for continuation of the contract relationship once it has been formed. Both common law and the UCC project a range of practical and doctrinal limitations which operate to restrain the parties from moving too quickly to the conclusion that contract duties have been discharged, whether by the failure of a condition or by a default of the other contracting party. Some of these limitations are discussed and particularized in the case-review that follows, though no attempt is made to exhaust the subject. Throughout, I think, we should bear in mind that the law imposes upon the contracting parties an obligation to act towards one another in "good faith". This extends not only to the performance of the contract but to the assertion and litigation of claims and defenses. "Subterfuges and evasions ... failure to cooperate ... conjuring up a pretended dispute ... harassing demands ... abuse of a power ..."[2]—these and other venal acts of strategy are condemned as contrary to the good-faith requirement even though perhaps not technically beyond the bounds of the contract. As noted earlier, lay people sometimes imagine that the law favors literal construction and strict formalism in the interpretation of contract terms. Lawyers know (or soon learn) better, and the requirement of good faith, which can be gravely cited to one's client as a well-established legal principle, makes it easier to counsel decent conduct on occasion and insist on caution and restraint.

Market Street Associates v. Frey[3], involving a sale and leaseback transaction, illustrates the "good faith" principle in action, and is

2. Restatement Section 205, Comments *d* and *e*.

3. 941 F.2d 588 (7th Cir. 1991), discussed in Rakoff, *Good Faith in Contract Performance:* Market Street Associates

worth a slightly detailed statement of the facts. For the reader's information, sales and leasebacks are common financing arrangements, roughly equivalent, though not identical, to conventional mortgage loans. Thus, Market Street, owner of a small shopping center, needs cash for various purposes. The General Electric Pension Trust (that's *Frey*) provides the same by purchasing the shopping center and promptly leasing it back to Market Street for an extended period. The annual rent paid by Market Street is calculated to repay the Trust's purchase price plus interest. In practical effect, it is very much as if the buyer-lessor (the Trust) were a lender, the purchase money a loan, and the lease a mortgage, with the property serving as security in case the seller-lessee (Market Street) should default.

There is, however, this important difference: unlike a mortgage-lender, the buyer-lessor takes title to, *i.e.*, owns, the property itself. Hence, on termination of the lease, the buyer-lessor (the Trust) is free to sell the property for whatever it is then worth or, more likely, lease it back again at a new and higher annual rent. But suppose Market Street at some point should need to borrow additional capital, perhaps to renovate or expand the shopping center. The Trust is really the only likely lender as long as it remains the legal owner of the property, because Market Street, having surrendered title, can no longer use the property as security for a mortgage loan from any other lending institution. Accordingly, the lease agreement between Market Street and the Trust included a clause—Paragraph 34—which provided that if Market Street should seek to borrow additional capital from the Trust, and if the Trust declined to make a further loan, then Market Street could repurchase the property from the Trust for an amount equal to the original sale price plus 6% a year for each year since the date of the sale. The 6% add-on was presumably expected to approximate the effect of inflation, in that way protecting the Trust from any loss in the real value of its principal should the option to repurchase ever be exercised.

In the present case the Trust purchased Market Street's store buildings in 1968, apparently for three or four hundred thousand dollars, and then leased the property back for a period of 25 years at an appropriately calculated annual rent.[4]

Time passed; the shopping center needed renovation. Accordingly, in June of 1988, Orenstein, president of Market Street,

Ltd. Partnership v. Frey, 120 Harv. L. Rev. 1187 (2007), and in Eisenberg, *The Duty to Rescue in Contract Law*, 71 Fordham L. Rev. 647 (2002).

4. The original seller-lessee was J.C. Penney, which subsequently assigned the lease to Market Street.

phoned Erb, a Pension Trust official, with a view to requesting a $2 million loan to be used for improvements and repairs. Erb, having bigger fish to fry, didn't take the call and didn't return it. Orenstein then wrote to Erb, expressing an interest in buying the property back and asking Erb to "review your files on this matter and call me so that we can discuss it further." Eventually, Erb's assistant called Orenstein and offered to sell the property to Market Street for $3 million, which Orenstein considered too high.

A month later, Orenstein wrote Erb a formal letter specifically requesting $2 million in additional financing. Erb made no response. In August, having heard nothing, Orenstein wrote Erb yet again demanding that "you advise us immediately if you are willing to provide the financing pursuant to the lease." Erb finally responded, also by letter, with a definite No, and somewhat snootily explained that a $2 million loan did not meet the Trust's "investment criteria" because the Trust was not interested in making loans for less than $7 million. Erb made no reference in his letter to Paragraph 34. Apparently (though one could not be sure), Erb was unaware that his refusal to make the loan would trigger Market Street's option to repurchase the property and terminate the lease.

Orenstein, of course, was very well aware of Paragraph 34 and must have calculated that the repurchase option could be exercised for about $1 million, even with the 6% add-on. The property itself was probably worth somewhere between $2 and $3 million, so that Orenstein presumably quivered at the thought that Erb had forgotten (if he ever knew) about Market Street's right to buy back the property at what was now a bargain price. Yet Orenstein hesitated. Was all this too good to be true? Did he have an obligation of some sort to alert Erb to Paragraph 34 and give the latter a chance to reconsider the loan request? Or should he say nothing and let Erb fall into a trap—one, to be sure, of his own making?

At this point let us briefly pause and suppose that we (you and I) are consulted by Market Street's board of directors in our capacity as company counsel. Which course should Orenstein follow (we are asked)? Should he, or must he, draw Erb's attention to Paragraph 34 and in that way save Erb from making a costly blunder? Or can he just keep quiet about Paragraph 34? Our answer: "Say nothing!" Market Street has no obligation, legal or ethical, to inform the GE Pension Trust about its own contract rights; Erb is a sophisticated money manager and the Trust has a large (if undistinguished) legal staff that is paid to protect its interests. If Erb is unaware of Paragraph 34, and if he fails to read the contract or have it read, then let him take the consequences. We would be mad to counsel otherwise. Don't you agree?

Actually, Orenstein went slightly beyond our good advice. Instead of keeping silent and simply exercising his $1 million repurchase option, Orenstein in August wrote Erb yet *another* letter expressing his disappointment about being turned down for the $2 million loan and stating (perhaps not entirely truthfully) that Market Street would seek financing elsewhere. This letter probably led Erb to dismiss the whole trivial business from his mind, which he was perfectly glad to do.

Finally, in September, Orenstein notified the Trust by registered letter that Market Street was exercising its Paragraph 34 option and would tender its check for $1 million in accordance with the 6% formula. The Trust, now wide awake, refused to sell, and Market Street brought an action for specific performance. From a decision granting summary judgment for the Trust, Market Street appealed.

The Seventh Circuit reversed and remanded, but only for the purpose of ascertaining Orenstein's "state of mind." Did Orenstein believe that Erb knew or would surely find out about Paragraph 34? Or, on the other hand, did he deliberately take advantage of what he perceived to be Erb's mistake by writing Erb "a lulling letter designed to convince the pension trust that the matter was closed and could be forgotten"? If the latter, as the Court apparently thought highly likely, judgment for the Pension Trust would be justified.

Writing for the Court, Judge Posner took pains to distinguish between private information that costs money to develop and results in bringing hidden values to light—the geologist who buys a farm knowing there's gold under the lettuce beds—and information of which the discovery favors the legally alert but has no research cost and adds nothing of value to the contractual undertakings. The former can be withheld, said Posner quite correctly, but the latter has to be disclosed under the good faith and duty-to-cooperate standards. "We do not usually excuse contracting parties from failing to read and understand the contents of their contract; and in the end what this case comes down to ... is that an immensely sophisticated enterprise simply failed to read the contract. On the other hand, such enterprises make mistakes just like the rest of us, and deliberately to take advantage of your contracting partner's mistake during the performance stage (for we are not talking about taking advantage of superior knowledge at the formation stage) is a breach of good faith."

So, as it turns out, our very confident legal advice was wrong and led Market Street to incur litigation expense for nothing ɔresumably the Trust is now obligated to provide the $2 requested financing). Well, we all make mistakes, as ___ modestly acknowledged. But, viewed more generally, how far would the Court's *formation v. performance* rationale take us? If X sells Y a 30–day option on certain property and learns that Y, busy with other matters, apparently believes it to be a 60–day option, is X obligated, in good faith, to tell Y on day 30 that the option is about to expire? A *yes* answer is almost inconceivable. Perhaps we would agree that there is a good-faith obligation to correct the other party's mistake if the mistake is merely clerical— a failure, say, to check a box on a form or even an obvious arithmetical miscalculation.[4a] But otherwise, commercial life moves too fast for the law to burden one party with a duty to keep the other informed about its own legal rights, unless, as in *Walker–Thomas* (p. 94), our concern is to protect consumers from "unconscionable" contract provisions.

In any case, the remand for a determination of Orenstein's "state of mind" was an open invitation (if not to perjury, then at least) to highly self-serving testimony. On the stand, Orenstein would be sorely tempted to say that Erb's snooty response to the initial loan request led him, O, to believe that the Trust was chiefly interested in terminating small loan accounts for reasons of administrative convenience. That would be a fib, I'm afraid, though hard to resist. What Orenstein actually said we don't know, but on remand the district court again found for the Pension Trust and held that Market Street was not entitled to specific performance.

A. Conditions

1. *Express Conditions.* Perhaps we should begin this topic with the traditional but somewhat confusing distinction between "conditions precedent" and "conditions subsequent". At stake, largely, are procedural matters such as burden of pleading and burden of proof. Yet the distinction may have substantive consequences as well. In *Howard v. Federal Crop Ins. Corp.,*[5] the plaintiffs, tobacco farmers, asserted that their crops, which were insured by the defendant, had been damaged by heavy rains, resulting in a loss of $35,000. Notice and proof of loss was promptly filed, but before an insurance adjuster could come and inspect the damage the plaintiffs plowed the tobacco fields under and prepared their land for another crop. Pointing to a provision of the insurance

---

4a. *Sumerel v. Goodyear Tire & Rubber Co.,* 232 P.3d 128 (Colo. App. 2009).

5. 540 F.2d 695 (4th Cir.1976).

policy which stated that "The tobacco stalks on any acre with respect to which a loss is claimed shall not be destroy͏ the Corporation makes an inspection", the defendant refused to pay and moved for summary judgment, which was granted by the lower court. Reversing and remanding, the Fourth Circuit held that the defendant's motion should have been denied for the reason that the inspection requirement was not a condition precedent to the defendant's duty to pay. Rather, that duty arose upon the filing of notice and proof of loss. While the defendant would afterwards be free to defend its refusal by proving that the plaintiffs' action had made it impossible to determine the extent of the loss, the plaintiffs might then respond by showing that the loss could have been evaluated without on-the-spot inspection, or that the plowing-under was necessary to prevent the spread of bugs ... or whatever. The larger aim of the insurance contract, in the Court's view, was to establish a right on the part of the insured to compensation for crop losses. That right having been established by the filing of a claim, the parties would then be left to determine the extent of such losses by inspection and other appropriate means. Treating the inspection requirement as a condition precedent would have meant that policy coverage was wholly forfeited even though there had in fact been rain damage; treating it as a condition subsequent properly placed the amount of the plaintiffs' damages in issue.

As there is no report of a decision on remand, I think we can assume that the defendant in *Howard* litigated the matter no further and simply paid or settled the plaintiffs' compensation claim.

In general, the function of a contractual condition is to place the risk of the non-occurrence of the critical event on one party rather than the other. One speaks of "risk" in this connection because the failure of a condition would often entail a loss, or at least a disadvantage, to one of the parties, with some sort of corresponding advantage or immunity to the other. If the parties bargained for that outcome—if the risk of non-occurrence was consciously assumed and priced into the deal—then, obviously, the law ought not to intervene and the disadvantaged party must simply take her lumps. Inevitably, however, there are instances in which the intention of the parties is less than clear. Where there is doubt about the meaning of the contract and the promisee has relied substantially on the expectation of the agreed exchange, the courts, as in the *Howard* case, usually seek an interpretation that avoids or minimizes the promisee's reliance loss. Supporting this effort, Restatement Section 227 states that in case of uncertainty with respect to the intended effect of a condition, the "preferred" interpretation is one that will reduce the risk of "forfeiture".

In *Gibson v. Cranage*,[6] the plaintiff was in the business of enlarging family photographs—presumably touching them up and coloring them in some ghastly manner. Having no doubt read about the death of the defendant's daughter in the obituary column of the local newspaper, plaintiff contacted defendant and offered to enlarge a snapshot of the daughter on the understanding that defendant would be obligated to pay for the work only if he was "perfectly satisfied" with the result. On being presented with the enlargement, defendant declared that he was *not* perfectly satisfied and declined to pay. Defendant apparently wouldn't state what his objections were, and he stubbornly refused to take a second look at the enlargement even after it had been returned to the "artist" for improvements. Quite obviously, the defendant had simply changed his mind about spending money on the enlargement and didn't care whether it looked wonderful or awful. Left with a worthless photograph, plaintiff sued for his fee.

The Supreme Court of Michigan held for the defendant on the ground that defendant's personal satisfaction had been made a condition of his duty to pay by express agreement of the parties. Others might consider the portrait an excellent one, but the parties themselves had stipulated that the defendant was to be the only person with a right to decide that question. To be sure, the plaintiff had spent time and money on the project. Even so, said the Court, since the plaintiff took a deliberate risk in giving the defendant a right to reject the photograph at will, "there is no hardship whatever ...".

The *Gibson* decision is generally regarded as correct, I think, although the notion that the defendant could arbitrarily declare himself dissatisfied and in that way impose a forfeiture on the plaintiff might in other circumstances seem unreasonable. Here, however, the plaintiff's unrecovered costs should probably be regarded as nothing more than an ordinary and necessary business expense. Allowing his customer to reject the product if not "perfectly satisfied" must be assumed to have been a marketing technique which the plaintiff consciously adopted as an aid to sales—in effect, the nineteenth-century equivalent of today's familiar money-back guarantee. Based on experience with customers, the plaintiff would have been able to predict quite accurately what percentage of his sales would ultimately fail of completion. The loss on uncompleted sales would simply be accepted as a cost of promotion and, like any

---

6. 39 Mich. 49 (1878). *Compare Mattei v. Hopper*, supra, p. 28.

other advertising outlay, would be reflected in the price at which the plaintiff regularly offered his services to the public. Putting the same point differently, the plaintiff actually made history of a sort by losing the case: if the decision had gone the other way and the defendant had been compelled either to pay for the portrait or give a "good faith" reason for rejecting it, the money-back guarantee, by now a time-honored marketing gimmick, would carry less conviction to consumers and would presumably have had to be abandoned.

In *Gibson,* as suggested, the question of whether "perfect satisfaction" did or didn't operate as a condition precedent was resolved by reference to the parties' intended allocation of risk: buyer and seller understood that the latter *meant* to offer his services on a money-back basis; hence, the buyer's "satisfaction" was a condition of his duty to pay. A similar analysis, but with a different outcome, was employed in *Peacock Construction Co. v. Modern Air Conditioning, Inc.,*[7] a casebook standby in this field. In *Peacock,* the defendant (Peacock) was the general contractor for a large building project and had entered into a subcontract (no doubt one among many) with the plaintiff to supply and install the heating and air conditioning. The subcontract provided that Peacock would make final payment to Modern "within 30 days after completion of the work ... and full payment therefor by the Owner." The Owner having gone bankrupt without paying Peacock for the subcontractors' work, Peacock refused to make final payment to Modern and the latter sued.

Affirming a grant of summary judgment for the plaintiff, the Supreme Court of Florida held that the clause just quoted was not intended to create a condition precedent to Peacock's duty to pay the various subcontractors, but served merely to fix a reasonable time for Peacock to make such payments, i.e., 30 days after the events named. While the contract language was admittedly open to more than one interpretation, the "fairest way" to deal with the issue was to recognize that small subcontractors would not ordinarily expect to take the risk of an owner's financial failure. Instead, presumably, the parties would expect the general contractor to assume that risk, because the general, having dealt directly with the owner, would be in the best position to appraise the latter's credit-worthiness and to insist on such security measures (*e.g.,* a payment bond) as the circumstances seemed to require. The Court noted that an agreement might be written otherwise, but if

7. 353 So.2d 840 (Fla.1977).

so, the intention to shift financial risk to the subcontractor would have to be clearly expressed, not left to inference.

As a final illustration of "conditions," let's return to the *Luttinger* case, cited at note 1, above. In *Luttinger*, the plaintiffs contracted to purchase the defendants' home for $85,000 and paid a deposit of $8,500. The contract of sale, which included a standard mortgage financing clause, provided that the buyers' obligation was "subject to and conditional upon the buyers obtaining first mortgage financing ... from a bank or other lending institution in an amount of $45,000 for a term of not less than twenty (20) years and at an interest rate which does not exceed 8½% per annum." The plaintiffs agreed to use "due diligence" in locating such a mortgage. In the end, having tried their best (so the trial court found), the plaintiffs could identify only one local bank that would lend as much $45,000 on a family residence. The loan, however, which would be for 25 years, would carry an interest rate of 8¾%, one-quarter of a point above the contractual limit. The plaintiffs in due course notified the defendants that the interest rate condition could not be met and demanded the return of their $8,500 deposit. The defendants refused and the plaintiffs sued.

The Supreme Court of Connecticut, holding that the language of the contract was clear and unambiguous with respect to the 8½% rate limitation, affirmed a decision for the plaintiffs. The rate limitation operated as a condition precedent to the plaintiffs' obligation to buy. Not having been met following a diligent effort to meet it, the condition failed and the plaintiffs were entitled to terminate the home-sale contract and recover their deposit. The Court refused to consider the effect of an offer by the defendants to make up the quarter-point difference through "a funding arrangement, the exact terms of which were not defined." Nor would the Court permit testimony as to the specific nature of the defendants' offer to "fund"; the condition precedent was altogether plain, it reflected the parties' intent, and hence "the offer was obviously irrelevant."

Not a very interesting case, I concede, but perhaps somewhat notable for the strict, not to say rigid, interpretation the Court gave to the home-sale contract. I remarked earlier at various points that contract interpretation often, even usually, admits of some flexibility, particularly where the operation of a condition imposes a hardship on one of the contracting parties. The monthly payment on a 25–year mortgage loan of $45,000 at 8¾% is about $369; at 8½% it would be $362, just $7 less. That being so, we can assume with confidence that the plaintiffs had simply changed their minds about buying the defendants' house and were only too glad to have a legal excuse for backing out. The defendants, having taken their house off the market for what may have been a critical selling period, and hoping to hold the plaintiffs to their promise, were presumably prepared (i) to be liable for and to pay that additional quarter-point per annum, perhaps depositing the necessary funds in an escrow account on which the plaintiff's could freely draw, or, alternatively, (ii) to accept a purchase-money mortgage from the plaintiffs at 8½% and in effect make the mortgage loan themselves in place of the bank, or even (iii) to knock a thousand dollars off the purchase price of the house, and thus reduce the plaintiffs' mortgage loan and monthly payments to what they would be under a $45,000 mortgage at the 8½% rate. Perhaps there were other ways of making the same concession. What is notable, as stated, is that Court regarded all such alternatives as "irrelevant."

Why so strict? One answer—perhaps *the* answer—is that a contrary decision would have impaired the simplicity and integrity of the printed contract Form by which all residential real estate (and even business real estate) is sold in the State of Connecticut. The Form, which can be purchased for a dollar at any legal stationers, was long ago worked out by the real estate section of the Connecticut State Bar Association with a view to fairly balancing the interests of sellers and buyers. As such, it requires little further input from the parties' lawyers and, like any standardized legal document, substantially reduces the costs associated with common and conventional home-sale transactions. Among other boiler-plate provisions, the Form contains a standard mortgage financing clause, which the parties can include or strike out as they may agree. Suppose, as in *Luttinger*, that the buyer insists on including a financing clause in order to protect himself against an unexpected rise in mortgage interest rates. If the Supreme Court had permitted that clause to be "interpreted" so as to allow the seller to overcome the interest rate condition by adopting a "funding arrangement" of some sort, the parties to a home sale would need to negotiate and engage in further drafting whenever a sale subject to a financing clause was made. The seller, like the defendant in *Luttinger*, would want to be free to absorb any additional interest cost by means of his own choosing—those mentioned above and perhaps others. The buyer would reject that idea or, at least, insist on limiting the acceptable alternatives. All this would add time and expense to what should be a very simple transaction, and in some cases might even be a deal-breaker.

Not a desirable development in Connecticut or anywhere else, which may explain the dismissive and peremptory tone of the Court's opinion.

Condition or Duty or Both. Yet another and a related issue in this field concerns the need, urgent on occasion, to distinguish between a condition precedent, a promise, and a so-called promissory condition. At stake, where the named event fails to occur, is the disappointed party's future performance obligation as well as that party's entitlement to damages. Thus—

If the event referred to in the contract is a condition precedent only, its failure to occur discharges the promisor from her own performance obligations but creates no claim for damages against the other party. In the *Gibson* case, providing perfect satisfaction was found to be a condition which the plaintiff-promisee had to meet, or "cause to occur", before the defendant-promisor would become obligated to pay for the tasteful enlargement. But the plaintiff had no "duty" to provide perfect satisfaction to the defendant and would not have been subject to a counterclaim for having failed to do so.

If the event referred to is a promise but not a condition precedent, failure constitutes a breach. While the injured party then has a claim for damages, its own performance obligations are not discharged unless the breach is "material" and the party in breach makes no reasonable attempt to "cure" in a timely fashion. Where a timely cure is effected, the injured party may have damages, but its performance is due despite the initial breach. Thus, a seller, having initially delivered the wrong merchandise to the buyer, promptly substitutes the right merchandise after being notified of its mistake. Seller's breach being cured, buyer is obligated to pay for the merchandise, although buyer may claim damages for any loss occasioned by the seller's delay.

Finally, if the event referred to is found to be a promissory condition—a condition precedent *and* a promise—failure of the event to occur both discharges the injured party from any future performance obligations—the condition precedent not having been met—and entitles the injured party to damages for its loss (if any). The well-known *River Brand* case, next discussed, is a slightly complex example.

In *Internatio–Rotterdam, Inc. v. River Brand Rice Mills, Inc.,*[8] the plaintiff, an exporter of commodities, contracted to purchase 95,000 pockets of rice from the defendant, a processor of rice, at a price of $8.25 per pocket. The contract was entered into in July for delivery in December. The plaintiff, which had already committed itself to supplying the rice to a foreign customer, was obligated to give the defendant shipping instructions—what port and what

---

8. 259 F.2d 137 (2d Cir.1958).

ship—two weeks prior to the delivery date. Taken litera
latter requirement meant that shipping instructions would ha,
be received by the defendant no later than December 17, since
instructions received after that date would push the two-week
period into January. As it turned out, the plaintiff met with
difficulties in (among other things) arranging for a ship and a dock
during what was evidently a busy export season in Texas and
Louisiana. These difficulties were overcome with respect to 50,000
pockets, which were duly delivered and shipped, but as to the
remaining 45,000 the plaintiff was unable to transmit shipping
instructions to the defendant until some time shortly after the
December 17 date.

Bright and early on the morning of December 18, no instructions having been received, the defendant notified the plaintiff that
the contract was rescinded as to the 45,000 pockets. The market
price of a pocket of rice had by that date risen to $9.75. Plaintiff
thereupon brought suit for the undelivered portion of its quota.

Finding for the defendant, the Court held that the plaintiff had
no legal right to insist upon delivery once the critical date had
passed. The provision for December delivery, the Court thought,
was fundamental to the defendant's obligation; hence, the giving of
shipping instructions by December 17 must be classified as a
promissory condition. Defendant had other contracts to fulfil in
January and there was evidence that it needed the protection of a
specified delivery date (*i.e.,* not later than two weeks before the end
of December) in order to avoid congestion of its storage facilities.

Equally important in the Court's view, allowing notification to
be effective after December 17 would give the plaintiff an "option"
to speculate on subsequent market-price fluctuations in the event it
decided to breach. Thus, if the market price of rice appeared to be
dropping, plaintiff could avoid giving any notification whatever and
simply wait and buy at the lower price. To be sure, the contract
would be breached by the failure to notify, but defendant's damage
claim would be limited to the difference between the contract price
and the market price on December 17, so that the subsequent
market decline would be entirely at defendant's expense. On the
other hand, if the market went up after December 17, plaintiff
would give notification within "a reasonable time" and would be
protected by the $8.25 contract price. The defendant, as the Court
said, apparently had no "reciprocal option". But presumably a
strategic disparity of this sort would not have been intended by the
parties. In effect, therefore, *time* "went to the essence of the
contract". It followed that notice of shipping instructions by December 17 was not merely a duty of the plaintiff but a condition as

well, and its failure to occur justified the defendant in treating its own performance obligation as discharged.

A shrewd analysis, some might say, yet the outcome in *River Brand* is, in a sense, upside down—or, at least, contrary to what must have been the parties' original expectation. Almost invariably, a rise in market price (relative to the contract price) is expected to mean a gain for the commodity buyer and a loss for the commodity seller. Here, we get just the opposite. The plaintiff's delay in issuing shipping instructions, apparently unavoidable, produced a gain for the defendant-seller in the amount of $67,500—$9.75, market price, minus $8.25, contract price, times 45,000 pockets of rice—and a corresponding loss for the plaintiff-buyer. Plaintiff and defendant took the usual market risk in agreeing to a price of $8.25 per pocket six months in advance of the delivery date. But they obviously had no intention of "gambling" on the state of available shipping, with the seller being the winner and the buyer the loser because dock facilities were then (temporarily) in short supply.

So, is the *River Brand* decision convincing? Not entirely. The plaintiff presumably argued that the contract should be treated as an ordinary merchandise-supply contract, in which case the "time" factor would be viewed more flexibly. If a wholesaler orders a quantity of goods from a manufacturer and the order is accepted, a brief delay in issuing shipping instructions would not usually be considered the failure of a condition entitling the seller to refuse performance. Or, turning the *River Brand* case around, suppose the plaintiff had issued its shipping instructions by December 17 as the contract required, but the defendant, owing to rail congestion, had delayed delivery until a few days after December 31. It is altogether unlikely that the plaintiff in such event could have refused payment on the ground that a condition of performance had failed to occur. In both cases, the delay would be regarded either as non-material in itself or, if potentially material, as susceptible to "cure" within a reasonable time.

3. *Oral Modification and Waiver.* As noted (p. 142), the parol evidence rule applies to alleged oral agreements entered into before the adoption of a written contract but has no application to oral agreements made subsequent to that event. In general, contracting parties are free by later oral agreement to modify or terminate their existing obligations and adopt different terms that better suit their present interests. Questions relating to duress, consideration, or the Statute of Frauds might afterwards be raised by one party or the other, but the mere fact that the subsequent agreement is oral and takes the place, in whole or part, of a prior written agreement is not of itself a ground for objection or exclusion.

But suppose the contracting parties, aware of the foregoing, actually wish to exclude any later attempt at oral modification and, indeed, to bar either party from even raising the question. Can they do that by providing in the contract that only written modifications shall be recognized and enforced? Or are they trapped by a kind of legal circularity? Thus, even if the original agreement contains an express no-oral modification clause, the parties apparently remain free to modify even *that* provision if they choose. Accordingly, can't one or the other argue that they did in fact later agree—orally—to waive or modify the no-oral-modification clause itself?

In *Universal Builders, Inc. v. Moon Motor Lodge,*[9] the plaintiff-construction company had entered into a contract with the defendant to build a motel and restaurant. Among other things, the contract provided that extras—additional work not called for in the original contract—would not be paid for unless done pursuant to a written change order signed by Moon or its architect. At some point while the job was underway, having detected a defect in the quality of the masonry supplied by a subcontractor, Moon "threatened" (the Court's word) to withhold progress payments and to kick Universal out unless the latter agreed to pay Moon $5,000 to make up for the defective masonry and do certain additional work for nothing. Apparently somewhat desperate, Universal signed a supplemental agreement in which it acceded to Moon's demands. The job was finally completed (a bit late), whereupon Universal, unable to collect all that it felt was due from Moon, went into bankruptcy.

Contending that it had done a good deal of extra work *beyond* that required by the supplemental agreement, Universal (or, rather, its trustee) sued Moon for the value of such alleged extras, about $42,000. Moon denied liability, pointing to the express contractual condition that change orders involving additional cost be submitted in advance and approved by it in writing. In reply, Universal asserted, and apparently proved to the trial court's satisfaction, that the extra work had been orally requested by, and had been carried out with the full approval of, Moon's agent—one Berger—who was at all times present at the construction site.

Affirming, a majority of the Supreme Court of Pennsylvania held for Universal. As a matter of law, the contractual requirement that change orders be in writing could be orally waived from time to time by the promisor's agent; in the alternative, the parties could authorize the extras by oral agreements separate from their written contract. It was reasonable, here, to infer that Moon *had* waived the requirement of a writing with respect to the extras in question,

9. 430 Pa. 550, 244 A.2d 10 (1968).

because its agent at the site both requested such extra work and watched while it was being performed. Citing the predecessor of Restatement Section 150, finally, the Court held that the Statute of Frauds was no bar to an oral (or tacit) waiver of a performance condition by a promisor where the waiver was relied upon by the promisee to its evident detriment.

One senses, in general, that the Court conceived no great admiration for Moon, which it apparently regarded as having bullied Universal into bankruptcy.

Justice Musmanno, in dissent, accused the majority of doing Moon "an injustice". Quoting affectionately from an earlier decision of his own, the dissenter warned that that "[c]haos would envelop the commercial world" if Universal's waiver argument were allowed to prevail, because the effect would be to treat written contracts as if they had been "penned in disappearing ink." The defendant, in Musmanno's view, was entitled to be protected by the no-oral-modification clause unless the clause itself had been waived prior to the attempted oral modifications. In any event, the "evidence failed to show that the work charged for was actually performed" or that the defendant had been given credit for items contained in the original contract but now allegedly changed and billed as extras. Pretty plainly, Justice Musmanno thought that Universal was engaged in an attempt to recoup its contract losses by fabricating extras long after the event—a danger which the no-oral-modification clause was specifically intended to guard against.

As so often in the Contracts field, the general question presented by the *Universal Builders* case is (a) thoroughly humdrum but (b) of considerable importance from a practical standpoint. On the one hand, the owner of the property, Moon, insists on written approval as a condition of any changes that involve an increase in the contract price. Its aim is to bar false claims on the part of the builder, Universal, and also, perhaps, to control its own agents in the field, who might otherwise be inclined to okay one proposed extra after another without counting the cost. On the other hand, there is obviously a need for flexibility in carrying out a large-scale, long-term building project. The original plans will almost surely have to be altered in minor ways from time to time even though additional costs may be involved; yet the need to obtain written authorization for each such alteration would be burdensome and often would be overlooked by people busy with the work itself. The dilemma is "solved" by the Court majority in *Universal Builders* by (i) subordinating the no-oral-modification clause and giving preference to the claim of waiver, but then (ii) requiring the builder to show that it did in fact receive oral approval for the extra work and actually incurred additional costs in reliance thereon. The builder gets some assurance that it will be paid for work that it has been told to do and has actually done, and the owner gets some protection against fraudulent claims. What drops out is the owner's *contractual* protection against over-hasty commitments by its on-site agents—Berger again, more or less casually saying yes to every change that Universal proposed.

B. Problems of Performance

1. *Constructive Conditions of Exchange.* We have no difficulty today in recognizing that the promises made by the parties to a bilateral contract are in almost every case "dependent". Each of the contracting parties regards performance by the other party as a condition of its own obligation to perform; failure to perform on one side obviously furnishes an excuse for non-performance on the other. Some contracts—those involving sales of real estate or securities, for example—plainly contemplate simultaneous performances by the parties. Thus, X and Y agree to the sale of Blackacre for $10,000, the closing to be held on June 1. On the closing date, X, the seller, is expected to deliver appropriate title documents and Y, the buyer, is expected to hand over her check. Check and title documents cross the table at one and the same moment; neither party would expect to surrender her property without equivalent action by the other. In other situations—sales of services, typically—one party, usually the buyer, would expect to become obligated to perform only after the other party's performance had been completed, whether in whole or part. Thus, A promises to pay B a stated sum for painting A's house, and B promises to paint. Apparently, B is expected to "go first"—B's performance is an implied or constructive condition of A's duty to pay—and it is plain that A is excused if the job is never done.

But while the idea of dependent promises now seems apparent to common sense, prior to *Kingston v. Preston*,[10] decided by King's Bench in 1773, the law evidently lacked a constructive conditions doctrine and instead treated the parties' promises as independently enforceable. Thus, unless the contract provided otherwise, the courts generally held that the failure of one party to perform did not, of itself, justify the other in withholding her own performance. X, above, could therefore seek payment from Y even though the deed to Blackacre was never delivered. Y might afterwards commence a suit against X to obtain title to the property, but of course there would be a fair chance by then that X would possess neither

10.   99 Eng.Rep. 437 (1773).

Blackacre nor other resources sufficient to meet Y's claim—to say nothing of the sheer waste of time and money involved in bringing multiple lawsuits.

Kingston v. Preston, which changed the law in this respect, appears to have involved a kind of small-scale leveraged buy-out. The defendant, in business as a silk merchant but eager to retire, had apparently induced the plaintiff to join the firm as an employee by entering into a contract with the plaintiff under which the latter, together with the defendant's nephew, was to purchase the assets of the business at the end of a year. The plaintiff agreed to pay for his share in monthly installments of £250, which presumably represented some portion of the anticipated cash-flow from inventory turnover. As assurance, the plaintiff further agreed, at or before the closing, to provide the defendant with "good and sufficient security" for his payment obligations, the same to be approved by the defendant himself. On the defendant's refusal to convey title at the closing date, the plaintiff sued, stating that he stood ready to make the installment payments as promised. In reply, the defendant asserted that he had no duty to perform, because the plaintiff had breached by failing to furnish the "good and sufficient security" that the contract required.

Not that it matters much at this late date, but I suppose we could wonder just what, beyond the inventory and accounts receivable of the business itself, such "sufficient security" was ever expected to consist of. Apparently, the defendant wanted the plaintiff to obtain additional collateral from other parties—a bank, perhaps, or another investor. The plaintiff, however, who conceded that his own net worth was zero and who had no outside source of capital, may well have assumed from the beginning that giving the defendant a security-interest in the firm's balance-sheet assets would satisfy the contractual condition; in effect, the defendant, like a mortgagee, would have a right to repossess those assets if the monthly installments weren't paid. But this issue (if it was an issue) never got debated. Electing simply to demur, plaintiff argued that the defendant's obligation to sell the business was independent of the plaintiff's duty to furnish additional security; if defendant *had* a remedy, he could pursue it in a separate action.

Holding for the defendant on the ground that the plaintiff's duty was a condition precedent, Lord Mansfield rejected the notion that the defendant's promise to transfer "his stock and business" was independently enforceable. The "greatest injustice" would result, his Lordship thought, if the defendant were required to trust to the "personal security" of the plaintiff, who was admitted to be "worth nothing".[11] In effect, the purpose of the transaction, together with the "evident sense and meaning" of the agreement, indicated that the parties, even without expressly so stating, had intended their promises to be conditional and mutually dependent. Without entirely discarding prior law, Mansfield quite clearly signalled that, for the future, a contract formed on the basis of an exchange of promises would be read to require an exchange of performances as well. Since, here, the plaintiff-purchaser had failed to perform by furnishing adequate security, the defendant-seller's performance obligations were excused.

As Lord Mansfield observed in *Kingston* (and as noted above), bilateral contracts can generally be divided into two subclasses— those that contemplate a simultaneous exchange of performances and those that assume a performance by one party in advance of, and as a condition to, performance by the other. The agreement in *Kingston* presumably belonged to the former subclass: evidence of the purchaser's security (e.g., a bank letter of credit payable to the seller in the event of default) and the seller's title documents were to change hands at the same moment in time, neither party being expected to act before the other. But in some cases the intention may not be quite so clear. In *Stewart v. Newbury*,[12] the plaintiff, a contractor, offered to do the excavation and concrete work on a mill building to be constructed by the defendants. The plaintiff submitted a written bid containing price quotations for various elements of the job, and the defendants accepted by telephone and then in writing. Neither the bid nor the acceptance said anything about *when* the plaintiff would be paid for his work, but the plaintiff testified that in their phone conversation he had said, "I will expect my payments in the usual manner," and the defendants had replied, "All right, we have got the money...." After working for two months the plaintiff asked for payment, claiming that the "custom" was to bill and be paid for 85% of the value of work performed on a monthly basis, with 15% being retained until the job was completed. The defendants, asserting that the work done was not in accordance with specifications, declined to pay anything at that point and apparently urged the plaintiff to get busy and complete the job. The plaintiff refused to proceed without payment

11. Question: what ever happened to the defendant's idle young nephew—for whose particular benefit, I would guess, the whole buy-out plan was intended? Maybe he gave up and quit the firm at some early point because he couldn't bear the hard work and long hours. Or maybe the plaintiff, older and more aggressive, somehow succeeded in pushing him out. In either or any event, the plaintiff, a stranger, now claimed sole ownership of the family silk business with no out-of-pocket cost to himself. Lord Mansfield, I imagine, seeing this, just wouldn't stand for it.

12. 220 N.Y. 379, 115 N.E. 984 (1917).

and the defendant notified the plaintiff that it considered the contract at an end, whereupon the plaintiff brought suit for the work billed to date, $896, plus $95 for loss of profits. Following a trial, the judge instructed the jury that "if there was no custom that was understood by both parties, and with respect to which they made a contract, then the plaintiff was entitled to payment at reasonable times." So instructed, the jury returned a verdict awarding the plaintiff the amount stated in his bill, though not the lost profits, and the defendants appealed.

Finding the trial court's instructions erroneous, the New York Court of Appeals reversed and remanded. The agreement between plaintiff and defendant was "an entire contract", meaning, presumably, a contract that called for a single completed performance, not a performance rendered in monthly installments. Absent anything in the agreement to the contrary, the common-law rule was that "the work must be substantially performed before payment can be demanded...." It followed, in the Court's view, that if the jury reached its verdict on the ground that the plaintiff was justified in abandoning the work because the installment had not been paid, then the verdict could not stand. While such verdict might be left intact if it simply reflected a finding that the defendant had breached the contract by preventing the plaintiff from going forward with the job, the jury's failure to have awarded loss-of-profits damages suggested that the former was true rather than the latter. The Court could not be certain, however, and hence a new trial was ordered.

Insofar as it pertains to service contracts generally, I suppose the *Stewart* decision is correct. Under ordinary circumstances, service providers are paid after their services have been performed. Thus, employees get their pay-checks at the *end* of a pay-period—a week or a month—for services performed during that period. In effect, the employee "loans" the value of his services to the employer until pay-day, and while this may sometimes be a bit tough on the employee, the alternative—payment in advance—is not likely to be acceptable to the employer, which would have no practical way of assuring itself that the employee will actually show up and perform. Employees with unique and highly valued skills—athletes, law-review editors—do occasionally receive advance signing bonuses, but for most service-providers the performance comes first and the compensation afterwards.

Restatement Section 234(2) reflects the rule of the *Stewart* case by providing that where the performance of one party to a contract requires a period of time, that party's performance is due at an earlier time than that of the other party, unless the contract "or

148

the circumstances" indicate the contrary. This no doubt, as stated, is the general understanding as far as employees and employers are concerned; employers are not expected to finance their employees' living and consumption expenditures by paying salaries in advance of services. The plaintiff in *Stewart,* however, was an employer himself with a crew of workmen and a monthly payroll to meet. In asking for periodic payments as the work progressed, the plaintiff sought to shift that payroll burden to the defendants—quite understandably given that the job would take considerable time to complete and would require a substantial outlay for labor and materials. Indeed, having been denied such payments, the plaintiff (had he continued the project) would apparently have had to finance the entire cost of the building's exterior structure. He would thus have become a lender to the defendant on a relatively large scale, a status which the parties probably never contemplated.

Though not mentioned by the Court in *Stewart,* the challenged jury instruction—"if there was no custom ... then ..."—allows yet a third interpretation of the jury's verdict; namely, that it *was* the custom for owners to pay builders on a periodic basis for work performed, and that the jury so found. One would think it must have been so, even as early as the year 1911. Today, at all events, the practice where construction contracts are concerned is to make *express* provision for progress payments; financing costs are almost invariably assumed by the owner, who will have borrowed the necessary funds on a short-term basis from a bank or other lending institution. Hence, whatever its value as a legal abstraction or in other fields, the *Stewart* decision probably has little continuing importance in the context in which it arose.

2. *Substantial Performance.* In *Kingston,* as noted, the transactional setting was one that contemplated simultaneous performances by the parties—title documents to be exchanged for cash and debt—at a given date in the future. In that circumstance, presumably, the parties have ample time to prepare themselves to meet the conditions expressed in the contract, and one would suppose that a fairly high degree of conformity would be expected of each. Even so, Lord Mansfield thought it relevant to emphasize the *importance* of the "sufficient security" requirement—"the essence of the agreement," he said, "was that the defendant should not trust to the personal security of the plaintiff"—and perhaps we might infer that Mansfield had made a kind of mental distinction, obviously one of degree, between conditions that go to "the essence" and conditions that appear to be trivial or incidental.

The need for such a distinction is evident, I think, in the case of an extended service contract under which the service-provider obligates himself to meet a long list of contractual requirements, of which, however, some are plainly more important than others. *Jacob & Youngs v. Kent*[13] presents the issue in classic form. The plaintiff, a contractor, agreed to build a large country residence for the defendant for a price of $77,000 (the year was 1914) of which $3,400 remained unpaid at the time the work was completed. Having moved in, the defendant discovered after about a year that the water pipes which the plaintiff had installed were not "of Reading manufacture" as the plumbing specifications clearly required, but had been made by "Cohoes" and other pipe manufacturers. Apart from brand-name, however, the quality, value, cost and appearance of Cohoes and Reading pipe were exactly the same; moreover, the mistake (using Cohoes pipe instead of Reading) was unintentional on the plaintiff's part. Although the Cohoes pipe was enclosed in the wall in many places, the defendant demanded that it be ripped out "from cellar to roof", presumably at great expense, and Reading pipe put in its place. When the plaintiff refused, the defendant's architect similarly refused to issue a certificate for final payment and the plaintiff sued.

Finding that there had been substantial performance of the contract, the New York Court of Appeals held (4–3) for the plaintiff. Writing for the majority, Judge Cardozo accepted that the plaintiff's default had been inadvertent rather than willful or fraudulent. That being so, it was appropriate to draw a line between "the important and the trivial" in the context of the overall contractual undertaking. If the default were found to be trivial—as, in the Court's view, the use of Cohoes instead of Reading pipe plainly was—then it ought not to be treated as the breach of a condition "to be followed by a forfeiture". Instead, the default would be "atoned for" by an award of damages for the resulting difference, or diminishment, in the value of the property. In many cases, perhaps most, the distinction wouldn't matter, because the difference in value would be measured by the actual cost of replacing the wrong item with the right one. Here, however, it obviously mattered very much, since the "cost of replacement"—tearing out all the plumbing—would be substantial. By contrast, "difference in value"—the effect on the market price of the house of having used Cohoes instead of Reading pipe—was "either nominal or nothing".

The outcome in *Jacob & Youngs* seems entirely reasonable on the facts given, but of course one's view of the decision does, ultimately, depend on whether one accepts the proposition that the brand-name on a water pipe (the two brands being otherwise

---

13. 230 N.Y. 239, 129 N.E. 889 (1921).

identical) is indeed a "trivial" matter. The dissenting judges didn't think so: "Defendant contracted for pipe made by Reading.... He wanted that and was entitled to it.... The rule, therefore, of substantial performance, with damages for unsubstantial omissions, has no application." Cardozo himself conceded that the permitted "margin of departure" on a sale of "common chattels"— a car, a TV set—would be less than with respect to "the construction of a mansion or a 'skyscraper'." Thus, an auto-dealer cannot substitute a Dodge for a Chevrolet even though the two cars have the same market value and even though mechanical characteristics are virtually identical. Advertising and brand-name preferences are basic to the choices that consumers make, and whether prompted by real or imagined distinctions among competing products, such preferences obviously cannot be set aside in the name of "substantial performance". Aware of this, Cardozo nevertheless, as noted, lumped "mansions" and "skyscrapers" together. Both are large, to be sure, and in that respect they have something in common. But there the resemblance ends. Skyscrapers are built by investors whose interest in the property is exclusively financial and who truly do not care whether the builder installs Reading or Cohoes pipe, everything else being equal. But houses, even mansions, are built to live in, and, as with other consumer choices, personal preferences count.

In a sense, therefore, the essence of the *Jacob & Youngs* decision resides in a kind of "finding" by Judge Cardozo that *some* consumer preferences are simply too remote and idiosyncratic to be taken seriously.[14] We all care deeply about brand-names when it comes to beer, breakfast cereal and even bathroom fixtures. As to the water pipes in the basement, however, Cardozo evidently concluded that no reasonable consumer feels anything but total indifference about competing brands, provided that one brand is as durable and functional and costs the same as the other. But how could he actually know that? How could he have been so sure about prevailing consumer attitudes, so confident that a reasonable consumer would be indifferent as between Reading and Cohoes pipe? The probable answer: self-scrutiny. On reflection, Cardozo realized that he himself didn't actually know what brand of plumbing had been installed in his *own* house—and even more important, that he did not wish to know. Thoughtfully consulting his own preference

14. Not to mention some doubt about Kent's bona fides, perhaps. As noted, Kent lived in the mansion perfectly happily for a year before bringing up the water-pipe nonsense. No doubt he would have settled for the $3,400 still due to the builder had he won the lawsuit, rather than actually requiring the pipes to be replaced. Just possibly, Cardozo saw the Cohoes/Reading claim as nothing more than a device for chiseling on the contract price.

on the question of pipe-brands, the good judge found that the choice between Reading and Cohoes was one that left him (and by extrapolation other sensible home-owners) absolutely cold.

In *Jacob & Youngs,* as stated, the defendant's home was a mansion. In *Plante v. Jacobs,*[15] yet another familiar home construction case, the residence in question was part of a standard suburban development—not very different, one supposes, from other homes in the same neighborhood. The plaintiff had contracted to build the residence for the defendants in accordance with "a stock floor plan" for the sum of $26,000. Having paid the plaintiff $20,000 during the course of the construction, the defendants finally declared themselves dissatisfied with the work done and refused to continue payment. The plaintiff thereupon halted construction and sued for the unpaid balance, claiming that the contract had been substantially performed. In reply, the defendants pointed out that the wall between the living room and the kitchen had been misplaced, narrowing the living room by more than a foot. To tear the wall down and put up a new one would cost $4,000. There were, in addition, a number of minor items—cabinets, closet poles, gutters and downspouts—which still remained to be furnished. Since the wall plus the minor items amounted to more than 25% of the total contract price, defendants argued that there had been no substantial performance on plaintiff's part and, hence, that the full cost of replacement—the wall as well as the minor items— should be offset against the balance otherwise due.

The Supreme Court of Wisconsin held for the plaintiff on the central question of substantial performance. The Court did not appear to deny or dispute that the defendants might reasonably have been dissatisfied with the placement of the living room wall. This, however, was outweighed by the "economic waste" that would result if the wall had to be torn down and rebuilt, because the plaintiff would then have to replaster and redecorate the walls and ceilings of at least two rooms, viz., the living room and the kitchen, at a cost that was "unreasonable and unjustified". Accordingly, while defendants would be compensated for the minor items on a cost-of-replacement basis, the misplacing of the living room wall fell "under the diminished value rule". All of the expert witnesses having testified that the market value of the house was the same whether the living room was a foot wider or a foot narrower, the defendants were entitled to no offset whatever for the builder's default in this respect.

15. 10 Wis.2d 567, 103 N.W.2d 296 (1960).

Assuming the reader agrees with the writer that living room dimensions are a good deal more important than the brand-name on a water pipe, the decision in *Plante* may be hard to accept. The Wisconsin Court appears to have taken the view that the consumer's preference can be disregarded if (a) the cost of satisfying that preference is relatively high and (b) the market value of the product is the same either way. But that line of reasoning leads ultimately to a rule that would allow builders to freely substitute one home-design for another if the experts say that they have equal value, which obviously goes too far. The Court, to be sure, announced no such "rule", although, as stated, it did not seem to challenge the legitimacy and sincerity of the defendants' preference for a wider living room. In the end, perhaps, the Court may have felt that it simply had to recognize the fact that developers of serviceable, middle-income housing face significant cost constraints with respect to labor and materials, and that those constraints make it difficult to furnish a product that is totally without shortcomings. As noted, the plaintiff built his homes on the basis of "a stock floor plan. . . . There were no blueprints. The specifications were standard printed forms. . . ." Under these limiting circumstances, the defendants would have to regard the contract as substantially performed despite some disappointment with the final product. The Court conceded that there "may be situations"—the reference, presumably, is to sales of higher-priced homes (more numerous of windows, superior of doors)—in which buyers can properly insist on precise room dimensions and other features "of great personal importance". But if what you want is a decent house for a mere $26,000, you will have to settle for "[s]omething less than perfection . . .", no matter how strongly you may feel about the size of your parlor. In effect, you cannot get hand-tailoring if the suit you buy is off-the-rack.

3. *Sales of Goods and Perfect Tender.* Contracts for the sale of goods—between "merchants" or between merchant and consumer—also present issues generally relating to shortfalls in performance, but here, as Cardozo observed in *Jacob & Youngs,* the tolerable "margin of departure" is likely to be much narrower than in the case of service agreements. One reason for this, perhaps, is that "goods" are more or less unitary in character; they present themselves as physical objects whose characteristics combine to create a single tangible article that either *is* the thing described in the contract or is something else. The article is either T or it is not T; logically, no other categories exist. The nature of a service, by contrast, is less susceptible to categorical definition; whether the work done on the portrait of the late Miss Cranage was or was not

153

ⁿ satisfactory would be a harder question to answer than
ι coffee-maker holds six cups or ten. Often, of course,
_ _nd goods are mixed together in a single contractual
setting and there is uncertainty as to which predominates. *Jacob &
Youngs,* I suppose, would be a fair example. Cardozo chose to
regard the great water pipe question as one that involved the
rendering of a service rather than a sale of "common chattels"; on
that basis he was able to locate a third category—call it nearly T—
that qualified as substantial performance. The dissenters evidently
viewed water pipes as "articles" like any other and, since Cohoes
wasn't Reading, thought the contract had been breached.

At common law, a buyer of goods possessed a legal right to
insist upon "perfect tender" by the seller. If the goods failed to
conform exactly to the description in the contract—whether as to
quality, quantity or manner of delivery—the buyer could reject the
goods and rescind the contract, which meant that the parties would
be returned to the positions they occupied before the contract was
entered into. By contrast, as has been seen, the doctrine of substantial performance would entitle, but also limit, the buyer to damages
measured by the difference between the value of the goods promised and the value of the goods delivered. If the market price of the
goods happened to have dropped between the contract date and the
delivery date, the buyer would obviously prefer to rescind and
purchase the goods at the lower market price from other sources.
Thus, suppose the contract price is $20 a widget but the market
price of widgets has fallen to $5 at the date of delivery. If the seller
delivers widgets that deviate from the contract description and have
a market value of only $4.90, the buyer will be exceedingly pleased
to rescind under the perfect tender rule and save $15, as compared
with a damage recovery of only 10 cents a widget if the substantial
performance rule applies. Under these circumstances, quite obviously, the buyer will resort to the remedy of rescission even though
the defect in the seller's tender is altogether trivial. Yet a change in
the market price of widgets is the very contingency to which the
agreement between buyer and seller is addressed: in agreeing to a
$20 contract price, the parties' aim is to protect themselves against
a later adverse change in the market price of widgets—the buyer
against a later rise, the seller against a later fall. In effect, however,
the rescission remedy deprives the seller of his contract protection
and, for the same reason, enables the buyer to do better than he
would have done if the contract had been performed to the letter.[16]

16. Priest, *Breach and Remedy for*   *Economic Approach,* 91 Harv.L.Rev. 960
the Tender of Nonconforming Goods Un-   (1978). And see, Wiseman, *The Limits of*
der the Uniform Commercial Code: An

On this analysis the common-law approach appear faulty and the reader may therefore be slightly surpri that the perfect tender rule, with accompanying right is in fact adopted by UCC 2–601—at least purportedly.[17] The reason for this, presumably, is that despite the danger of opportunism on the buyer's side, there is an equal or perhaps a greater concern about how sellers would behave if buyers *lacked* a right to reject imperfect merchandise and were limited to a claim for damages (10 cents a widget in the illustration above). With little to lose, sellers would be expected to be less concerned with the need to conform precisely to the requirements of the contract; some, indeed, hoping the buyer will find it too burdensome to pursue a damage claim, might be tempted to deliberately substitute non-conforming goods for the goods described. A careless or a bad-faith seller who knows that he can defend on grounds of substantial performance might therefore seek to enforce a sale even though the goods delivered depart from the contract description and even though the seller was aware of the non-conformity at the time the goods were shipped.

The UCC attempts to resolve the conflict between buyers' and sellers' interests in this context through a kind of strategic compromise. As indicated, UCC 2–601 provides that a buyer may reject the goods supplied by his seller "if the goods or the tender of delivery fail in any respect to conform to the contract". Thus, facially, no distinction is to be made between more important and less important deviations from the contract or between a material and a non-material failure to conform. But while expressed in absolute terms, the buyer's right of rejection is actually somewhat less than absolute. Under 2–602(1), a rejecting buyer must "seasonably" notify the seller of his intention. Such notice having been given, 2–508(1) provides that the seller may respond by notifying the buyer of his intention to "cure" and may then make a conforming delivery if the time for performance has not yet expired. Presumably, then, in the widget case above, while the seller cannot prevent the buyer from treating the non-conformity as grounds for rejection, he can avoid the loss resulting from the slump in market price by promptly making delivery of conforming goods. The effect, roughly, is to protect the buyer from having defective merchandise dumped in his lap with no recourse other than a damage claim, while at the same time affording the seller a kind of second chance to meet his contract obligations.

A buyer's right to reject non-conforming goods may even survive his acceptance of the goods in question, "acceptance" being

---

Vision: Karl Llewellyn and the Merchant Rules, 100 Harv.L.Rev. 465, 526 (1987).

17. White and Summers, *Uniform Commercial Code* 303 (2d ed., 1980).

defined as a failure to reject after a reasonable opportunity for inspection. Here, however, the buyer encounters additional statutory limitations which presumably reflect a further effort to balance the parties' legitimate interests. Under 2–608(1), a buyer who has accepted non-conforming goods may subsequently revoke his acceptance and reject the merchandise only if (a) the non-conformity "substantially impairs its value to him" and (b) either he had reason to assume that the non-conformity would be cured by the seller (but it hasn't been) or the defect could not have been discovered on initial inspection (e.g., the widgets looked great but they shrank after washing). Moreover, a buyer who decides to accept and perhaps even use the non-conforming goods for some purpose cannot simply change his mind at a later date. Under 2–608(2), revocation of acceptance must occur within a reasonable time after the defect was or should have been discovered and before any alteration occurs in the condition of the goods other than that resulting from their own defect. In effect, then, while a buyer is not bound by his acceptance of non-conforming goods, he can thereafter revoke only if the non-conformity is substantial, only if he accepted without knowledge of the defect or in expectation of a cure, and only if the revocation is prompt and timely.

If non-conforming goods are accepted and the acceptance is not revoked, the buyer obviously loses his right to reject and must keep and pay for the goods. He does not thereby give up his right to conventional contract damages, however. The terms of the contract describing quantity, quality, function, etc., together constitute an "express warranty" on the seller's part that the goods delivered shall conform to such terms in all respects. If they do not, there is a breach. Under 2–714, the buyer may recover as damages the difference in value between the goods described in the contract and the goods actually delivered—e.g., 10 cents a widget—plus incidental and consequential damages as provided in 2–715.

4. *UCC Warranties.* A *description* of the goods sold by a seller is treated as an "Express Warranty"—that is, a promise to the buyer that the goods will conform to that description—if the description is "made part of the basis of the bargain." UCC 2–313. Whether the description is made part of the basis of the bargain depends on whether it is reasonable to infer that the seller intends to bear the risk of nonperformance if the goods fall short of their described function. There is, of course, near endless litigation as to whether particular contractual language constitutes an "express warranty" or is merely a recommendation or, indeed, mere "puff-

ing." In the *Bayliner* case[18], for example, the seller of
fishing boat stated in its sales literature that its model ᴜᴄ̣
"delivers the kind of performance you need to get to the prime
offshore fishing grounds" and then back home by nightfall. Claiming breach of an express warranty, the disappointed buyer asserted,
and apparently proved, that such "performance" required a speed
of 30 miles an hour whereas in fact the boat could do no better
than a sluggish 24. Holding for the defendant boat-seller, the Court
found that the quoted statement was "merely a commendation of
the boat's performance ... simply ... [an] opinion ... and did not
create an express warranty" that formed "the basis of the bargain"
under section 2–313.

Apart from section 2–313, the UCC provides protection to
buyers in the form of two Implied Warranties, the warranty of
"merchantability" and the warranty of "fitness", both of which are
deemed to be part of the seller's contractual obligation to the buyer
unless disclaimed. To be "merchantable" under 2–314, the goods
sold must be such as "(a) pass without objection in the trade ...,
(b) are of fair average quality ..., and (c) are fit for the ordinary
purposes for which such goods are used...." The warranty of
"fitness" in 2–315 implies a promise on the seller's part that the
goods shall fit the *particular* purpose for which the goods are
required where the seller knows of the buyer's purpose and knows
also that the buyer is relying on him, the seller, to use that
knowledge in selecting goods that are appropriate. Under 2–316, a
seller may limit or disclaim both of the implied warranties by
specifically so stating or by providing that the goods are sold "As
Is," meaning that the buyer, not the seller, assumes responsibility
for the quality and suitability of the goods sold. In the *Roto–Lith*
case at p. 76, the glue-seller disclaimed "all warranties ... whatsoever" because of the "variable conditions under which these goods
may be ... used." The glue didn't glue, but the warranty disclaimer relieved the seller of liability.

The warranty of merchantability is well illustrated (negatively,
as it turned out) by the *Flippo* case[19], of which the first paragraph
of the Arkansas Court's opinion is worth quoting:

"This litigation is occasioned by a spider bite. Gladys Flippo
... went into a ladies clothing store in Batesville, operated by Rosie
Goforth, and known as Mode O'Day Frock Shops of Hollywood.
Mrs. Flippo tried on two pairs of pants, or slacks, which were

---

18. Bayliner Marine Corp. v. Crow, 257 Va. 121, 509 S.E.2d 499 (1999).

19. Flippo v. Mode O'Day Frock Shops of Hollywood, 248 Ark. 1, 449 S.W.2d 692 (1970).

shown to her by Mrs. Goforth. The first pair proved to be too small, and ... when Mrs. Flippo put on the second pair, she suddenly felt a burning sensation on her thigh; she immediately removed the pants, shook them, and a spider fell to the floor which was stepped upon.... Mrs. Flippo was subsequently hospitalized for approximately 30 days. According to her physician, the injury was caused by the bite of a brown recluse spider...."

Mrs. Flippo brought suit against Mode O'Day asserting "that there was an implied warranty that the slacks were fit for the purpose for which they were purchased, though actually not fit, because of the poisonous spider concealed therein." Holding for the defendant, the Court found that the implied warranty of merchantability had no application "to a case of this nature." The pair of pants, said the Court, "was fit for the ordinary purpose for which stretch pants are used ... and there is no evidence that [the defendant] had any control of the spider, or caused it to be in the pants.... Perhaps our position can best be made clear by simply stating that the spider was not part of the manufactured article, and the injury to Mrs. Flippo was caused by the spider—and not the product." Mrs. Flippo's other asserted grounds for recovery, largely tort claims, were also dismissed. Lacking was any proof that the spider had found its recluse in the Batesville store rather than on the premises of the manufacturer far away.

5. *Material Breach.* As noted earlier, there is an apparent opposition between the strict rule that failure to perform constitutes a breach which properly excuses the injured party from her own performance obligations and, on the other hand, a fairly strong sense that the law should do what it reasonably can to prevent or deter the break-down of contract relations. Like the UCC, the Restatement seeks to achieve a practical balance of interests by (a) asserting the absolute right of the injured party to treat non-performance as a breach, but then (b) calibrating the legal consequences by reference to the gravity of the offense. Thus, Restatement Section 235 provides that when performance of a duty under a contract is due, "any" non-performance by the obligor is to be regarded as a breach. If the obligor's failure to perform is not "material" in character—a minor departure from plan-specifications by a builder, for example—the injured party is required to continue performance but may claim damages for whatever loss has been sustained. If the failure *is* material, then, under Sections 225 and 237, the injured party may treat the failure as equivalent to the non-occurrence of a condition and, depending on the circumstances, either suspend her own performance or regard herself as having been discharged in full. If it is reasonable to expect that the party

failing to perform will resume performance and "cure" her failure in a timely fashion, the injured party's duty to perform will be suspended until a cure takes place; but if no cure is possible, or if none is effected, then, at last, the injured party may regard her obligations as discharged. In the latter event, the injured party is entitled to damages for "total breach"; in the former, to damages for "partial breach", meaning, presumably, any loss incurred by reason of the obligor's delay in effecting a cure.

In applying these (or similar common-law) rules to particular cases, the important questions, quite obviously, are: what constitutes a "material" as opposed to a non-material failure to perform, and when is the injured party justified in considering her own performance duties discharged? *K & G Construction Co. v. Harris,*[20] decided by the Maryland Court of Appeals, furnishes an illustration of the issues. In *K & G*, the plaintiff, owner and general contractor for a housing subdivision, entered into a contract with the defendant to do the excavation and earth-moving work for the project. The contract called for the plaintiff to make monthly progress payments to the defendant (less a retainage of 10%), with each such payment being due on the 10th day of the following month. The defendant agreed to perform "in a workmanlike manner, and in accordance with the best practices", and further agreed to carry liability insurance for any property damage that might occur while the work was in progress.

Excavation proceeded satisfactorily through the month of July, but on August 9 a bulldozer operator employed by defendant drove his machine too close to a house, causing the collapse of a wall and other damage. The defendant, and more particularly its insurer, refused to repair the house and denied liability for the damage—presumably on the ground that there had been no negligence in the operation of the bulldozer. The plaintiff thereupon refused to make the payment otherwise due on August 10 for work that had been done during the preceding month. The defendant nevertheless continued to work on the project until September 12, at which date it stopped work and left the site because the plaintiff again refused to make payments either for July or for August. Although the defendant notified the plaintiff (by registered letter) that it was willing to return to work if the overdue payments were made, the plaintiff finally hired another excavating firm to complete the job and was obliged to pay the latter $450 above the contract price.

Plaintiff sued for the property damage caused by the bulldozer and for contract damages of $450. Defendant counterclaimed for

20. 223 Md. 305, 164 A.2d 451 (1960).

the back payments plus its own lost profits, a total of $2,824. In a separate proceeding before a jury, the plaintiff was awarded $3,400 for the bulldozer damage, which defendant's insurer apparently paid. The parties' contract claims were then submitted to the trial judge, who held for the defendant and allowed its counterclaim in full.

Reversing the trial court on the contract issue, the Court of Appeals denied the defendant's counterclaim and awarded damages of $450 to the plaintiff. The Court found that negligent operation of the bulldozer by defendant's employee constituted a material breach of defendant's duty to perform "in a workmanlike manner...." This, in turn, left the plaintiff with an option to regard the defendant's failure as a "total breach", in which event the plaintiff would have been discharged and free to sue for damages, or to treat the defendant as being in "partial breach" only, in which event the defendant, though unpaid, would be expected to continue its work and complete the contract. Plaintiff obviously chose the latter course. Accordingly, the defendant *again* breached the contract—this time totally—when it walked off the job on September 12, and it thereby became liable to the plaintiff for the increased cost, $450, of having the excavation finished by another subcontractor.

Despite the jury's finding of negligence on the defendant's part, the decision in *K & G* seems questionable. While "workmanlike" performance was plainly a condition precedent to the plaintiff's duty to make monthly progress payments, it seems well arguable that isolated accidents were not intended to be regarded as violating that condition since such occurrences (if found to be due to negligence) would be covered by the defendant's repair obligation or by insurance. In any case, the defendant's overall performance *was* workmanlike; the bulldozer accident was not part of a pattern of careless job-performance and one would not have supposed that a single event, by itself, would amount to a breach. Even if it were so regarded, there would be a real question as to whether it should be considered "material" given that in all other respects the excavation was proceeding in a wholly satisfactory way. Finally, even assuming that the bulldozer accident was a material breach, it appears that a "cure" was assured to the plaintiff through resort to the insurance fund if and when the defendant should be found liable for negligence. From the standpoint of orderly conduct, one's impression is that plaintiff and defendant should have gone forward with their respective contract responsibilities—as defendant declared itself ready to do if progress payments were resumed—and that the parties should have treated the damage issue as one to be resolved separately, whether by suit or settlement, after the excavation work had been completed and paid for.

The plaintiff's decision to suspend progress payments on August 10—the day after the bulldozer accident—was undoubtedly taken in haste and without consulting counsel. This was fortunate for the plaintiff as it turned out, because plaintiff's lawyer, had she been consulted, would very likely have found the legal and factual questions too close and too numerous to feel safe in advising her client that it would be legally proper to withhold the payment otherwise due. *Was* the defendant's performance so "unworkmanlike" as to constitute a material breach? It would have been difficult, I think, to say yes with confidence or to go beyond a highly qualified prediction as to the outcome of any future litigation. As has often been observed, the lawyer's counselling job in these and similar circumstances is really quite chancy. If she advises her client that the latter may suspend performance because the other party has committed a material breach, and if that advice is acted upon but turns out to be wrong, then it will be the client who will have committed the first breach and the other party who will have a claim for contract damages. No doubt with this risk in mind, the defendant in *K & G* adopted what most would say was the better and more cautious tactic when it chose to continue working without pay for a second month and then—almost certainly on the advice of counsel—indicated its willingness to complete the job if payments were resumed. Defendant's aim, pretty clearly, was to leave it to the plaintiff to repudiate the contract and take responsibility for the final rupture. Ironically, this wise and well-considered strategy didn't succeed. Probably it should have.

Much the same point—namely, that "the injured party's determination that there has been a material breach, justifying its own repudiation, is fraught with peril"—is well illustrated by *Walker & Co. v. Harrison*,[21] yet another casebook standby. The defendant, Harrison, proud owner of a neighborhood dry-cleaning establishment, purchased a large and beautiful outdoor advertising sign (18'9" by 8'8", no less) from the plaintiff, Walker & Co., which was in the business of building and servicing signs and billboards. The contract between plaintiff and defendant—essentially a conditional sales contract—called for the defendant to pay $148.50 a month for 36 months, following which the defendant would take title to the sign. Failure to make timely payments entitled the plaintiff-seller to recover the entire unpaid amount for the remaining term of the contract. Plaintiff, for its part, agreed to "maintain and service the

21. 347 Mich. 630, 81 N.W.2d 352 (1957).

.. such service to include cleaning and repainting . . . as often
:emed necessary . . . to keep sign in first class advertising
ᴄᴏ.. ition and make all necessary repairs to sign and equipment. . . ."

Along with the proprietor's name in flashing neon lights, the
sign featured a large electric clock, presumably fixed in place high
above the street. After duly making the first monthly payment of
$148.50, Harrison noticed that little boys in the neighborhood had
scribbled naughty sayings on the sign and, even worse, that somebody with a pretty good arm had hit the clock itself with a ripe
tomato. Vexed and dismayed, Harrison at once called Walker, told
the company about the tomato and the naughty scribbles, and
demanded prompt "maintenance," especially cleaning, in accordance with the service agreement. Walker listened politely but
otherwise failed to respond. Harrison angrily called again, and
again and again. Still Walker did nothing. Finally, after two full
months had passed, having made no monthly payments beyond the
first, Harrison sent Walker a telegram (probably drafted by counsel) asserting, in effect, that Walker's failure to provide maintenance as promised constituted a material breach, and stating that
he, Harrison, would make no further payments and considered the
contract to be "Voided." Walker did send out a service crew a week
later, but Harrison stuck by his position and refused to resume
monthly payments. Ultimately, Walker sued, claiming damages
equal to the full amount still due on the purchase price, about
$5,200.

Holding for the plaintiff, the Supreme Court of Michigan first
listed the criteria for materiality, (a) through (e), that now appear
in Restatement Section 241. It then speedily concluded that Walker's failure to clean the sign, however irritating to Harrison, "was
not of such materiality as to justify repudiation of the contract."
On this central issue the Court affirmed an equivalent finding by
the trial court, but it did so entirely without discussion and without
further reference to the Restatement. It did not explain why none
of the criteria in Section 241 had been met, and most particularly
why Section 241(a), which refers to "the extent to which the
injured party will be deprived of the benefit which he reasonably
expected," had no application from Harrison's standpoint. Apparently, the Court did not think Harrison had been "deprived" of
benefits reasonably expected. Again, however, that conclusion was
reached without explanation and appears to have been altogether
intuitive.

While, on the whole, one shares that intuition, even so it might
have been appropriate for the Court to have devoted some analysis

to the likely or intended scope of Walker's maintenance and service obligation, which, as noted, was "to keep sign in first class advertising condition." Tomato splatter obviously made the sign look ridiculous and certainly not "first class," however defined. That being so, why shouldn't the desecration of the clock-face have been enough to trigger Walker's duty under the contract?

The answer, perhaps, is that outdoor advertising inevitably attracts graffiti, and anyone who buys such advertising has got to expect exactly that. Almost any billboard within reach of passing strollers gets its daily share of spray-paint, naughty scribbles and other mutilation more or less as a matter of course. That, I would say, is common experience. Putting the point in present context, if the tomato was thrown at the clock on Monday, and if Walker had cleaned it off on Tuesday as Harrison demanded, it would surely have been up there again on Wednesday or Thursday unless Walker posted a 24–hour guard to chase the kids away. Plainly, however, Walker's service obligation could not have contemplated a duty to clean and repaint the sign on a daily basis, which is what it would have had to do as long as the local lads found target practice amusing.

It follows, I think, that Walker's maintenance obligation should reasonably be understood to require service at regular intervals only—say bi-monthly—despite the inevitable graffiti attacks that would occur between service calls. The implied contractual duty, it would seem, was that cleaning, painting and repair would be performed (if "deemed necessary") on the occasion of such regularly scheduled service calls, but not before, and not simply on demand. And, of course, Walker's crew did clean Harrison's clock in due course as promised. On this view, the issue in the case was not so much whether Walker's failure to respond when Harrison called was a "material" breach as whether it was a breach at all.

Winning the case, on whatever ground, was obviously important from Walker's standpoint—not merely because of the dollars involved, but because of the implication a contrary outcome would have had for the company's entire portfolio of customer service contracts. The Court, one would guess, perceived that the lawsuit actually posed a threat to Walker & Co. that went well beyond this sign, this clock and this tomato. The Court could, and perhaps should, have been more explicit about what it thought the seller's duty was under a standard billboard service contract—as suggested, to provide maintenance at scheduled intervals despite the daily dose of graffiti. Instead, it took the easy way out by treating Harrison's particular complaint as non-material.

Driven by pique, Harrison, or his counsel, took a step that was aught with peril" and paid a price for acting hastily. On the plus ~ de, Harrison now owns the sign free and clear, and he can get up there and clean the clock himself if he is able.

6. *Anticipatory Breach.* The legal and factual issue in *K & G* and in *Walker & Co. v. Harrison*, as has been seen, was whether the plaintiff or the defendant should be held to have breached by failing to render performance at the time such performance fell due. A slightly different and seemingly simpler question is presented if one of the contracting parties expressly repudiates her contractual obligations in *advance* of the time performance is due, in effect advising the promisee that no such performance will be forthcoming. Thus, A and B enter into a contract on April 1 under which B agrees to work for A for a three-month period beginning June 1. A is planning a trip abroad and wants B to come along as a kind of messenger boy and all-around flunkey. On May 11, A informs B that he has changed his plans and will not need B's services after all. On May 22, B brings an action against A for breach. Should B's suit be dismissed as premature? Viewed in strictly formal terms, the answer might be yes: A has promised to employ B on June 1 and he cannot logically be found to have broken that promise until the June 1 date has come and gone. Statements made by A before the June 1 date, however ominous, do not in themselves constitute a failure on A's part to perform his duty under the agreement. Practically speaking, however, it is plain that in repudiating his obligation to B, A has impaired, indeed destroyed, B's employment expectations and has made it necessary for B to scurry about and find other employment without delay. B cannot wait until June 1 to find out whether A might still provide him with a paycheck, and he obviously cannot live on the distant prospect of a damage recovery.

In *Hochster v. De La Tour,*[22] on the facts stated in the preceding paragraph, Queen's Bench held that A's repudiation operated to discharge B's duties under the employment agreement, which left B free to find himself another job for the three-month period and in effect precluded A from changing his mind yet again and repudiating his repudiation. Apparently deeming it a necessary corollary, the Court held also that the plaintiff had a right to commence an action for damages immediately, that is, prior to the scheduled beginning of performance on June 1. The latter holding, as many have pointed out, was something of a *non sequitur:* the Court could have dismissed B's suit for damages as premature, while still

22.   118 Eng. Rep. 922 (1853).

confirming his right to rely on A's repudiation by tr
obligation to work for A as having been cancelled. T!
notwithstanding, the twofold rule of the *Hochster* decision is gꞈ.
ally followed by the courts and is adopted by Restatement Section
253. In the end, the rather unsurprising point is that the anticipatory repudiation of a promise to perform, no less than a failure to
perform at the time performance is due, may constitute a total
breach. In either case the injured party has a claim for damages
and may assume that her own performance obligations have been
discharged.

Apart from the injured promisee's right to sue, the *Hochster*
rule, treating repudiation as equivalent to total breach, may also
have the "virtuous" consequence of reducing the cost of contract
failure. Two related reasons can be mentioned. First, the injured
party is presumably required to mitigate at the time of, or reasonably soon after, the act of repudiation instead of delaying until
actual performance would be due. Mitigation would take the form
of "cover" or "resale" where, as in the *Olaffson* case below, the
repudiated contract involves a sale of goods, or of a substitute
employment where, as in *Hochster*, a service contract is involved.
Second, the injured party should halt what would otherwise be
wasted reliance outlays, a problem noticed in connection with the
Luten Bridge case at p. 203. Repudiation in advance of the performance date may thus in some circumstances minimize the cost of
breach.

Actually, the legally appropriate time for cover or resale where
advance repudiation involves a sale of goods has been a litigated
issue. Ordinarily, if a seller fails to deliver goods when due, the
buyer may "cover" under UCC 2–711(1) by purchasing equivalent
goods in the market and under 2–712 have damages equal to the
difference between the cost of cover and the contract price. If the
contract price is $1 a unit and, following the seller's failure to
deliver, the buyer covers at a cost of $1.25, the seller is liable to the
buyer in the amount of 25 cents times the number of units
promised under the contract. All perfectly simple. Suppose, however, that the seller expressly repudiates the contract well before the
delivery date. Are the buyer's damages limited to the difference
between the market and the contract price at the time the seller
repudiates, or is the market-minus-contract differential to be determined at the later date when the seller's performance would
otherwise come due? The buyer will obviously prefer the later date
if the market price of the goods goes up following the seller's
repudiation; the seller's preference will be the reverse.

In *Oloffson v. Coomer*,[23] the plaintiff was a grain dealer who, in April, entered into a contract with the defendant, a farmer, for the purchase of 40,000 bushels of corn at about $1.12 a bushel. 20,000 bushels were to be delivered by the defendant in October, 20,000 in December. In June, when the price for future delivery was $1.16, the defendant notified the plaintiff that he had decided not to plant corn that season—the weather was too wet, he said—and he therefore advised the plaintiff to obtain the corn elsewhere. The plaintiff disregarded that advice and instead continued to request delivery of the corn, which requests the defendant ignored. Finally, the scheduled delivery dates having passed with no corn delivered,, the plaintiff covered by purchasing 40,000 bushels of corn in the market at an average cost of $1.42 a bushel and sued the defendant for 30 cents ($1.42—$1.12) times 40,000 bushels, or $12,000. The defendant conceded his breach, but insisted that the plaintiff's cover damages should be limited to 40,000 times the difference between the contract price and the market price per bushel at the earlier date of repudiation, $1.16—$1.12 = 4 cents, or only about $1,600.

The Illinois court held for the defendant. Recognizing that the UCC supplied no very clear direction, the court found that the plaintiff's failure to cover at the time he learned of the defendant's repudiation—instead, waiting until the later delivery date, by which time the market price of corn had gone up sharply—was contrary to the established and accepted "usage of trade" in the grain business, and therefore lacked good faith. If the plaintiff had complied with the usage of trade, said the court, he would have permitted the defendant to cancel and buy his way out of the contract by paying him, the plaintiff, the difference between the contract and the market price on the day of cancellation, *i.e.*, 4 cents a bushel or $1,600. The plaintiff was aware of such "usage" and, knowing the defendant was not, should have disclosed the same to the defendant and in that way given the latter an opportunity to minimize his liability for breach.

The outcome in the *Oloffson* case seems correct, though perhaps not absolutely inevitable.[24] If Oloffson, the buyer, could wait to establish his cover price until the later delivery date, then the breach would be entirely in his favor: if the market price of corn rose between the repudiation and the delivery date, as it did in the case itself, Oloffson would recover from Coomer the amount of such

---

23. 11 Ill.App.3d 918, 296 N.E.2d 871 (1973).

24. *See* Jackson, *"Anticipatory Repudiation" and the Temporal Element of Contract Law*, 31 Stan.L.Rev. 69 (1978). *But see* White & Summers, *Uniform Commercial Code* § 6–7 (3d ed. 1988).

increase; if the market price fell below the contract price following repudiation, Oloffson (freed from his obligation to buy from Coomer) would buy at the lower price in the spot market. On his side, Coomer would have to compensate Oloffson for a rise in the market price of corn, but would get no benefit from a price decline. In effect, anticipatory repudiation would put Oloffson in a better position, prospectively, than if Coomer simply waited until the delivery date to decide whether to perform. Repudiation in advance of the delivery date—an appropriate action, it seems, once the farmer realized that he would have no corn to deliver—would thus overcompensate the buyer by permitting him to speculate risk-free at the seller's expense.

To be sure, Coomer himself could have hedged against future market changes at the date of his repudiation by entering into an equivalent purchase contract with another farmer at the then market price of $1.16—precisely what he advised Oloffson to do when he, Coomer, decided to repudiate. At least arguably, Coomer, being the party in breach, should have acted to minimize his own risk of loss by finding a substitute source of supply—that is, by purchasing an offsetting "call" on 40,000 bushels of corn at $1.16 a bushel. Had he done that, there would have been no need for him to repudiate or make any kind of fuss at all. But Coomer was a farmer, a man of the soil, not a market adept. By contrast, Oloffson was an active and sophisticated grain dealer with wide knowledge of alternative supply sources. Dealers know many things, farmers only one. Presumably, therefore, Oloffson was in the best position to arrange a substitute supply contract, and to avoid delay and added cost in doing so.

7. *Demand for assurance.* In *Hochster* the promisor expressly repudiated the contract, but of course repudiation may be inferred from the promisor's conduct even if no statement is made. Thus, A agrees to sell a house to B, the deed to be delivered and the purchase price to be paid on June 1. On May 1 A sells the house to C. The latter act is obviously a repudiation even though A says nothing to B directly. Complicating the issue slightly, suppose B learns (on May 1) that various mechanics liens have been filed on the property which, unless satisfied before June 1, would violate A's obligation to transfer clear title. Assume further that B has reason to doubt whether A can find the money to satisfy the liens. At least arguably, the resulting uncertainty "impairs the value of the contract" from B's standpoint and leaves B in rather a quandary as to how she should proceed—e.g., whether she should or shouldn't commit herself to a lender, whether she should or shouldn't spend time looking for another house to buy, and so on. Restatement

,ion 251, which echoes UCC 2–609 in this respect, offers B a
 ,ctical solution by providing that a promisee who has "reason-
ᴜ.le grounds" for believing that the contract will be breached may
"demand adequate assurance of due performance" from the promisor and suspend her own performance until such assurance is
received. Failure to provide adequate assurance may be considered
by the promisee to be the equivalent of a repudiation, in which
event the promisee, like the messenger-boy in *Hochster,* may sue
for damages and regard her duties under the contract as discharged.

What qualifies as "reasonable grounds" for insecurity on the
promisee's part, and what should then be taken as "adequate
assurance" by the promisor, must of course depend on the particular facts and circumstances of the case at hand, which suggests that
the parties and their counsel, like the litigants in *K & G,* will
sometimes find themselves in the uncomfortable position of having
to make nice judgments in a hurry. Thus, a promisor may decide
not to respond to a demand for assurance because she or her
counsel consider that the promisee lacked "reasonable grounds" for
making that demand; similarly, a promisee who has received an
assurance of some sort from the promisor may decide that such
assurance is less than "adequate" and conclude that her own
contractual obligations are cancelled. In either case, of course, the
decision could turn out to be "wrong" in the later view of a court or
jury, which would be asked to decide not whether there had been
an *actual* failure to perform on the promisor's part, but whether
the prospect of such a failure was sufficiently threatening to justify
the promisee in taking self-defensive action in advance.

Doubts about getting paid by a buyer is obviously a reason for
"insecurity" on the part of a committed seller. Presumably the
seller satisfied itself about the buyer's credit record at the time it
accepted the buyer's order. Since that time, however, the seller has
learned or heard rumors that other suppliers have failed to receive
payment when due and are now insisting that the buyer put up
cash in advance of delivery. Can the seller on that ground demand
"adequate assurance" and suspend performance? It might be argued that accepting the buyer's order includes accepting the credit
risk as well, but I suppose ordinary day-to-day dealings would then
be complicated by the seller's need to qualify its acceptance or
require security unless it knows the buyer well. In any case, the
"default rule" is generally otherwise: a seller who has reasonable
grounds for feeling insecure about the buyer's ability to pay is
entitled under UCC 2–609 to demand assurance, usually in the
form of a letter from the buyer's bank or an updated credit report,

and to regard the buyer as having repudiated the contract if such assurance is not forthcoming.

But not always. In *Pittsburgh–Des Moines Steel Co. v. Brookhaven Manor Water Co.*,[25] a case arising under UCC 2–609, the plaintiff, PDM, had contracted to build a tank for the defendant for $175,000, payment to be made 30 days after construction. The parties evidently understood that the defendant would obtain a loan to pay for the facility. Having learned that the defendant had been unable to complete arrangements with one prospective lender, the plaintiff advised the defendant that it would suspend performance unless the defendant placed the purchase price in escrow or unless the defendant's president gave his personal guarantee of payment. Subsequently, neither action having been taken, the plaintiff charged the defendant with repudiating the contract and sued for damages. The defendant, charging repudiation on the plaintiff's part, entered a counterclaim.

The Court held for the defendant. The issue, in the Court's view, was whether there had been a change for the worse in the defendant's financial condition after the contract was entered into sufficient to establish "reasonable grounds for insecurity" within the meaning of UCC 2–609. The defendant's inability or unwillingness to borrow money from a particular lender did not prove that such a worsening had occurred, and in fact the defendant's credit status, of which the plaintiff's comptroller conceded that he had had complete information, was no different, and no weaker, than it had been at the contract date. In effect, the Court surmised that the plaintiff-seller had simply changed its mind about extending credit to the defendant-buyer and had decided that it did not wish to go forward without additional security. On this view, the plaintiff's demand lacked good-faith and was nothing more than a backdoor attempt to rewrite the terms of the original agreement.

25.   532 F.2d 572 (7th Cir.1976).

Chapter 7

MISTAKE AND IMPOSSIBILITY

The question of contract breach most often arises by reason of the conduct and behavior, overt or implicit, of the parties themselves. One party is complained of by the other either for actively doing something he shouldn't have done or, more commonly, for failing to do something he should have done, and the issue to be resolved is whether the circumstances reasonably support the complaining party's position. In the cases considered in this Chapter, by contrast, it is some exterior event—one that lies beyond the direct control of either party—that is said to explain and justify the apparent breach. The non-performing party admits his non-performance but argues, in effect, that facts or events not known to him at the time the agreement was entered into, or that took place afterwards, made performance impossible or impracticable both actually and as a matter of law.

The discussion that follows is divided into two sections, as the title implies. The two topics relate in the sense that the element of demonstrable fault is lacking in each. Thus, the cow in *Sherwood v. Walker* was not the cow, or at least not the kind of cow, that buyer and seller had in mind; but neither party intended to mislead or deceive the other (apparently). Similarly, while the big parade never took place in *Krell v. Henry,* neither landlord nor tenant could be blamed for the King's appendicitis. In both cases, however, there were losses—including actual out-of-pocket expenditures— that would have to be suffered by someone. Yet if no one was to blame, how do we decide which party should be made to take the consequences?

A. Mistake and Impracticability

1. *Restatement Section 152.* Discussing the good ships *Peerless* in Chapter 2, above, it was observed that parties who misunderstand each other's initial intentions may find that they have no contract at all, that their apparent relationship does not exist and never did. The formation of a contract presupposes mutual assent, so that if each party assents to a different proposition, there is nothing to enforce and the contract is void.

But *Peerless*-type cases are surely rare. Somewhat more common, I would guess, are cases in which the contracting parties fully

agree as to the identity of the particular property to be ex
but one or both are mistaken in what they understand tha
ty to be. When the reality finally emerges and the natu
property is seen in its true light, one party finds it advantageous to
seek enforcement, the other to resist. Minds (however misguided)
met at one level, so that at least conceptually the threshold question of whether there ever *was* a contract appears to be answered.
Yet the fact that the parties (either or both) erred in making a basic
assumption about the character of the transaction obviously raises
doubts about whether such a contract merits enforcement.

   Sherwood v. Walker,[1] long a vehicle for weary classroom hu-
mor, presents the issue in the context of what appears to have been
a *mutual* mistake. The defendant, an importer and breeder of
Angus cattle, offered to sell a certain cow (known by name and
pedigree) to the plaintiff, a local bank executive. Defendant advised
plaintiff that the cow in question was barren and could be purchased for $80, which represented her value as sirloin steak. By
contrast, had the cow been capable of breeding her market value
would have been $1,000. Plaintiff made a visit to defendant's cattle-
pen, looked at the cow and liked what he saw, and therefore
promptly accepted defendant's offer. Before plaintiff could take
delivery, however, defendant learned from his ranch foreman that
the cow was in fact "with calf" and refused to hand her over.
Plaintiff then brought an action in replevin seeking to obtain
possession of the animal, now known to be a breeder, at the $80
contract price.

   Reversing a lower court judgment for the plaintiff and remanding the case for a new trial, the Supreme Court of Michigan held
that if at the time they entered into their agreement both parties
did in fact believe that the cow was barren and forever useless for
breeding, then the defendant had a right to rescind and refuse
delivery. Under well settled law, said the Court, a contract cannot
be enforced if the "whole substance" and "very nature" of the
merchandise sold is different from that which the parties bargained
for, if the mistaken identification was mutual, and if the dollar
consequences to the disadvantaged party are significant. Apparently
each of those criteria was satisfied in the Court's view, and one
assumes that the plaintiff abandoned his claim once the decision
was announced. A dissenting Justice argued that the majority
opinion overstated the strength of the parties' original convictions:
defendant "thought" the cow would never breed, but plaintiff
"thought" she might, neither being perfectly sure. The parties were

---

1.   66 Mich. 568, 33 N.W. 919 (1887).

not mistaken in a legal sense, merely ignorant or uncertain, and each took his chances. Accordingly, the banker should have his cow.

There are, I think, dark shapes and suspicions running through the *Sherwood* case.[2] Taking the facts presented by the Court at face, however, the decision is hard to accept. Certainly we must have a doctrine of "mistake". If B agrees to buy the contents of boxcar #306 from S at a price which reflects the assumption that the boxcar carries a shipment of soybeans, when in fact it carries a shipment of gold bars, no sensible legal rule would deny S's right to rescind or reform the contract by showing that what he intended, and what B understood him to intend, was boxcar #206, which happens to contain the soybeans. A contrary position would convert administrative and other quasi-clerical errors into acts of forfeiture and would be appropriate only if the law were viewed as a mindless ritual. Where, however, as in *Sherwood,* the transaction relates to property that has been particularized by the parties (the cow had a glorious name, as noted), and where appraisal of the property's value is a function of the seller's professional expertise, a different conclusion seems proper. The circumstances in *Sherwood* really suggest a misjudgment on the defendant's part rather than a mistake, and it is that, I think, that leaves the reader feeling doubtful about the outcome.

Perhaps even the term "misjudgment" concedes too much. A dealer in specialized property—antiques, paintings, pedigreed cattle, real estate—invests what he regards as an appropriate amount of time and money in ascertaining the value of his inventory. The dealer operates on the assumption that in general sales are final and cannot be reversed, but presumably he recognizes the possibility that he may, occasionally, arrive at too low an appraisal for some article and give the lucky customer a bargain. He knows from experience, however, that this will happen only rarely. To be sure, the number of such mistakes or misjudgments could be reduced even further, perhaps wholly avoided, by spending still more time and money on the appraisal process, but as a business matter it

---

2. Sherwood was not a butcher but, as noted, a banker and perhaps a gentleman farmer. As such, why would he want to purchase a single head of beef cattle from Walker, i.e., just one non-producing cow? Whatever the reason, one marvels at his luck at having picked this particular cow out of a number of non-breeders that were being offered for sale. But was it luck? My own guess (just a guess) is that Sherwood paid a "fee" to someone at the cattle-pen who knew very well that the cow was with calf and who was looking for a way to turn that inside information into cash. If the Michigan Court suspected such a thing ("She was evidently sold and purchased on the relation of her value as beef, unless the plaintiff had learned of her true condition, and concealed such knowledge from the defendants...."), then the decision might possibly be explained as an exercise in judicial realism (upper Midwest variety).

really isn't worth it. Quite simply, the dealer calculates that he will lose $X through misappraisals unless he spends $X *plus* $Y to hire another appraiser. Since the cost of employing additional personnel exceeds the expected benefit, the dealer wisely decides not to take that step. But having made that decision, he cannot also claim that he has made a "mistake" and should be permitted to rescind when the rare event occurs. In effect, he *figured* it would happen (sometime) and rationally chose to assume the risk rather than pay to avoid it. If, nevertheless, he *is* allowed to rescind, then the dealer gets a financial benefit that is undeserved—very much as if he somehow became entitled to the proceeds of an insurance policy (call it "misappraisal insurance") without ever having had to pay any insurance premiums.

The best reason for allowing rescissional relief in a mutual mistake case, I suppose, is that otherwise one party would receive a windfall while the other would suffer a penalty. This is certainly true in the case of boxcar #306, mentioned above. In *Sherwood,* however, as I have tried to argue, there really is no element of penalty, and the "windfall" is entirely up for grabs. Enforcing the contract would have given buyer an unexpected benefit, but rescinding did just the same for seller. With neither party having any moral claim to the difference between the contract price and the true value of the property, the fact that the seller could have "insured" but didn't, together with a general preference for treating transactions as final rather than reversible, pretty strongly suggests that enforcement would have been the better result.

Though largely disregarded in *Sherwood,* the factor of risk-assumption is treated by most modern authorities as an integral feature of the doctrine of mistake. Restatement Section 152 provides that a contract based on mutual mistake is voidable unless the adversely affected party bears the risk of the mistake under a reasonable view of the circumstances, and the Supreme Court of Michigan, indicating that *Sherwood* might be decided differently today, has expressly accepted the Restatement position. As suggested below, the question of which party *should* reasonably be said to bear such risk might be thought debatable in some cases, but where the seller is a professional dealer and the buyer is a mere customer the question, once raised, would seem to answer itself. Briefly put, experts dealing with non-experts cannot make "mistakes" as to the intrinsic value of the property being sold.

What about experts dealing with experts? In the *Beachcomber Coins*[3] case, the plaintiff, a retail dealer in rare coins, sought to

---

3. *Beachcomber Coins, Inc. v. Boskett*, 166 N.J.Super. 442, 400 A.2d 78 (1979).

rescind the purchase from defendant, another dealer, of a dime that bore a certain mark—"D" for Denver mintage—which, if genuine, gave the dime special value to collectors. Having completed the purchase, the plaintiff, on the point of reselling the dime at a profit to a retail customer, submitted the coin for certification to the American Numismatic Society in accordance with regular practice. In due course the Society reported that it was counterfeit. Finding that the transaction reflected a "mistake" on the part of both dealers, the Supreme Court of New Jersey held for the plaintiff and allowed the transaction to be rescinded. The mistake was mutual, apparently, because the defendant had paid a high price for the coin when *he* bought it, obviously supposing it to be the genuine article.

The outcome in *Beachcomber* can be explained, somewhat mechanically, by pointing to the circumstance that plaintiff and defendant were equally expert in appraising coins; hence, neither was more "at fault" than the other and neither bore the greater burden of risk. The case then presents itself, almost uniquely, as one of pure mistake. Yet even here one is left to wonder why the plaintiff didn't check the coin with the Numismatic Society at the time of sale, or make the sale contingent on certification, or require a representation of some sort from defendant as to genuineness . . . or *something*. Presumably, an expert purchaser should be expected to exhaust the available means of inspection and authentication before crying "mistake" (as opposed to fraud and misrepresentation, from which even he deserves protection), whether his seller is another expert or an amateur. As suggested in discussing the *Sherwood* case, a professional dealer would be presumed to spend as much on self-protection as his business experience appeared to justify; if he still gets stung on rare occasions, he deserves it. While the doctrine of mistake might literally apply to the facts in *Beachcomber,* there is surely something odd in extending relief on that ground to a coin dealer whose very occupation consists of distinguishing between the true and the false.

Searching for another explanation for the outcome, I might suggest that the Court in *Beachcomber* was really using the doctrine of mistake as a rule of prophylaxis or prevention. Its aim, perhaps, was to stop or deter worthless objects from being passed from hand to hand under cover of apparent authenticity. The Court was not in a position to identify the very first vendor of the phony dime—the counterfeiter, presumably—so as to place responsibility where it actually belonged. It did the next best thing, however, by halting the chain of transactions at the point of earliest discovery.

In effect, *no* purchaser, however expert, bears the risk of unmasking a counterfeit; and I assume that the seller could now rescind as to *his* vendor if that person could be located. And so on back to the source. The "rule", then, is that you cannot shed yourself of a counterfeit coin (painting, precious stone, etc.) by passing it along in ignorance or by citing the buyer's expertise. What you can do, however, is return it to the person you got it from. Whether on grounds of fraud or misrepresentation (when that can be shown) or mistake (when it can't), sales of counterfeit articles are simply void.

Sherwood and *Beachcomber* are cases of mutual mistake—buyer and seller shared the same error—leading, as has been seen, to voidable contracts. The same result may follow, however, where the mistake is confined to one of the parties only. The notion, presumably, is that there can be no contract unless the minds of both parties coincide on a single subject-matter. A fundamental mistake may therefore result in a voidable contract even though the mistake is unilateral, provided, as usual, that the mistaken party does not bear the risk of the mistake under the circumstances. Once again, clerical error would be the typical instance of voidability. Thus, where a contractor submits a winning bid on a construction contract but inadvertently omits a major cost item from the total, the courts almost always allow the contractor (provided he acts before the other party has relied on the contract in some substantial way) to rescind or reform his bid on the ground that enforcement would be unconscionable.[4] The outcome would, of course, be otherwise and the contractor would be bound by his bid if the "mistake" was really a business misjudgment, e.g., underestimating the cost of the material and labor required for the job.

A much more interesting case of unilateral mistake—also easily resolved, but worth brief comment—is that of a seller who simply doesn't know as much about his property as the well-informed buyer to whom he sells it. Thus, suppose a farmer sells 100 acres of farmland to a shrewd purchaser who, based on geological tests that he has performed on neighboring tracts, believes—perhaps knows—that the land contains valuable mineral deposits. It in fact does, but the price paid to the farmer reflects the farmer's basic assumption that the land was useful for farming only. Can the farmer rescind? Certainly not, the reason commonly given being that the "adversely affected" farmer bore the risk of the "mistake". This, however, seems rather fanciful: the farmer is hardly in a position to discover the true value of the property by carrying out the same geological

---

4. *Elsinore Union Elementary School Dist. v. Kastorff*, 54 Cal.2d 380, 6 Cal. Rptr. 1, 353 P.2d 713 (1960).

tests for himself. He knows about seeds and fertilizer, but geology he's never heard of.

Probably, though, the real reason for barring rescission has as much or more to do with the geologist's interests and outlook as with the farmer's. The geologist, obviously, is in the business of converting low-value farmland into high-value mining property. Although most of us, as we drive along the turnpike, would rather gaze at a green and pleasant farm than an ugly mining operation, the plain fact is that people in general, otherwise known as the "market," have a greater need for copper and sulfur than they do for lettuce and tomatoes. It follows that the purchaser performs a socially valuable service, one from which we all benefit, when he does his geological survey, and he has to be rewarded for his time and effort. It may be odd, even slightly repellent, to say that the reward should come from the poor benighted farmer, but there appears to be no ready alternative. If, for example, we required the purchaser to share the value of his discovery with the seller in some measure, we would effectively discourage the purchaser from investing as much in research and discovery activities as he appears to be willing to invest, and we would then presumably have more lettuce and tomatoes, but less copper and sulfur, than we seem to want. While the farmer *might* go into the mineral prospecting business on his own, he can't do it by leaning on his hoe. He will have to make the same investment in skills and equipment that the purchaser has made, and if he does that he will quickly cease to be a seller and become a purchaser in his own right. The conclusion, which is really inescapable under present arrangements, is that we cannot allow contract rules—and certainly not the modest doctrine of mistake—to reduce or eliminate the rewards claimed by those who invest in information gathering[5]. Like an inventor's patent, the purchaser's information can be viewed as *his* property and, as such, entitled to the same protection as the farmer's title to his land.

The decided cases and the Restatement appear to confirm that the farmer would be treated as having made a "mistake" when he sold his land at a bargain price, but then deny his claim for relief on the ground that he assumed the risk. Taking a longer view of the matter, the farmer's mistake, if you want to call it that, was in deciding to grow lettuce rather than study geology in the first place. He made his bed, however, and the law leaves him with nothing but a feeling of regret (plus the proceeds of the sale). Actually, the term

5. Kronman, *Mistake, Disclosure, Information, and the Law of Contracts*, 7 J. Legal Studies 1 (1978). And see, Kull, *Unilateral Mistake: The Baseball Card Case*, 70 Wash. U.L.Q. 57 (1992).

"mistake," which implies an error or an oversight rather than a fundamental career choice, is somewhat misleading in this context.[6]

Summarizing the obvious, it is plain that contract law needs a rule or principle that affords relief in cases involving clerical mistakes, arithmetical blunders, misidentification of persons or property, and the like. The rule itself, however, needs to be confined to cases of *just* that sort, and the question is how to express and then apply an appropriate limitation—one, roughly speaking, that separates inadvertent errors from misjudgments. The law attempts to answer that question by stressing the notion of risk-assumption, which appears to be correct as a policy matter, though somewhat ponderous and uncertain in operation. If we were drafting a statutory provision in this area, or yet another restatement, we might consider whether we would not do better to *reverse* the structure of the rule, i.e., by declaring that "mistake" shall not, in general, be grounds for relief, *except* in the case of clerical or arithmetical error, misidentification, etc. The challenge, of course, would be to enumerate our exceptions so as to eliminate the ambiguity present in the risk-assumption concept, but without denying relief to those "adversely affected parties" to whom we really think it ought to be extended.

2. *Existing Impracticability.* Restatement Section 266 provides that "performance" under a contract may be excused if, at the time the contract is made, such performance is "impracticable . . . because of a fact of which [the performing party] has no reason to know and the non-existence of which is a basic assumption on which the contract is made". Section 266 borders closely—perhaps too closely for easy distinction—on the "Mistake" provisions just discussed. Thus, under Restatement Section 152, "mistake" is a ground for excusing the contracting parties' obligations unless the

---

6. The same standard analysis could explain the outcome in *Wood v. Boynton*, 64 Wis. 265, 25 N.W. 42 (1885). Wood, a young girl, sold a "pretty stone" to Boynton, a jeweler, for $1. Buyer and seller both apparently believed that the stone was an almost worthless topaz, but of course it turned out to be an uncut diamond worth $700. In a suit by the seller to rescind the transaction and recover the stone, the court held for the buyer despite the element of mutual mistake. Presumably, jewelers, antique dealers and other experts in rare objects are entitled—expected, really—to use their expertise to make bargain purchases from the unaware, in that way earning a reward for bringing the true value of such objects to light. Like it or not, that is their business. Being in "the business," bargain purchases that are accidental or lucky (for the buyer) probably merit the same treatment. One weeps for Wood; but if Boynton would have been within his rights in making a shrewd purchase had he *known* the stone was a diamond, it is hard to see how his legal position could be worse because he *didn't* know. Put otherwise, Wood, like the farmer in the text, assumed whatever risk was involved in sparing herself the cost of an independent appraisal.

"adversely affected" party "bears the risk of the mistake". Evidently, "reason to know" in Section 266 and "bears the risk of the mistake" in Section 152 are intended by the Restatement to mean two different things, but the difference, if any, is not entirely obvious at first reading. Both appear to suggest that a party claiming "mistake" or "existing impracticability" is *not* excused from his apparent contract obligations if the troublesome "fact" is one he should have known or should have taken steps to find out about.

The two well-known cases described below are both approved by the Restatement—*Stees v. Leonard* under Sections 152 and 154, *Mineral Park v. Howard* under Section 266—apparently on the ground that the contractor in *Stees* knew or should have known about the quicksand, while the road builder in *Mineral Park* was excusably ignorant of the underwater gravel problem.

In the *Stees* case[7], the defendant, a contractor, agreed for a certain price to erect a building on the plaintiff's property in accordance with plans and specifications provided by the plaintiff. Having built the structure up to three stories, the whole thing collapsed and disappeared into the ground beneath it. It turned out that the ground itself was made of quicksand, "damp and porous," and as such would not support a three-story building. Very discouraging, you would think. Even so, and apparently undaunted, the defendant tried to build a second time—first the first story, then the second, then.... But the third story again proved to be one story too many. Just as it had before, the structure collapsed at that stage and was sucked into the deadly quicksand (damp and porous), leaving not a trace behind. Presumably, this process could have continued more or less indefinitely. After the second collapse, however, the defendant refused to go on. The plaintiff then sued, insisting that it was the builder's obligation, at whatever large expense, to dig up the quicksand, dry it out somehow, and then build the building as promised under the contract.

The Minnesota Court held for the plaintiff. "If a man bind himself, by a positive, express contract, to do an act in itself possible, he must perform his engagement.... No hardship, no unforeseen hindrance ... will excuse him from doing what he has expressly agreed to do." The defendant could have qualified his obligation by including in the contract a requirement that the land be stable enough to bear the building's weight. But he didn't. Rather, said the Court, he "improvidently assumed an absolute".

7.   20 Minn. 494 (1874).

Hence his obligation to build or pay damages (in some unstated amount) would be enforced.

The decision is pretty tough on the defendant, though why the defendant would go ahead and build on the same quicksand twice is a bit of a puzzle. Actually, the question in this early (1874) owner-builder case is not so much what happens under the law of contracts "If a man bind himself ... etc., etc.," as it is: who is responsible—owner or builder—for evaluating the ground conditions when the contract says nothing on that subject? The Court's seemingly strict approach to contract obligation in effect yielded a "default rule," to-wit: the risk and responsibility for determining whether the property is suitable for the planned construction falls on the builder, not the property owner, when the contract is silent. As such, the default rule seems entirely reasonable, and my impression (not verified) is that the same default rule applies today. The builder has the technical skill and experience to make a judgment on the suitability of ground conditions and would normally be expected to make that judgment before commencing to build, whereas the owner, not typically anything but an investor, obviously lacks such skill and experience. The defendant in *Stees v. Leonard* asserted that he received assurance from the plaintiff that the quicksand problem had been taken care of, but that appears to have been an afterthought and the evidence was unconvincing.

Stees v. Leonard can be compared with the California Court's decision in *Mineral Park Land Co. v. Howard*[8], a case that may have launched the "impracticability" defense in this country. Mineral Park (the plaintiff) owned gravel property from which the Howards, road builders, agreed to take *all* the gravel they would need for the planned construction of a road and bridge under a contract with public authorities. The amount of gravel needed for the road construction was estimated to be 101,000 cubic yards. The Howards agreed to pay Mineral Park 5 cents a cubic yard for the first 80,000 cubic yards, nothing for the next 10,000 (for some reason), and 5 cents a cubic yard for the balance. Removal of the gravel would be done by the Howards at the Howards' expense.

In the end, the Howards took only 50,131 cubic yards of gravel from Mineral Park because, as it turned out, only 50,131 cubic yards were accessible and removable. The remaining gravel on Mineral Park's property was actually under water and would have cost the Howards ten to twelve times as much (the Court found) to dredge it up from the bottom and haul it away. As a consequence,

---

8. 172 Cal. 289, 156 P. 458 (1916). My discussion of *Mineral Park* follows   Goldberg, *Framing Contract Law: An Economic Perspective* 370–5 (2006).

bought the 50,869 cubic yards still needed from an
 er. Claiming, nevertheless, that the Howards were
 bligated to take from it *all* the gravel needed for the
 lineral Park sued the Howards for damages in the
 43.45.

Holding for the defendants, the Court found that the cost to
the Howards of taking the underwater gravel would have been
"prohibitive." Faced with a "prohibitive" cost, performance under
the contract was "impracticable." "Impracticable" is legally equivalent to "impossible." Performance being "impossible," it followed
that "the situation is not different from that of a total absence of
. . . gravel"—not different, that is, from how it would be if there
had been no gravel at all on Mineral Park's land beyond the first
50,131 cubic yards.

The background facts in *Mineral Park* are not disclosed in the
Court's opinion. We do not know whether, for obvious example, the
Howards were aware or unaware of the underwater problem at the
time they made their contract with Mineral Park. One likely
possibility is that the Howards needed to assure themselves of a
gravel supply at 5 cents a cubic yard no matter how costly removal
might turn out to be. Another is that the Howards never thought
they would really need as much as 101,000 cubic yards and felt safe
in ignoring the underwater problem. Another . . . well, who knows.

Whatever the reason for the Howards' commitment to Mineral
Park, they did in fact commit themselves to pay 5 cents a cubic
yard for all the gravel they required, and one might suppose
(quoting *Stees*) that "If a man bind himself, by a positive, express
contract, to do an act in itself possible, he must perform his
engagement. . . ." That, presumably, is the accepted rule of law.
Notwithstanding, the Court in *Mineral Park* found that it was
"impracticable" for the Howards to perform, and in consequence
held that nothing was due from the Howards to Mineral Park. The
Restatement, which, as noted, adopts the "impracticability" excuse
in Section 266, expressly approves the *Mineral Park* decision.

But should it be approved? As noted, the Court in *Mineral
Park* found that the Howards faced a removal cost of 50 or 60 cents
a cubic yard ("prohibitive") if the contract was enforced. That
would be true, I suppose, if the remedy sought by the plaintiff had
been specific performance. But the plaintiff had no right to specific
performance, and actually had no interest in specific performance.
Mineral Park's claim was *not* that the Howards must actually
remove the underwater gravel. Rather, what it asked for—and was
apparently entitled to under the contract—was that the Howards

180

pay the "royalty" or stand-by fee of 5 cents a cubic yard for all the gravel used on the road building project, whether taken from Mineral Park itself or from some other supplier. Put differently, Mineral Park was completely indifferent as to where and how the Howards got their gravel, *provided* that the Howards paid Mineral Park a 5–cent fee for every cubic yard used, whatever its source.

So did the underwater problem render the Howards' contract obligation "impracticable"? Not really. If no outside gravel supplier had been available, the Howards would presumably have been forced to dredge up the underwater gravel despite the "prohibitive" cost—not because of any obligation to Mineral Park, but because the alternative would have been to halt its road building work for lack of gravel, thus breaching its contract with the public authorities. That, most likely, would have been even more costly in damages and lost reputation than dredging up the gravel.

Happily, 50,869 cubic yards of gravel could be purchased from an outside supplier whose price was obviously far less per cubic yard than the cost of underwater dredging. The Howards quite sensibly chose to buy their gravel from the outsider. Indeed, the Howards would *always* buy their gravel from an outside supplier as long as the outsider's price per cubic yard was less (even if only a penny less) than the cost per cubic yard of dredging. That would be true *whether or not* the Howards also had to make a payment of 5–cents per cubic yard to Mineral Park. To make the last point clear (with apologies), suppose dredging up Mineral Park's gravel cost 9 cents a cubic yard, while the outside supplier offered gravel at 8 cents a cubic yard. If the Howards *did* have to pay Mineral Park 5 cents under the contract at issue, the cost of removing Mineral Park's gravel would be 14 cents a cubic yard (9 plus 5), while the cost of the outsider's gravel (8 plus 5) would be only 13 cents. Buying from the outsider would always be the obvious choice. Mineral Park, however, gets its 5–cent royalty in either event.

The legal issue in Mineral Park had nothing to do with "impracticability" because the contract imposed no performance obligation (other than to pay the 5–cent fee) on the defendants. A duty to pay money can never be "impracticable." The Court, I believe, and perhaps the Restatement, simply misunderstood the deal.

B. Impossibility and Frustration

The "impossibility" problem is a remarkably persistent one in contract law, going steadily back from the still remembered *Transatlantic* litigation, which involved the closing of the Suez Canal, to the destruction of the rickety old music hall in *Taylor v. Caldwell,* and far beyond. The reasons for this, alluded to earlier, have mostly to do with the limitations of human foresight and with the fact that the negotiation of contract details has to come to an end at some point. Every future contingent state of the world cannot be predicted, and lawyers are often faulted for spending too much of their clients' time and money quibbling about risks and hazards that will probably never materialize (although, as the reader may one day learn, that is absolutely nothing to the criticism they hear when contingencies *not* covered by the contract actually fall in). But even if the contract is planned and drafted with the greatest care and patience, "things" may happen that are not explicitly dealt with and that make performance difficult or impossible to carry out. And, of course, many routine transactions are expected to begin and end quickly—the two-day apartment rental in *Krell v. Henry,* for example—so that detailed and extended negotiations by batteries of lawyers would simply be too costly to justify.

The inevitable question is: who pays? In *Taylor v. Caldwell,*[9] decided by King's Bench in 1863, plaintiff rented the Surrey Gardens—a music hall and outdoor dining area—from defendant for four separate days during the summer months at a rental of £100 a day. Plaintiff, who seems to have been a sort of roving impresario, planned to stage musical events and other entertainments for the local folks and with this in view spent a substantial sum on promotion, advertising and general preparation. Before any of these entertainments could be offered, however, the Surrey Gardens caught fire and burned to the ground. The disaster was no one's fault; it just happened. Claiming that defendant had breached by failing to make the Gardens available on the agreed dates, plaintiff sued to recover an amount equal to his promotional expenditures and related outlays, now wasted. Defendant responded by arguing that he should be excused as a matter of law, performance having obviously become impossible.

The Court held for the defendant. The central question, it indicated, was one of intent. To be sure, the contract itself said nothing about what should happen in the event of disaster, and evidently neither party raised the issue in the course of negotiations. Even so, the parties must have known that the contract could not be fulfilled if the music hall was destroyed by fire. They undertook their mutual obligations on the assumption that the Surrey Gardens would be there, physically, when the time came to use it. That circumstance was plainly essential to performance on

9. King's Bench, 1863, 3 B. & S. 826, 122 Eng.Rep. 309.

either side. Looking at the contract as a whole, therefore, and in the absence of any express provision to the contrary, the continued existence of the music hall must be regarded as a condition "by law implied." Since without fault the premises had ceased to exist, the contract was discharged and both parties, but especially defendant, were legally excused.

The decision in *Taylor v. Caldwell* appears correct, but nothing in the Court's opinion really helps very much in resolving the critical issue of "intent." It is certainly true, as the Court says, that the defendant could not have been expected to make the Surrey Gardens available to the plaintiff once the facility had perished. But it does not necessarily follow that defendant's *financial* obligation to plaintiff was expected to perish as well. Thus, suppose we took a contrary position and insisted that the intention of the parties—somehow divined—was to require defendant to perform at all events. This would *not* mean that defendant must by some magic rebuild the Surrey Gardens in time for the first of the scheduled entertainments—that indeed would be impossible and, hence, could not have been intended. Rather, the inference would be that defendant, finding himself unable to furnish the music hall as promised, must do the next best thing, which is to sit down and write a cheque to cover plaintiff's losses. Nothing could be easier and "less impossible" than that, and the question, therefore, is whether the parties intended that he should.

Lacking any affirmative evidence that they did so intend, I think the fairly clear presumption is that they did not. Thus, what should we take to be the obligation of a landlord, here the defendant, where the destruction of the leased premises through fire or other casualty results in property losses to his tenant? Suppose, for example, that the plaintiff in *Taylor* had had tangible property on the music-hall premises at the time the fire occurred—costumes and stage-sets, say—and that those assets were likewise consumed by the flames. As the plaintiff's loss would then be attributable to the fire itself rather than to the defendant's non-performance, the only question would be whether, under the terms of the lease, the landlord had undertaken to insure his tenant for casualty losses not due to the landlord's negligence. To be sure, the property in *Taylor* was the plaintiff's investment in customer goodwill—an intangible, obviously, and hence perhaps less readily identified as "property". But the question is really no different. Just as the fire destroyed the defendant's music-hall, so it destroyed the valuable interest that the plaintiff had created through his promotional expenditures. Under these circumstances, is it likely that a landlord would be obligated to compensate his tenant's loss?

One would hardly think so. The defendant presumably had fire and casualty insurance covering the value of the music-hall itself, and I suppose he *might* have been willing to assume liability for the value of his tenant's property and business expectations as well. But that would be unusual. The tenant, being in the best position to estimate his own financial exposure, would normally be left to make his own protective arrangements, whether through insurance or by some other means. In any case, if there *had* been such an undertaking on the defendant's part, the plaintiff would surely have been required to specify the amount and the limit of the liability so assumed and, probably, to add a premium to the rent. Apparently, however, no evidence was offered to suggest that matters of that sort had even been discussed, and without such evidence I think it would be very difficult to resolve the critical issue of "intent" in the plaintiff's favor. The Court framed the issue somewhat differently by asking whether the parties meant the contract to be performed even if the music-hall should be burned to the ground; but the outcome, or the answer, was the same.

Canadian Industrial Alcohol Co. v. Dunbar Molasses Co.[10a], a case that finds its way into many of the Contracts casebooks, is an almost equally well-known *anti*-impossibility decision. In *Canadian*, the defendant, Dunbar, agreed to supply the plaintiff with 1,500,-000 gallons of "refined blackstrap molasses" from the expected output of a particular refinery, namely, the National Sugar Refinery of Yonkers, N.Y. Dunbar was obviously acting as a middleman and no doubt expected to earn a commission per-gallon delivered from Canadian. It seems very likely (in any case I assume) that the contract between Canadian and Dunbar included a stated price—$x a gallon—although the dollar amount actually agreed to by the parties is curiously omitted from Judge Cardozo's sketchy opinion. Somewhat surprisingly, Dunbar took on its obligation to Canadian with one leg lifted, so to speak, because it made no offsetting supply contract with National Sugar, presumably expecting on the basis of experience that National Sugar would provide the required quantity of 1.5 million gallons in due course at or below the $x price.

Alas for Dunbar. In the end, National Sugar cut back its output of blackstrap molasses to the point where Dunbar was able to acquire only 344,000 gallons and thus fell 1,166,000 gallons short of its contractual obligation to Canadian. Canadian thereupon sued Dunbar for damages. Dunbar's defense was "that its own duty ... was proportionate to [National Sugar's] willingness to supply [mo-

[10a]. 258 N.Y. 194, 179 N.E. 383 (1932).

lasses]," and that its duty to Canadian was discharged when the supply source failed.

The Court held for Canadian. "We may assume," said the Court, that Dunbar would be discharged of its duty to Canadian if National Sugar's short supply could be explained by any one of the following: (a) the refinery had been destroyed; or (b) the sugar crop had failed; or (c) ravages of war; or even (d) breach of contract by National Sugar itself. Apparently, none of those factors was present—certainly not (d) because, as stated, Dunbar never entered into a supply contract with National Sugar in the first place. In Cardozo's view, Dunbar's legal vulnerability had nothing to do with "impossibility" or "commercial impracticability" or even the failure of an implied condition. Had Dunbar made a supply contract with National Sugar at the time it did its deal with Canadian, it would now have a claim that could be pressed against National Sugar for Canadian's benefit or even assigned to Canadian itself. Instead, Dunbar evidently "put its faith in the mere chance that the output of the refinery would be the same" as it had been in earlier years. That faith was misplaced, as it turned out, and Dunbar would have to take the consequences.

Actually, apart from a vague reference to "hard times" and "high labor costs", the *Dunbar* opinion tells us nothing about why National Sugar suddenly decided to reduce its output of molasses, although the reason for the cutback—if not (a) through (d) above, then why?—would seem, at least potentially, to be a matter of considerable legal interest. Perhaps we can assume that the price of its inputs—e.g., sugar—having unexpectedly increased, National Sugar simply found that it would lose money if it continued to sell blackstrap molasses to Dunbar at $x a gallon, that being the highest price that Dunbar was prepared to pay, or willing to pay, given its obligation to resell to Canadian at the $x price. But then could Dunbar have overcome the short supply problem by offering National Sugar a higher price than $x—perhaps a much higher price, say three or four time $x or even more? We don't know, but nothing in the fact-recital suggests that Dunbar ever made such an offer.

UCC 2–615 provides, in effect, that a seller in Dunbar's position may be "excused" from its contractual obligation to the buyer by the failure of a contemplated source of supply. But "[t]here is no excuse," the Code commentary adds, citing the *Dunbar* case itself, "unless the seller has employed all due measures to assure himself that his source will not fail."[10b] The phrase "all due measures" is

---

10b. UCC 2–615, Note 5.

defined, but I suppose that Dunbar's initial failure to supply contract with National Sugar would be taken as Dunbar's part to have taken "all due measures," as the statute evidently requires.

The so-called frustration-of-purpose cases have a good deal in common with *Taylor v. Caldwell* but also differ in important ways, and the question is whether the similarities or the differences ought to count most in the result. *Krell v. Henry*,[11] one of the famous coronation cases, will serve to make the point. Queen Victoria having at long last gone to her reward, the coronation of her son, soon to be Edward VII, was jubilantly planned for the end of June, 1902. The coronation procession, in all its magnificence, was to pass along Pall Mall on June 26 and June 27, so that individuals having apartments overlooking the procession route were greatly envied. Apparently caring more for money than pageant, Krell, the owner of a flat so situated, agreed to let his chambers to Henry for the two daytime periods at a fee of £75, of which £25 was paid in advance as a deposit. To everyone's disappointment, Edward suffered a sudden attack of appendicitis and the coronation had to be postponed. Henry, in consequence, refused to pay the balance of the rent, and Krell sued.

Finding the issue controlled or at least dominated by *Taylor v. Caldwell*, the Court of Appeal held for the defendant. Concededly, Krell's apartment, unlike the Surrey Gardens, continued to exist, and Henry could have gone in and spent two days looking at the vacant streets if he wanted to. But the undebatable purpose of the agreement was to provide a view of the great procession. That goal having been frustrated by the King's illness, the foundation of the contract was eliminated. Performance effectively became impossible; hence the contract was discharged.

Edward VII's coronation, including the procession along Pall Mall, did take place in August, just six weeks later. While one might suppose that the parties would have agreed to transfer their arrangement to the later date, they obviously didn't. Henry may have lost interest in the meanwhile (the August ceremony was apparently less well attended than the earlier one would have been), or, of course, Krell, then considering himself free to let his chambers for a second time at the same premium, may have rejected any idea of a rain-check.

Restatement Section 265 specifically approves the result in *Krell v. Henry*, treating the case as one of "supervening frustration". Writers on the subject are not unanimous, however, and a

---

11. Court of Appeal, 1903, 2 K.B. 740.

contrary decision was reached on related facts in another of the coronation cases.[12] One reason for feeling doubt about the Court's decision, I suppose, is that the two-day lease of Krell's apartment *could* be viewed as nothing more than a speculation in Henry's hands. The lease was apparently transferable, and if things had turned out differently, it might have been Krell rather than Henry who wound up suffering the bitter pangs of frustration or, at least, of lost opportunity. Thus, demand for a vantage-point overlooking the big parade might have increased stupendously as coronation day approached, so that Henry could have found himself holding a very hot ticket indeed. In effect, Henry was "long" 1 two-day lease on a flat in Pall Mall. Whatever his original aim might have been, if the coronation had gone forward as scheduled and the day had been especially fine, he might finally have chosen to sell his lease at a profit—say double his purchase price—and then contented himself with reading about the coronation in the *Times*. Even a spectator can become a speculator if the price is right.

Putting the same point more generally, it might be argued that the situation in *Krell v. Henry* was really just a very special instance of a common configuration with which the law deals swiftly under ordinary circumstances. Thus, a typical buyer and seller agree today upon a price for goods or services to be delivered in the future. Each of the parties knows that the actual market price on the delivery date may be higher or lower within some predictable range, with the upside and downside probabilities being roughly symmetrical on either side of the contract price. The contract will, of course, be enforced *whatever* the outcome—the law is properly indifferent between the parties—and indeed, as explained much earlier, the willingness of the parties to enter into a contract in the first place depends on a legal remedy being available if performance is refused. Why should Krell and Henry be treated differently? While the King's illness was certainly unexpected, star performers do get sick from time to time. Such a development can never be regarded as entirely remote—"unexpected" is not the same as "unforeseeable"—and I would imagine that a modern insurance company could tell you exactly what the chances were that a person of the King's age (and habits) would get sick today, next month or a year from now. Neither Henry nor Krell was a modern insurance company, but this does not mean that they were wholly incapable of weighing relevant contingencies, including the very familiar contingency of illness and mortality.

12. *Chandler v. Webster*, 1 K.B. 493 (1904).

The effect of all this argumentation is to leave one in some doubt about whether it really is correct to place *Krell v. Henry* within the general ambit of the impossibility doctrine. If we take the position, as the Court apparently did, that the staging of the coronation on the expected date was a condition on which the parties intended Henry's rental obligation to depend, then, obviously, the coronation having been cancelled, the rental fee should be refunded or forgiven. But that, in a sense, begs the question. Krell, after all, was not the sponsor or producer of the event and had no responsibility for anything except the availability of his well-situated flat. Looked at from another standpoint, Krell was merely the seller (and Henry the buyer) of negotiable viewing rights, which rights might be regarded as a marketable commodity like any other.

As a final observation, it might be noted that Henry cross-claimed (successfully in the court below) for the return of his £25 deposit, but for reasons not given withdrew that claim on appeal. A possible inference is that Henry was prepared to view the deposit as a kind of liquidated damage figure—as if the parties had agreed that Krell could retain that amount (but would receive no more) even if the big parade was cancelled—and that the Court, in effect, approved what it took to be a reasonable settlement of a difficult controversy.

Transatlantic Financing Corporation v. United States,[13] which arose on the seller's rather than the buyer's side of the equation, is a well-known modern illustration of the "impracticability" problem. The plaintiff, a shipping company, had entered into a contract with the United States to carry wheat from Galveston to a port in Iran. The contract price for the shipping service was $305,000, a figure that reflected the parties' shared assumption that the cargo ship would make the voyage—some 10,000 miles—by way of the Suez Canal, which was the customary and the shortest route. While the ship was on the high seas, Egypt was attacked by Britain, France and Israel and responded by closing the Canal and blocking passage to all vessels. Following inconclusive discussions with the Department of Agriculture, plaintiff's ship was rerouted around the Cape of Good Hope, arriving in Iran several weeks later than expected, and having added 3,000 miles to the trip. Plaintiff never sought to be excused from its contract obligations—the ship did go on to Iran—but it subsequently asked the government for an additional $43,000 to cover the expense of the longer voyage. The government refused. Arguing that performance of the original

13. 363 F.2d 312 (D.C.Cir.1966), discussed in Posner & Rosenfield, *Impossibility and Related Doctrines in Contract Law: An Economic Analysis,* 6 J. Legal Studies 83 (1977).

contract had become "impossible" because of the C
plaintiff sued in *quantum meruit* for the sum just

In an opinion much-admired for its thoughtful trea
topic, the D.C. Court of Appeals held for the govern___
elements, said the Court, were necessary to justify the plaintiff's
impossibility claim. These were (i) an unexpected occurrence, (ii) a
failure to have allocated the risk of that occurrence by agreement
or by custom, and (iii) "commercial impracticability" with respect
to the performance of plaintiff's obligations. Running down the list,
Judge Wright agreed with plaintiff that both parties expected the
ship to follow the usual and customary route, which, as stated, was
through the Canal. Hence the need to travel around the Cape
qualified as an "unexpected occurrence". As to risk-allocation,
however, the Court felt that tensions in the Middle East, which
were present long before the joint attack on Egypt, must have
alerted plaintiff to the presence of "abnormal risks" in any voyage
that was routed through Suez. To be sure, the United States would
have been no less aware of those risks and tensions; hence it would
be difficult to say that one party rather than the other was in a
better position to make predictions about the possibility of war. But
assuming that the parties were equal in that respect, it would still
follow that the plaintiff, as an experienced shipping company,
would be better able to estimate the added cost of performing by
alternative routes. In effect, both parties knew that there was some
risk of a Canal shutdown. But only plaintiff would know exactly
how much its own additional expenses would amount to if a trip
around the Cape became necessary. In any event, the actual variation in cost was fairly modest—only $43,000, less than 15% of the
total contract price of $305,000—so that performance could not be
said to have been "commercially impracticable" from a purely
financial standpoint. "While it may be an overstatement to say that
increased cost and difficulty of performance never constitute impracticability, to justify relief there must be more of a variation
between expected cost and the cost of performing by an available
alternative than in the present case, where the promisor can
legitimately be presumed to have accepted some degree of abnormal
risk, and where impracticability is urged on the basis of added
expense alone."

The Court noted, finally, that there was an inconsistency in
plaintiff's litigating position. Thus, plaintiff sought to enforce the
basic contract itself—it still wanted $305,000 for carrying the
freight from Galveston to Iran—but then also demanded non-
contractual relief in the form of *quantum meruit* to cover the
additional cost. The claim of "impossibility," however, is all-or-

nothing. Either the contract should be treated as wholly discharged—in which event the entire voyage would be compensated at a *quantum meruit* rate—or the contract should be viewed as binding and the plaintiff should be limited to the contract price for its services. Apparently, however, as the Court slyly observed, the contract price was just too good to give up. The *quantum meruit* rate seems to have been a little more than $14 a mile ($43,000/3000 miles). The extended voyage, Cape route included, was 13,000 miles in total, so that *quantum meruit* for the whole trip would have been only about $182,000.

Although steadily supported by the Restatement, the doctrines of "supervening frustration" and "supervening impracticality" have not often been invoked by our courts to excuse performance by a disadvantaged buyer or seller. In crude terms, the reason is that post-contractual change in the market price of promised goods or services is generally an expected element in any forward exchange. Once again, the odds that the buyer or the seller will turn out to be the advantaged party must be assumed to be about equal, with the contract price representing something like a midpoint between the foreseeable high and low. Future events that "merely" affect the market value of the thing promised—whether a two-day right of occupancy or an ocean carriage contract—would almost always be presumed to have been anticipated by the parties when they settled on their terms initially, even if the particular event is both unexpected and impracticable or frustrating.

The impossibility doctrine invariably breeds confusion in the minds of students, and it is commonly observed that the cases tend to slip through one's fingers when an attempt is made to apply them to new situations.[14] The reasons for this (though hardly the cure) may be twofold. First, there is the problem of classification just alluded to. Thus, which of the two *kinds* of cases are we talking about in a given instance? Is the case one in which the critical event has rendered performance physically impossible, or is it one in which the event has reduced the market value of performance, or increased its cost, in a way that no one appears to have anticipated? *Krell v. Henry* might be seen as an impossibility or supervening frustration case, the big parade having been cancelled because of the King's appendicitis; *or,* it might be seen as a market-value case, Henry having taken a speculative risk and being at all times free to trade on the value of the occupancy rights that he acquired from Krell. If *Krell v. Henry* is a market-value case—one speculator selling tickets to another, in effect—a court is likely to hold that

14. White and Summers, *Uniform Commercial Code* 155 (3d ed. 1988).

190

there is no "impossibility" as such, and then go on to enforce the contract by awarding damages to the injured promisee. If it is an impossibility or frustration case, on the other hand, the promisor can obviously set up a defense on that basis, as of course he did in the case itself. The classification question is pretty much up for grabs in *Krell,* and perhaps it can never be resolved with perfect confidence.

But there is a second and equally troublesome problem. Even if we agree that the case before us is an impossibility or frustration case, that in itself only begins the inquiry. As suggested in discussing the *Taylor* case, we are still obliged to decide which of the parties was intended to bear the risk that performance would in fact be rendered impossible by the particular event. The contract itself is silent on that point, so that we must ultimately try to determine the parties' probable intent by putting ourselves in their place *ex ante.* How *would* the parties have decided to deal with the contingency in question if it had been discussed between them at the time they entered into their agreement? In *Taylor,* it seems unlikely that the parties would have intended the defendant to be responsible for the plaintiff's losses for the reason, as suggested, that the plaintiff would have been in a better position than the defendant to estimate its own insurance and other self-protection needs. That, however, is merely a supposition—an "economic story"—that one is inclined to accept on grounds of plausibility and likelihood. In other cases it may be harder to develop any *single* story that is equally plausible. How and to whom the risk of impossibility or frustration would have been allocated in *Krell v. Henry* or in the *Transatlantic* case is not so easy to surmise. Judge Wright's opinion in *Transatlantic* takes the question up in specific terms, and that is a virtue, but the story he finally adopts—that the shipping company would have had a better idea of the additional cost than the government and therefore qualified as the "superior risk bearer"—is really only marginally convincing. No doubt the plaintiff had a different story to tell—*viz.*, that "via the Suez Canal" was a condition of performance so clearly understood that it did not need to be specified—and as between the two competing scenarios it might have been hard to state in advance just which, or whose, the Court would choose to credit. Then, however, the question of intent begins to look somewhat artificial. If nothing was foreseen—neither the closing of the Canal *nor* the Court's decision in the litigation that followed—how can we say, even hypothetically, that the parties "intended" that one or the other should bear the risk and absorb the resulting loss?[15]

---

15. *See* Kull, *Mistake, Frustration, and the Windfall Principle of Contract Remedies,* 43 Hastings L.J. 1 (1991).

Indeed, looking back at the decisions discussed in this section (just a sample, to be sure), it could be argued that the court in each instance merely left the losses where they fell, more or less as if the contract ceased to have enforceable meaning in the face of an event that had never been within the parties' active contemplation. The impresario in *Taylor v. Caldwell* got no compensation for its wasted advertising expenditures; the shipping company in *Transatlantic* got no reimbursement for its additional mileage costs; the owner of the well-situated flat in *Krell* lost his claim for rent when the coronation parade was canceled, though in the end he did retain the £25 deposit that his lessee had already paid. The result in each case would be the same, it seems, had the court, like the court in *Peerless*, stated simply that it had no basis for intervening on behalf of *either* party once contractual performance had been halted or rendered futile by the unexpected event.

Chapter 8

REMEDIES

A. Expectation Damages

1. *Damages or Specific Performance.* Assuming a failure or unwillingness to perform on the part of a promisor, the law customarily provides a remedy to the promisee in the form of money damages based upon the promisee's expectation interest. As suggested in Chapter 1, the aim and the effect of the prevailing damage rule can be described as forward-looking as well as remedial. Two parties contemplating an exchange obviously need to be assured that their commitments are mutual and that neither party will be free to receive the performance of the other while withholding his own. Lacking such assurance the parties might be reluctant, perhaps unwilling, to make deals on the basis of mere promises and would find themselves unable to project their plans into the future with the necessary degree of confidence. The larger purpose of contract law is to supply that assurance by requiring each party to meet the expectations of the other, if not through willing performance then by forced surrender of the equivalent in hard cold cash.

Calculating expectation damages is easy in theory, though not, I think, always so in practice. The object of the exercise, once again, is to give the injured party the benefit of his bargain, that is, to put him in as good a position as he would have been in had the contract been performed in accordance with its terms. Briefly stated, this formulation means that the injured party is entitled to a damage recovery equal to (a) the value he has lost by reason of the other party's default, plus (b) the expenditures he has made (if any) in carrying out his own obligations under the contract. To illustrate simply, suppose that C, a contractor, agrees to build a house for O for $100,000. C figures that the job will cost him $80,000 and hence looks forward to a $20,000 profit. After the house is partly built and C has spent $50,000 on wages and materials, O repudiates the contract. C is entitled to damages of $70,000 – $20,000 for the lost profit, plus $50,000 to compensate for the expenditures he made in reliance on the contract. Another way of reaching the same result is to measure C's damages by reference to the difference between the full contract price of $100,000 and the $30,000 of "cost avoided" by C in not having to complete the work. I should add that C would have a damage claim even if O had repudiated before C spent anything on the project, but then, of course, C's recovery would be limited to his $20,000 profit expectation, since his anticipated cost of $80,000 would have been "avoided" entirely.

Turning the illustration around, assume that it is C who repudiates the contract and O who has a claim for damages. Since O is entitled to a house for $100,000, O's recovery would be measured by the difference between the contract price and any greater amount that he might have to pay another builder to do, or to finish, the work. If, for example, O had already made progress payments to C of $50,000, and if O now has to pay a second contractor $55,000 to get the house completed, then O has suffered a loss of $5,000 in the value of his expectation interest and would be entitled to recover that amount from C.

The UCC applies essentially the same damage rule to the purchase and sale of marketable goods. Thus, assume Seller agrees to deliver certain merchandise to Buyer at price of $1 a unit but subsequently fails to make delivery or repudiates the contract. Under Section 2–712, Buyer may "cover" by making a purchase of substitute goods and have damages from Seller equal to the difference between the "cost of cover" and the contract price. If Buyer (without unreasonable delay) acquires like merchandise by paying another seller $1.50, his damage claim is obviously 50 cents a unit. Buyer thus obtains the goods that he requires at a net cost of $1 a unit just as if Seller had performed as promised.

A seller's remedies in the event of breach by a buyer are largely parallel. If it is Buyer who breaches by repudiating the contract or refusing to accept the goods when tendered, Seller may resell those goods to other buyers "in a commercially reasonable manner" and, under 2–706, claim damages equal to the difference between the contract price and the resale price. The matter does not quite end there, as our discussion of the "lost volume" seller at p. __, infra, will suggest. In general, however, the effect of the Code provision, at least the aim, is to put the injured seller in as good a position as he would have been in if the buyer had accepted the goods and paid the price called for by the contract.

The availability of a substitute transaction—an owner hiring another contractor after the first has defaulted, a buyer resorting to "cover" after the seller has failed to deliver—makes the damage calculation look pretty straightforward, but in some cases the simple act of substitution may not be possible or feasible. Suppose, for example, that A agrees to sell B certain specialized equipment which is not available, or at least not readily available, from other sources. Although eager to perform, A finds that he cannot obtain the equipment, or cannot make timely delivery, and hence is compelled to breach. If B is not able to cover or to ascertain the cost of substitute equipment by reference to "the market," B's damage claim will have to be measured by looking at his own individual expectations with respect to the value of the promised performance. This, however, seems somewhat open-ended and, depending on the circumstances, one might have some concern for the extent of *A's* financial exposure, even though A is the non-performing party and presumably took a conscious risk when he entered into the contract. The problem would not seem too serious if B were a jobber whose aim was simply to resell the equipment to end-users at a conventional mark-up. Assuming A was aware of B's role as a middleman, the net profit that B would have realized on resale would be a proper measure of B's expectation interest and A's liability. But suppose B himself is the end-user and asserts that A's failure to deliver the equipment resulted in the shut-down of a major manufacturing division and the loss of 6 months' operating income. Although B's loss of earnings is plainly a consequence of A's breach, the scope and extent of B's potential loss might not have been known by A, or even have been foreseeable, at the time the transaction was agreed to. The question, then, is whether A's state of expectation should serve as a limitation on B's recovery rights, though A is the party in breach and B is the victim of A's default. This issue, which is one of some conceptual importance in the contracts field, is discussed at p. 214, infra, in connection with the famous case of *Hadley v. Baxendale.*

Moving briefly to a more general policy level, I think students are sometimes troubled by the rather stark fact that the law does not actually require a promisor to keep his promise, but instead treats the payment of money damages as a wholly adequate remedy for breach. In effect, the law says that a party to a contract is free either to perform or not to perform, provided only that if he breaches he shall be obliged to pay the injured party an amount in cash sufficient to give the latter the benefit originally expected. In everyday life, to be sure, we regard breaking promises as more or less dishonorable. By contrast, in the largely commercial setting with which contract law is concerned, keeping or breaking one's word appears to be an ethically neutral event, of which the proof, perhaps, is that punitive or exemplary damages are not recoverable by an injured promisee.[1]

---

1. Restatement Section 355. And see, White v. Benkowski, 37 Wis.2d 285, 155 N.W.2d 74 (1967). On damages generally, see Kornhauser, *An Introduction to the Economic Analysis of Contract Reme-* *dies,* 57 U.Col.L.Rev. 683 (1986). And see, Goetz and Scott, *The Mitigation Principle: Toward a General Theory of Contractual Obligation,* 69 Va.L.Rev. 967 (1983).

The explanation generally given for this apparent state of moral indifference is that the law, in permitting (even encouraging) a promisor to breach and compensate the promisee with money, promotes an efficient disposition of material resources. Assuming the breaching promisor has acted rationally, there is, or should be, a net social gain to the parties; yet no one is left worse off as a consequence. The point is customarily illustrated in the following way. Suppose Ursula contracts to sell Gerald a certain customized machine for a price of $100,000, delivery and payment in 60 days. The machine is worth $120,000 to Gerald, who intends to use it in his business. Prior to the delivery date, Rupert offers Ursula $150,000 for the machine. Assume that Ursula reacts by deliberately breaching her contract with Gerald and selling the machine to Rupert. To be sure, Ursula then owes damages of $20,000 to Gerald. Even after paying Gerald's damage claim, however, Ursula nets $130,000 instead of the measly $100,000 she would have had if she had kept her promise. In the end, Ursula is better off to the tune of $30,000, Gerald is as well off as he expected to be when the contract was entered into, and the machine is ultimately acquired by the person for whom it has the highest economic value, namely, Rupert. Accordingly, there is a net social gain, and no harm to anyone, by virtue of Ursula's deliberate act of breach.

One's doubts about Ursula's morality in breaking her promise are thus overcome by awe and admiration for the elegance of the result. Or are they? Actually, a rule of specific performance that absolutely *required* Ursula to sell the machine to Gerald for $100,000 would lead to an equally efficient outcome, but the $30,000 of overplus would wind up in Gerald's hands rather than Ursula's. Thus, Rupert, on learning of Gerald's contractual right to pay $100,000 for the machine, would be just as glad to offer Gerald (rather than Ursula) $150,000 for a transfer of title to the machine (or to offer Gerald $50,000 for an assignment of his contract rights). Assuming he accepted, Gerald would obviously be $30,000 richer than he expected to be, Ursula would be no worse off than *she* expected to be, and the machine would go to the highest-value user just as above. Finally, specific performance would make it unnecessary to put a dollar value on Gerald's expectations—Ursula simply has to go ahead and deliver the machine. The need for and cost of a judicial determination with respect to the amount of an injured party's damages are avoided, as is the quite considerable danger that a court might, in the end, underestimate such damages in Gerald's case and in that way deny him a complete remedy.

As a practical matter, Ursula, being in the business of selling machines, would be more likely than Gerald to receive an inquiry from Rupert and may be in a better position than Gerald to get Rupert's highest bid. If so, the effect of a specific performance rule would simply be to prompt Ursula to negotiate with Gerald for a buy-out of his contract rights. Gerald would then get some portion of the $30,000 in question—just how much would depend on how good he is at haggling—with Ursula retaining the balance as a reward for her superior market expertise. Efficiency goals would be met—Ursula and Gerald would both be better off—but the legal rule would lead to a negotiated settlement rather than a breach.

All this argumentation should not be taken by the reader to suggest that there is any fundamental doubt about the state of the present law of remedies in this field: both at common law and under the UCC, the remedy that is normally and generally available to a disappointed promisee is money damages, with specific performance being granted only if the contract involves "unique" property—typically, real estate. Nevertheless, there is said to be a tendency, encouraged by Restatement Section 359 and by UCC 2–716, to "liberalize the granting of equitable relief by enlarging the classes of cases in which damages are not regarded as an adequate remedy."[2] What constitutes adequacy or inadequacy for this purpose obviously depends on circumstances—among other things, on the ease or difficulty of proving damages with reasonable certainty, on the availability of a suitable substitute in the market, and on the need, if any, for continuing judicial supervision if equitable relief is granted. The "modern approach," according to the Restatement, is to *compare* money damages with equitable relief in order to determine which form of remedy best serves the ends of justice.

In *Walgreen Co. v. Sara Creek Property Co.,*[3] the well-known drugstore chain had leased space in the defendant's shopping mall under a lease agreement which barred the defendant from renting mall space to a competitive drugstore concern. A major tenant of the mall having gone broke and being about to close up, Sara Creek advised Walgreen that despite the prohibition in the lease, which still had some 10 years to run, it intended to replace that tenant with Phar–Mor, another large drugstore operator. Walgreen at once brought suit seeking an injunction against bringing Phar–Mor into the mall. Sara Creek apparently conceded that renting to Phar–Mor

---

2. Rest. Sec. 359, Comment a. And see: Bishop, *The Choice of Remedy for Breach of Contract,* 14 J. of Legal Studies 299 (1985); Shavell, *The Design of Contracts and Remedies for Breach,* 99 Q.J.Econ. 121 (1984); MacNeil, *Efficient Breach of Contract: Circles in the Sky,* 68 Va.L.Rev. 947 (1982); Schwartz, *The Case for Specific Performance,* 89 Yale L.J. 271 (1979). Compare Kronman, *Specific Performance,* 45 U.Chi.L.Rev. 351 (1978). *See also,* Farnsworth, *Legal Remedies for Breach of Contract,* 70 Columbia L.Rev. 1145 (1970).

3. 966 F.2d 273 (7th Cir.1992).

would be a breach but contended that equitable relief would be improper and that Walgreen's remedy should be limited to money damages based on estimated loss of future profits. Holding that damages would not adequately compensate Walgreen for its exclusivity right, the trial court enjoined the Phar–Mor deal until expiration of the Walgreen lease.

The Seventh Circuit affirmed, finding the grant of injunctive relief "broadly consistent with a proper analysis...." Ever the pedagogue, Judge Posner provides us with a textbook comparison of the two remedy alternatives. Granting an injunction (he observed, in effect) essentially leaves the working-out of the parties' conflict to the parties themselves. Once enjoined, Sara Creek would presumably commence to bargain with Walgreen for the release of the contract prohibition. Walgreen won't take less than its lost profit expectation; Sara Creek won't pay more than the value to it of getting Phar–Mor into the mall. Ultimately, the parties will or should agree upon a price at which the "purchase" of the injunction by Sara Creek, and its "sale" by Walgreen, leaves both parties feeling better off, very much as would the purchase and sale of any other property right. The bargaining process takes time and money, but in the end the cost to the parties, actual and imputed, might well be less than the cost of a full-fledged court proceeding with its tedious and expensive parade of expert witnesses. Most important, the price the parties finally agree upon must reflect the true value of their respective interests in their own estimation, and it is bound to be a more accurate measure of costs and expectations than an abstract damage figure determined by a government functionary (that is, a judge) having nothing personally at stake.

But there is, or there can be, a downside to equitable relief. In the first place, as the court noted, the bargaining process just referred to may break down and result in an impasse. The vaunted efficiency benefits that would otherwise attach to private agreement are lost in such event, and damages may then be the only way of arbitrating a solution. Second, equitable relief calling for performance on the part of the breaching party often requires judicial supervision and enforcement, which may be costly and burdensome. Continuing intervention is avoided if the remedy afforded to the injured party is a lump-sum money judgment. A damage award terminates the court's role in the dispute.

Taking all these elements into account, the *Walgreen* case offered a very plausible occasion for equitable relief. Calculating the plaintiff's anticipated loss of profits over a 10–year period was obviously a matter of considerable uncertainty, expert testimony notwithstanding. The absence of a market substitute for the plaintiff's exclusivity right was equally apparent. Finally, and perhaps most important, the injunction against the Phar–Mor deal was negative in its effect on the defendant. Sara Creek was simply enjoined from leasing space to Phar–Mor. No act or performance was demanded of it, merely forbearance; hence judicial oversight would be unnecessary.

2. *Cost Avoided and "Overhead"*. The point has been made that the "cost avoided" by an injured party as a result of being excused from performance by the other party's breach is necessarily subtracted from the injured party's damage recovery. "Cost avoided" would obviously include anticipated outlays for labor and materials, now "avoided" owing to the breach. Beyond those outlays, I suppose we could ask whether "cost avoided" also should be taken to refer to the so-called business "overhead" that would have been allocated to the particular contract (at least in accounting terms) had the project been carried on to completion. Is "overhead" an added element of "cost avoided"? The question is a bit obscure as posed, but perhaps a brief discussion of the well-known *Vitex*[4] decision will make it clearer.

Back in the 1960's (we learn from the Third Circuit's opinion), the United States generally imposed high tariffs on the importation of foreign wool products. Under a special exception, however, if such goods were first imported into the Virgin Islands and there processed in a substantial manner, the tariff on re-import into the U.S. would be eliminated. While Virgin Islands wool processors were thus enabled to profit quite handsomely, there was concern, locally, that the overall volume of imports from the Virgin Islands might increase to the point where Congress would be "stirred" to withdraw the beneficial tariff concession. Accordingly, the Islands legislature established an annual quota restriction on local processors—only so much re-importable woolen cloth for each processor.

Vitex Corp., a Virgin Islands company whose business was chemically water-proofing imported woolen cloth, presumably existed and made money solely or largely by virtue of the tariff concession just described. In 1963, finding itself with unused plant capacity and not yet having exhausted its quota allowance, Vitex entered into a contract with Caribtex, the defendant. Caribtex was in the business of importing cloth into the Virgin Islands, arranging to have it processed there in order to qualify for the tariff exception, and then exporting it to the United States. Under the contract, Caribtex was to furnish 125,000 yards of woolen material to Vitex

4. Vitex Manufacturing Corp. v. Caribtex Corp., 377 F.2d 795 (3d Cir.1967).

and Vitex was to process that material at a price of 25 cents a yard, or $31,250 in total. Vitex thereupon reopened its plant, recalled workers, ordered chemicals and generally made ready to do the water-proofing. Caribtex, however, apparently having encountered difficulty in meeting customs standards, never delivered the woolen goods and in effect repudiated the contract. Vitex then sued to recover the "profits" lost by reason of Caribtex's breach.

Holding for Vitex, the trial court awarded damages against Caribtex of $21,114: $31,250, the total contract price, minus $10,136, the labor and materials cost that Vitex would have incurred had it performed the contract, but avoided because of the breach. On appeal, Caribtex seemed to concede the breach but argued that the "cost avoided" number should be increased (and thus the net damage award reduced) by so much of Vitex's overhead expenses as would properly be allocated to the contract if the contract had been performed. Just what Caribtex meant to include as "overhead" is not made clear, but the term itself, though a bit old-fashioned ("fixed costs" would be the current version), is generally taken to refer to that category of expenses which the firm is obligated to pay as long as its business operations continue, irrespective of how much business it actually does in a given period. Obvious examples would be rent owed to a landlord under a long-term lease, interest owed to bondholders, real estate taxes owed to the city, and salaries owed to top managers under long-term employment contracts. In each case, the expense is a constant obligation that has to be paid (short of bankruptcy) and does not vary with the level of output. By contrast, "variable costs"—typically, wages and materials that relate to some particular project—rise and fall with the company's business volume and, as with the Caribtex contract, would be reduced or eliminated if for some reason business volume shrinks.

Affirming the $21,114 damage award, the Third Circuit held that "overhead should be treated as a part of gross profits recoverable as damages, and should not be considered as part of the seller's costs." Vitex's overhead, the Court reasoned, bore no direct relationship to any particular transaction and would have remained the same whether or not Vitex entered into a contract with Caribtex and whether or not it did the water-proofing work in question. The Court noted that UCC 2–708(2), although not then in force in the Virgin Islands, embodied the same rule—that "the measure of damages is the profit (including reasonable overhead) which the seller would have made from full performance by the buyer...." Being the product of "the foremost modern legal thought," the UCC was deemed by the Court to be persuasive.

The decision in *Vitex* was undoubtedly correct, at least as far as the question of "overhead" was concerned. By way of simple illustration, assume V, a manufacturer, enters into a contract with C, an exporter, to produce and supply certain goods. C repudiates the contract prior to any performance by V. Assume V annually pays $40,000 rent for its factory space, of which 20%, or $8,000, would be allocable to the C contract if C hadn't repudiated. Using roughly the numbers above—

Expected contract revenue	$31,000
Expected cost of Wages and Supplies	10,000
Expected gross profit	$21,000
Allocable factory rent	8,000
Expected net income	$13,000

How much in damages is V entitled to from C? Obvious answer: $21,000, that is, expected revenue less variable costs avoided. If the factory rent, which is owed to the lessor of the factory space, were treated as an addition to "cost avoided," then such rent would in effect be credited to C through a reduction in its liability for breach, as if C were somehow entitled to an $8,000 share of the gross profit that V expected to earn from the contract. Not so, of course. The factory lease is, in effect, a senior security entitling the holder (the lessor) to a limited share (the rent) of the gross profit generated by V from its business operations. Once the lessor's prior claim is satisfied, the residual claimant, V's owner, gets what is left, here $13,000. But C, the buyer in my illustration and the party in breach, has no place whatever in the line of takers.

As a final comment on the *Vitex* case itself, it seems to me that the term "profit" is thrown about rather loosely in the Court's opinion. Vitex's "profit" from a contract of $31,250 is found to be $21,114—better than 67 cents on the dollar—which makes it a very lucrative deal indeed, almost too lucrative. One explanation may be that the $21,114 figure included compensation for various expenses—the cost of reopening the plant, etc.—that were actually paid by Vitex before Caribtex breached the contract. In that event, for the sake of clarity if nothing else, the Court might have separated the damage award into two parts, (i) reliance and (ii) profit expectation, which would make the $21,114 figure look a bit more plausible.

Another possibility, however, is that the "large profit" (the Court's words) to be realized by Vitex reflected the premium price that Vitex was able to get from Caribtex because it, Vitex, still had available an unused portion of its allowable processing quota.

Perhaps other Virgin Islands processors had exhausted their quotas or were demanding an even higher premium. If so, the breach by Caribtex not only relieved Vitex of the further cost of labor and materials, but also restored to Vitex the quota allowance that it would otherwise have used up in performing the contract. Whatever that quota was worth, Vitex presumably got it back and, for a price, could make it available to another buyer in Caribtex's position. Having been returned unused, therefore, its value should properly have been included in calculating Vitex's cost avoided. Whether that would have reduced the damage award appreciably one cannot tell. Caribtex, which vainly argued that the contract price had been "unconscionable," was apparently convinced it would.[5]

The discussion that follows is divided into three sections. Section B describes the principal limitations on the expectation damage rule. Section C examines the chief alternatives to expectation damages, namely, damages based on the promisee's reliance and restitution interests. Section D, finally, considers whether and to what extent the parties may contract for a damage measure in advance of any breach instead of leaving the matter for judicial determination after a breach occurs.

B. Limitations on Expectation Damages

1. *Avoidability and Mitigation.* An injured promisee cannot recover damages for losses that, with reasonable effort, he could have avoided after the promisor's breach became known. In effect, the injured party is under a legal obligation to take (or else be presumed to have taken) reasonable steps to avoid waste and minimize the cost of breach. So stated, the rule, or limitation, applies both to the reliance feature and to the lost-profit feature of the injured party's claim. Having become aware of the promisor's non-performance, the injured party is expected to suspend or terminate his own performance and has no claim for expenditures made in reliance on the contract beyond that point in time. Going further, the injured party is expected to minimize his lost-profit claim by making reasonable efforts to substitute other arrange-

5. Yet another possibility is that the tariff exception expired or was tightened in some way before Caribtex was able to take advantage of it. The question, then, would be whether Vitex or Caribtex should be deemed to have taken the risk that such might occur. *Compare Krell v. Henry, supra,* p. 186.

ments—another job, another seller or buyer—for those provided in the contract. In effect, he cannot recover the value of lost benefits if and to the extent that there are opportunities to mitigate the loss by doing similar worthwhile things with his time and resources.

Following are three familiar illustrations of the "avoidability and mitigation" rule, all commonly featured in the contracts casebooks.

(1a) *Piling up damages.* In *Rockingham County v. Luten Bridge Co.,*[6] the plaintiff, Luten, in January entered into a contract with the County Board to build a bridge which was to be part of a newly constructed County road. There was public opposition to the project and in February, after one of the County commissioners had resigned (but then quickly attempted to rescind his resignation), the Board reversed itself (by a bare majority vote) and notified the plaintiff, which had by then spent $1,900 on labor and materials, that the contract was now regarded as unauthorized and invalid. The plaintiff, apparently believing that the later notice was itself invalid because the Board was illegally constituted, chose to disregard that notice and continued to build the bridge in accordance with the terms agreed upon. By November, the plaintiff had expended more than $18,000 and, its request for payment being refused, sued the County for that amount.

Reversing the trial court, which had held for the plaintiff, the Fourth Circuit found that the February notice possessed a kind of de facto legality and should have been taken by the plaintiff as a repudiation of the contract. At that point the plaintiff should have halted its own performance rather than piling up damages by "proceeding with the erection of a useless bridge." In the present action, therefore, the plaintiff was entitled to recover $1,900—its outlays up to the date of the notice—plus anticipated profit. It could not, however, claim reimbursement for expenditures made after it had become aware that the County had breached.

The rule of the *Luten* case—that the victim of a breach has a duty to avoid actions that increase the other party's damages—is well accepted and obviously correct. On the other hand, we might wonder what Luten's position would have been if it *had* halted performance on receiving the February notice and if the de facto legality question (to which the Court devoted four full pages of its opinion) had been decided differently. Then, perhaps, Luten itself might have been regarded as the party in breach and disentitled even to recover its $1,900 outlay (especially if the road project had finally gone forward). The February notice advised Luten that its

6.   35 F.2d 301 (4th Cir.1929).

contract "was not legal and valid", which was plainly false, and Luten might well have considered that the notice, hastily issued by a rump Board, could not be taken as definitive. As indicated, the Court held for the County by reciting the familiar and well-acknowledged rule that an injured party has no right to "pile up damages". But the real issue in the case, I think, was whether Luten faced an honest or a phony dilemma regarding the effect of the February notice, and if the former, whether its decision to continue working on the bridge was reasonable or capricious. As to this factual question, the Fourth Circuit had nothing whatever to say, although, as stated, one might suppose that it would have been seen as fairly critical.

1(b). *Personal Services.* Minimizing loss through mitigation is a self-executing obligation when the subject-matter of the contract is commodities or other fungible merchandise, because the injured party's damage claim is capped, in effect, by the market value of equivalent goods. In other situations, particularly where the contract calls for specialized services, the question of equivalence or substitutability may be much less certain. In what is perhaps the best known of all "duty to mitigate" cases—*Parker v. Twentieth Century–Fox Film Corp.*[7]—the plaintiff, Shirley MacLaine, in 1965 had entered into a contract with Fox to play the lead role in a movie version of the Broadway musical *Bloomer Girl.* The much coveted role would provide an opportunity not only to "act", but also to sing, dance and otherwise exhibit oneself to advantage. MacLaine's fee was guaranteed at $750,000 for 14 weeks' work. For reasons unknown, Fox decided to cancel *Bloomer Girl* before production had begun. In order "to avoid any damage to you," however, Fox offered in writing to employ MacLaine as the leading actress, at the very same fee, in a western film tentatively entitled *Big Country, Big Man,* giving her one week to say yes or no to the offer. The female lead in *Big Country* would presumably have involved little more than standing about in a flimsy frock tearfully begging Big Man to settle down and leave his guns at home. MacLaine said no and sued for her fee.

Holding (with one dissent) that MacLaine was under no legal obligation to mitigate damages by accepting the western role, the Supreme Court of California affirmed the trial court in granting her motion for summary judgment and awarded damages of $750,000 against the studio. The Court majority acknowledged the general rule that the measure of recovery for a wrongfully discharged employee is the salary agreed upon *less* the amount that

7. 3 Cal.3d 176, 89 Cal.Rptr. 737, 474 P.2d 689 (1970).

the employee earned or with reasonable effort could have earned from other employment. This, however, did not mean that the wronged employee must simply take any job in the economic universe; rather, the "other employment" must be comparable and not "of a different or inferior kind". By "no stretch of the imagination", said the Court, could a silly part in a cowboy movie be considered the equivalent of the lead in a major song-and-dance production. As to comparability, therefore, there was simply no factual issue whatever—no need to take testimony or to hear the views of experts—and hence the trial court's action was correct.[8]

The dissenting Justice, concerned that the majority opinion might encourage plaintiff-employees to ignore the general duty to mitigate and thus increase the cost of contractual failure, thought that there should have been a trial to determine whether the differences between the two jobs really were substantial enough to justify MacLaine in treating the later offer as "inferior" in kind. One suspects that the dissenting Justice viewed MacLaine's conduct in rejecting the substitute role as distinctly egoistic. The dissenter may also have experienced a certain visceral shock when he perceived that MacLaine would now receive $750,000 (more than $4,000,000, I guess, in 2012 dollars) for sitting home and doing nothing.

The outcome in the Shirley MacLaine case obviously invites comparison with the result reached by the New York Court of Appeals in *Jacob & Youngs v. Kent,* discussed in Chapter 6. In the latter, the promisor's breach—installing Cohoes instead of Reading pipe—was dealt with under the diminished value rule, presumably because the cost of curing the defective performance would have been so much greater than the very small loss in economic value suffered by the promisee. In the Shirley MacLaine case, apparently, the Court majority made the opposite finding: the loss to MacLaine of professional standing and future career opportunities resulting from the cancellation of *Bloomer Girl* was so great that it could not be compensated by a dollar amount smaller than the entire fee that had been promised her. In effect, and by implication, the Court seemed almost to believe that MacLaine would not have substituted the female lead in *Big Country* at any price. That could not literally be true, one would think, even for the proud MacLaine; and while the task of proving otherwise in the face of her sworn denials would

---

8. MacLaine's contract could have been read to require Fox to pay MacLaine her fee at all events, that is, solely in consideration of her 14-week time commitment. Fortunately for the casebooks, MacLaine's counsel seems to have accepted the proposition that she had a general duty to mitigate, and to have confined his argument to the comparable employment question.

have been difficult, one might suppose (along with the dissent) that the defendant should at least have been given a chance to show the jury that the *Big Country* part was not so inferior as to be wholly non-substitutional. My guess is that the Court's willingness to let the issue go on summary judgment reflected a conviction (which the trial judge may have shared) that the studio was not in good faith when it offered MacLaine the role of a cowboy's cowgirl—*and* gave her just one week to take it or leave it. Did the studio people truly expect that she might take it? Perhaps; yet the language of the offer itself—"to avoid any damage to you"—sounds more like the conscious product of a legal mind intent on laying the basis for a mitigation defense than it does the gravelly voice of a movie executive eager to convince MacLaine that the role was exactly right for her.

Mention of Shirley MacLaine leads the author to add yet another celebrity dispute, this one involving Michael Jordan—he of the unstoppable jump-shot—"considered to be one of the most popular athletes in the world."[8a] In 1995 Jordan entered into a 10–year (!) endorsement agreement granting MCI the right to use his name and personal services to promote MCI's telecommunications products. In addition to a $5 million signing bonus, Jordan was to receive $2 million dollars a year in exchange for making himself available for brief periods—actually, no more than four 4–hour days a year—to do promotional work for MCI. From 1995 to 2001 Jordan appeared in various television commercials and a number of print ads on behalf of MCI, but in 2002 (for reasons not relevant here) MCI ceased to make the $2 million annual payments required by the endorsement agreement and in effect terminated the contract. Jordan then sued for the four omitted annual payments–2002—2005–a total of $8 million.

Breach by MCI having been conceded, the issue before the Court was limited to the calculation of Jordan's damages. Over Jordan's strenuous objection, the Court held that Jordan had a duty to mitigate—to make, or try to make, other endorsement deals in place of the four years remaining under the MCI agreement. The burden was on MCI, however, to produce "evidence" showing whether, and if so by how much, Jordan's claim would have been reduced had he made "reasonable efforts" to arrange other endorsements. "It is not clear," said the Court, "that Jordan could have found an endorsement agreement . . . that paid him $2 million a year [that is, for just four half-days]. . . . It is also unlikely that

---

8a. *In re Worldcom, Inc.*, Bankrupt-cy, Southern District N.Y., 361 B.R. 675 (2007).

Jordan would have been obligated to accept a large number of endorsements of smaller value to make up the $2 million, owing to the dilution effect such a number would have, because such efforts would likely be unreasonable."

So, both Shirley and Michael were found to have a legal duty to mitigate. Shirley's duty was virtually self-liquidating. Michael fared less well, yet I think it would have been almost as hard, practically speaking, for MCI to find evidence of equivalent opportunities involving the same 4–day, 4–hour time commitment for the same $2 million fee.

Nothing further being reported in the Jordan case, one assumes the parties settled.

1(c). *Coal and gravel.* As the above mention of *Jacob & Youngs* should suggest, the "mitigation" principle can be taken to refer broadly to the prevailing notion that the law ought to do what it reasonably can to minimize the cost of contract breakdown—subject, however, to the constraint that the injured party's expectations be fully compensated by the party in breach. *Groves v. John Wunder Co.,*[9] yet another casebook classic, provides a fairly challenging illustration both of the minimization goal and of the constraint. Groves (a corporation) owned 24 acres of suburban real estate which, though zoned as industrial property, was being used by it for the excavation of sand and gravel. In 1927, Groves leased the land, together with related equipment, to John Wunder Co., also engaged in sand and gravel excavation, for a 7–year term. Wunder paid Groves a lump-sum rent of $105,000 and agreed that when the lease expired it would restore the land to Groves "at a uniform grade, substantially the same as the grade now existing at the roadway...." Seven years later, however, having turned the property into a choppy mess, Wunder refused to carry out its grading obligation and chose instead to deliberately breach the contract.

In the litigation that followed, Wunder conceded that Groves had a valid claim for breach, but it urged that the proper measure of damages was the difference between the current market value of the property if the grading work had been done as promised, only $12,000, and its value as a choppy mess, roughly zero. Groves, by contrast, argued that damages should be measured by the actual cost of grading—doing the work itself—which, as it turned out,

9. 205 Minn. 163, 286 N.W. 235 (1939). And see, Farnsworth, *Your Loss or My Gain? The Dilemma of the Disgorgement Principle in Breach of Contract,* 94 Yale L.J. 1339 (1985); Muris, *Cost of Completion or Diminution in Market Value: The Relevance of Subjective Value,* 12 J. Legal Studies 379 (1983).

would have been more than $60,000. Using *Jacob & Youngs* terminology, Wunder sought the application of a "diminished value" rule, while Groves sought "cost of replacement". Underlying the dispute, quite obviously, was the advent of the Great Depression: land values in suburban Minneapolis had simply collapsed between the commencement and termination of the lease.

The Supreme Court of Minnesota held (3–2) that Wunder was liable to Groves for an amount equal to the "reasonable cost" of grading the property, presumably $60,000. Groves, said the Court, was entitled to the promised performance (or its money equivalent) since that was what the contract called for. The diminished value rule would properly apply where the cost of remedying a defect in a completed structure was excessive relative to the loss in value attributable to the defect—that, indeed, would entail "economic waste"—but it could have no application to a contract to *construct* an improvement, "particularly where, as here, the delinquent [Wunder] has had full payment for the promised performance." In any case, as Cardozo emphasized in *Jacob & Youngs,* the doctrine of substantial performance and diminished value could not be appealed to by a promisor when the act of breach was willful and deliberate. In effect, therefore, Wunder must go ahead and spend $60,000 to generate property-value of $12,000—or else, of course, settle with Groves for a payment in cash. The dissenters urged, to the contrary, that the correct damage measure was Groves' loss ($12,000), not Wunder's cost ($60,000), and that willfulness had nothing to do with the question.

According to report, Wunder did in fact settle following the decision, paying Groves $55,000 cash in lieu of actual performance. What Groves did with the money one doesn't know, but if it still had faith in the future of suburban real estate it could have purchased nearly five times the acreage it started with at the depressed market price then prevailing. Should we therefore regard the Court's decision as having provided a "windfall"—that is, an undeserved benefit—to Groves and a corresponding penalty to Wunder? Answer: no. As the Court implied, Groves, as lessor, had really paid in advance for the grading work when it agreed to accept a rent of $105,000. If Wunder had *not* undertaken to grade the land at the expiration of the lease, then, obviously, Groves would have had to look forward to doing that job itself and at its own expense. In the latter event, the rent initially agreed to by the parties would necessarily have been higher. If, for example, Groves foresaw that the cost of grading at the end of 7 years would be about $60,000, it would have demanded an additional amount equal to the present value of the anticipated outlay (i.e., a sum which, at current interest rates, would grow to $60,000 in Groves' hands over the 7–year term). No one would regard that "fund" as a windfall to Groves; Wunder would have no claim to recapture any portion of it just because land values had fallen; and Groves would be free to use the fund for any purpose it chose, whether to grade the land, buy new property, or make unrelated investments. Having decided that the grading work would be carried out more efficiently by Wunder, Groves in effect forbore to demand additional rent and, in so doing, gave up an equivalent sum to Wunder for later expenditure on Groves' behalf. If the cost of grading varied from the parties' original expectation, one or the other would enjoy a benefit, so that they did indeed "gamble" with each other on that factor. But there was no evidence whatever that they intended their duties to be affected by ups and downs in the real estate market (or the stock market or the economy in general).

Finally, although presented as a case involving "contract damages", it may be more accurate to regard *Groves* as a problem in restitution. If the proposition suggested above is accepted—namely, that Groves "paid" for the grading work in advance—then Groves was entitled under Restatement Sections 370 and 373 to the reasonable value ($60,000, apparently) of the benefit that it had "conferred" on Wunder by reason of the prepayment. There really could be no "waste" in enforcing Groves' claim against Wunder: the actual grading work would not be done in any event, because Groves would always prefer a cash settlement greater than $12,000 to actual performance. The only question, then, was whether Groves had a right to recover the full amount of its prepayment ($60,000) or just the lesser sum that reflected the value of the land if re-graded ($12,000).[11] Put differently, the question would be whether Wunder, having elected to breach, should be permitted to keep the disputed balance of $48,000 or be required to give it back. As suggested, the majority's answer—give it back—seems quite correct.

My views notwithstanding, the *Groves* decision was rejected by the Supreme Court of Oklahoma in the well-known *Peevyhouse*[11a] case, largely on what the Court deemed the reasoning and authority of *Jacob & Youngs*. The facts in *Peevyhouse* resemble the facts in *Groves*. The Peevyhouses, owners of farm land containing coal

11. From Groves' standpoint, the grading contract was really a "losing contract"—Groves paid $60 to get $12 as it turned out—and hence perhaps the case itself belongs to the category of restitutionary disputes discussed at p. 231, below. Here it is the service-buyer (Groves) that is the injured party and the service-seller (Wunder) that commits the breach. Those positions are reversed in the example discussed at p. 231, but the issue seems pretty much the same.

11a. 382 P.2d 109 (Okl. 1962).

deposits, entered into a 5–year strip-mining lease with the Garland Coal Mining Company. Under the lease, which called for a stated royalty per ton mined, Garland agreed to restore the land by filling in the pits and other desecrations once the strip-mining work was finished. In the end Garland refused to do the land restoration work, of which the cost (perhaps unexpectedly) would have been more than $25,000. The value of the land as restored would have increased by a mere $300. The Peevyhouses sued for $25,000; Garland offered $300.

The case was tried to a jury, which received a curiously ambiguous set of legal instructions from the trial judge. Instructed that it must return a verdict for the plaintiffs, the jury was also told that it had a choice as to damages: it could award the plaintiffs either "the cost of performance," presumably $25,000, or "the diminution in value of plaintiffs' farm," presumably $300. Having deliberated, the jury found that the Peevyhouses were entitled to damages of $5,000, a number that corresponded to no legal rule whatever but probably reflected the jury's irritation with Garland and sympathy for the Peevyhouses—in other words, rough justice.

On appeal by both parties, the Supreme Court held for Garland and reduced the damage award to $300. The Court seems to have been slightly hypnotized by the notion of "economic waste," which it evidently associated with Cardozo's *Jacob & Youngs* opinion. The Court apparently viewed Garland's duty to restore the farm land as an "incidental" feature of the mining lease and as somehow equivalent to the trivial difference between Reading and Cohoes water pipes. The idea that the Peevyhouses may have "prepaid" Garland to do the restoration work by accepting a lower royalty rate than they would have accepted if left to do the restoration work themselves was given no consideration, although it seems likely, or at least plausible, that the Peevyhouses made the same sort of cost calculation that was made by the landowner in *Groves*.

In virtually escaping its contractual obligation, Garland both increased its net profit from operations and likewise managed to avoid what may have been a serious underestimate of the actual cost of filling in the pits. Neither, I believe, could have been said of the contractor in *Jacob & Youngs* when it more or less inadvertently substituted one identical brand of water pipe for another.

2. *The Lost–Volume Seller Exception.* Under UCC 2–706, as noted, where a buyer of goods repudiates or wrongfully refuses to accept delivery the seller's damages are measured by the difference between the contract price and the price—presumably lower—at which the same goods are or can be resold in the market. But

suppose the seller resells at exactly the *same* price; the buyer's reason for repudiating is simply a change of heart—he no longer wants the goods in question—rather than a drop in market price. If the second contract is regarded as a substitute for the first, the seller would have suffered no loss by reason of the breach and would apparently have no damage claim whatever. But how do we know that the second contract *was* a substitute for the first? In the well-known *Neri* case (below), the New York Court of Appeals apparently made the assumption that the disappointed seller, in the ordinary course of business, could have expanded its inventory more or less at will and was prepared to sell to as many buyers as might care to buy, indeed the more the better. If that was true in *Neri*, or is true in general, then there is something not quite right about the idea of regarding one customer as a substitute or replacement for another. If customer A, having agreed to buy, later repudiates his purchase agreement, the seller would hardly feel that the "profit" he expected to realize from the sale to A had been recouped or replaced because customer B walked in a little later and purchased goods of the same sort at an identical price.

Recognizing that the contract-minus-resale measure may not be appropriate in these circumstances, UCC 2–708(2) establishes an exception for so-called lost volume sellers. In effect, if the standard damage measure is inadequate to put the seller in as good a position as performance would have done because the buyer's breach entails the loss of a profitable sale, then the seller's damages shall instead be "the profit (including reasonable overhead) which the seller would have made from full performance by the buyer...." *Neri v. Retail Marine Corp.*[12] is illustrative. In *Neri,* the plaintiff contracted to purchase a new boat from the defendant, a dealer, for $12,500 and put down a deposit of $4,250. Within a week the plaintiff's lawyer notified the defendant that the plaintiff was rescinding the purchase contract because of illness, but the defendant, having by then ordered and received the boat from the manufacturer, refused to return the plaintiff's deposit. Four months later the defendant sold the same boat to another buyer at the same $12,500 price. The plaintiff sued to recover his deposit, and the defendant counterclaimed under 2–708(2) for lost profit of $2,500 plus incidental expenses.

The Court of Appeals held for the defendant. "The conclusion," said the Court, "is clear from the record—indeed with mathematical certainty—that 'the [contract-resale] measure of damages ... is inadequate to put the seller in as good a position as performance

---

12. 30 N.Y.2d 393, 334 N.Y.S.2d 165, 285 N.E.2d 311 (1972).

would have done' ... and hence ... that the seller is entitled to its 'profit' ''. The second customer would not be regarded as having replaced the first nor the later transaction the earlier. The defendant could have obtained sufficient inventory to supply all available customers, and it would therefore have had two sales instead of one if the plaintiff hadn't breached.

The lost-volume rule has provoked a very earnest scholarly debate in recent years,[13] with some writers suggesting that the seller's expected "volume" is in fact unknowable and in any case may be wholly unaffected by the buyer's breach. If, for example, the plaintiff in *Neri* had gone through with the unwanted yacht purchase, he might have turned around and resold the yacht to the second buyer, in which event Retail Marine would have had only one sale, not two. Arguably, also, a seller operating in a strictly competitive market—a retailer, for example, selling standard-price goods—generally attains an optimum volume of sales by selling all the goods at the prevailing market price that he can profitably dispose of. Additional sales, including the one "lost," would not be made, because the marginal cost of displaying and selling one more unit of merchandise—renting additional store-space, say, or paying the salary of another sales-clerk—would exceed the revenue to be realized from that additional sale.

This line of analysis, if accepted, suggests that what the injured seller really loses when a buyer breaches is not the "profit" from one more sale, but the "selling costs" that were incurred in making the *particular* sale which the buyer repudiated. The wholesale cost of the merchandise itself is recouped by the seller when, as in *Neri*, the same merchandise is sold to another customer. But what the seller cannot recoup is the time (talking to the customer) and money (investment, rent, advertising and other amortizable outlays) expended in making the repudiated sale. Such selling costs are lost when the first buyer breaches and cannot be recovered by selling the same merchandise at the same price to a second buyer for whose "benefit" the same selling costs will be incurred a second time. On this view, what the injured seller is entitled to recover from the breaching buyer under the lost-volume rule is not "lost profit," but "incidental" damages equal to the added cost of selling the same merchandise twice.

13. *See, e.g.,* Cooter & Eisenberg, *Damages for Breach of Contract,* 73 Calif.L.Rev. 1432 (1985); Goldberg, *An Economic Analysis of the Lost–Volume Seller,* 57 S.Cal.L.Rev. 283 (1984); Goetz & Scott, *Measuring Sellers' Damages: The* *Lost–Profits Puzzle,* 31 Stan.L.Rev. 323 (1979); Speidell & Clay, *Seller's Recovery of Overhead Under UCC 2–708(2): Economic Cost Theory and Contract Remedial Policy,* 57 Cornell L.Rev. 681 (1972).

There is, however, a problem. Although the formulation just offered is precise in terms, as a practical matter the amount in question is likely to be difficult if not impossible to determine with accuracy, and in most cases the accounting and related expense of making that determination would simply be too large to justify. But perhaps the "lost profit" calculation serves the same end. A retailer's selling costs (it is argued) are likely to be equivalent, roughly, to the retailer's gross sales margin—in *Neri*, the excess of the retail price of the yacht over its cost to the dealer. Put differently, the markup on the dealer's wholesale cost—his "lost profit" under UCC 2–708(2)—should approximate his actual and imputed retailing costs, again roughly speaking. If that is true, then "lost profit," which can be calculated relatively easily, may serve as a substitute or proxy for the seller's "incidental" damages, and may be the best way, or at least a practical way, of compensating the seller for the buyer's breach.

Whatever the merits of the lost-volume rule, my impression is that the issue presented in *Neri*—whether breach by a retail customer results in recoverable damages to the retailer—does not arise very often in practice. If that impression is accurate, the reason may be that retailers generally make their order-cancellation policy known to their customers in advance. A high-class department store might have a policy that not only permits cancellation prior to delivery but allows its customers to return merchandise within a specified period after delivery. A discounter, by contrast, sells for cash or requires a deposit for big-ticket items and permits no return or cancellation once you leave the premises. In either case, the terms of dealing are pre-announced by the retailer, and in that sense pre-negotiated, and hence disputes that result in claims under 2–708(2) are rare. It goes virtually without saying that the department store with a "liberal" cancellation policy also has higher selling costs than the discounter and will recoup those costs at its customers' expense; the discounter has an "all sales are final" policy but obviously sells for less. The customer can have it either way, depending on where he chooses to do his shopping. The Court in *Neri* made no determination with respect to the parties' understanding on this question, and of course it may be that they had none. On the other hand, the seller did require the buyer to make a cash deposit at the time of sale. While the amount, $4,250, somewhat exceeded the seller's profit margin, the parties may well have intended thereby to establish both the existence and the limit of the buyer's liability in the event that he later changed his mind about the boat.

Although one generally thinks of the lost-volume rule in connection with retail sales and other merchandise transactions, its application, or its "penumbra," is probably somewhat wider. Thus, suppose X, a construction company, contracts with Y to build a factory for $1,000,000. If Y subsequently repudiates the contract, X will almost certainly be entitled to recover damages that would include its expected net profit even if X subsequently enters into a contract to build a similar factory for somebody else at the very same price. Y might defeat X's damage claim by proving that X lacked the resources to profitably undertake both building jobs at the same time, but in most circumstances such a factual showing would be difficult for Y to make since the relevant "evidence" is pretty much within X's control.

Where the repudiated agreement is an employment or personal service contract, the general rule is otherwise. A wrongfully discharged employee cannot claim to be able to fill two jobs simultaneously. Hence, injured employees and other personal service performers are usually obligated to mitigate damages (whether actually or presumptively) by seeking substitute employment of an appropriate character. In the *Shirley MacLaine* case, for example, the plaintiff apparently conceded that she had a legal duty to mitigate, the only issue being whether one movie role was a suitable substitute for the other. But where the promisee functions as a "firm"—the building contractor being the most familiar example—the same legal obligation is not likely to be deemed applicable.

3. *Foreseeability.* In *Hadley v. Baxendale*,[14] decided by the Court of Exchequer in 1854, the plaintiffs, operators of a flour mill in Gloucester, sued the defendants, a firm of carriers, for their failure within the time promised to deliver a broken millshaft to the manufacturer in Greenwich, which needed the broken shaft to use as a model for making a replacement. Since the broken shaft was delayed in getting to Greenwich, its replacement was similarly late in getting back to Gloucester. As a consequence, the flour mill had to be shut down for five days, during which period the plaintiffs paid wages and assertedly lost business profits. From a jury verdict awarding damages to the plaintiffs for lost profits, the defendants appealed.

Speaking through Baron Alderson, the Court held that, although they had breached the carriage contract by their delay, the defendants were not liable for the very sizable losses that resulted from the five-day shut-down of the mill. "Where two parties have

14. 156 Eng.Rep. 145 (Court of Exchequer 1854).

made a contract which one of them has broken, the damages which
the other party ought to receive ... should be such as may fairly
and reasonably be considered either arising naturally, i.e., according to the usual course of things, or such as may reasonably be
supposed to have been in the contemplation of both parties, at the
time they made the contract...." The five-day shut-down would
not have been considered as arising in the "usual course", the
Court thought, since one's natural assumption, "in the great multitude of cases of millers sending off broken shafts", would be that
the miller had another shaft in reserve or otherwise had made
provision for continuing his business. Here, as it turned out, there
were "special circumstances"—plaintiffs *didn't* have another shaft
in reserve, so that any delay in getting a replacement would cause a
total shut-down of the mill. No doubt the defendants heard a great
deal about the need for on-time delivery *after* the breach had
occurred. At the time the contract was entered into, however, the
plaintiffs said nothing, or at least not enough, to make the defendants aware of how dire the consequences would be. Had there
been sufficient communication at that time, the defendants might
have done a number of things, of which one (and the most likely)
would have been to insist that the contract contain "special terms
as to the damages"—meaning, presumably, limitations on defendants' liability for breach. And "of this advantage," the Court said,
"it would be very unjust to deprive them."

The rule of the *Hadley* case—that damages are not recoverable
for loss that was not known to or reasonably foreseeable by the
party in breach at the time of contracting—can be linked to the
familiar proposition that "contract", unlike tort, is a species of
absolute liability. An unexcused failure to perform results in liability for the promisor even though such non-performance is unintended and inadvertent and cannot be blamed on the promisor's negligence or on his failure to meet an ordinary standard of care.
Coupling absolute liability for breach with exposure to unlimited
consequential damages, however, could be devastating to the promisor and especially in the case of routine over-the-counter transactions like the carriage contract in *Hadley* would impose a risk upon
the promisor which far outweighs the modest benefit that he might
expect to realize from the transaction itself.

The point can be expanded slightly. Like any producer, a seller
of goods or services—in *Hadley,* the carrier—needs to calculate his
costs when he sets a price on his performance. Such costs would
include not only the standard bookkeeping outlays (wages, fuel,
docking fees), but also a reasonable reserve for contingent expenses
where there really are adverse contingent events to worry about. If,

for example, experience shows that Event X will occur 10% of the time and will result (if it does occur) in an unavoidable expense of $1,000, then, no doubt, the seller will add $100 to his cost estimate and price his performance accordingly. In the case of a freight-carrier, perhaps the adverse event that is most likely to occur would be the seller's own inadvertent failure to make deliveries on time. If so, the seller's reserve for contingencies would have to reflect his potential liability to the buyer, discounted by the probability of occurrence. Quite obviously, the greater such potential liability the greater must be the seller's contingency reserve and the higher the price he will demand for his product or service. The buyer, who faces a similar set of considerations in dealing with his own customers, is of course aware of all this and, as a result, has an incentive not to disclose any unusual damages that might result from the seller's non-performance *until* the contract price has been agreed to and it is too late for the seller either to negotiate a higher figure or to insist on liability limitations. The effect, if this tactic succeeds, is to add a large insurance-like obligation to the seller's undertaking without his knowledge. But as that would be "very unjust," the Court in *Hadley* effectively eliminated the benefit of a non-disclosure strategy by excluding unanticipated losses from the final damage calculation.

Viewed from yet another angle, the foreseeability doctrine can be said to encourage the promisee to behave in an efficient, cost-saving manner *before* the promisor breaches. Thus, anyone reading the *Hadley* opinion will quite naturally find himself wondering why the mill-owner didn't have a couple of extra millshafts around the place somewhere. If the continued operation of the mill was entirely shaft-dependent, so to speak, then it seems imprudent not to have maintained an inventory of spare parts. The explanation, presumably, is that the mill-owner wished to avoid investing money in spare parts and preferred instead to rely on the shaft-manufacturer's ability to furnish a quick replacement when one was needed. Then, however, as the Court suggested, it became necessary to inform the carrier in the clearest terms that an on-time delivery was essential. Had the mill-owner made its "special circumstances" known, the carrier might have reacted (a) by adding extra personnel or by using a separate vehicle to assure that the shaft arrived on time, or (b) by refusing the contract unless the mill-owner obtained loss-insurance (whether from the carrier itself or from a third-party) in case delivery failed. Either alternative, to be sure, would ultimately be reflected in higher freighting cost to the mill-owner, but I think it is plain that neither would be as costly as the loss that might be expected to result from a prolonged shut-down of the whole mill operation. The finding in *Hadley* that the mill-owner's losses were "unforeseeable" is thus equivalent, in practical effect, to a finding that the mill-owner was in the best position (prospectively) to minimize damages, but that he failed to do so.

Put differently, the foreseeability doctrine creates what has been described as "an implicit duty to premitigate".[15] The mill-owner could have met that obligation either by carrying an inventory of replacement parts or by informing the carrier about his special circumstances "at the time they made the contract". Having done neither, recovery was barred.

Restatement Section 351 adopts the "foreseeability" limitation of the *Hadley* case. Subsection (3) reflects a particular concern that consequential damages for breach by sellers may overcompensate buyers when "loss of profits" is included in the damage calculation. The *Village Plaza* case discussed below might be an example. To avoid that risk, the parties in a commercial setting may "contract around" the foreseeability problem by limiting or excluding liability for consequential damages. UCC 2–719 expressly authorizes such liability limitations, though in the case of consumer goods 2–719(3) treats a "Limitation of consequential damages for injury to the person"—see *Henningsen* at p. 100 as "prima facie unconscionable."

4. *Certainty.* As a general rule of limitation, damages for breach are recoverable only to the extent that the injured party's loss can be established with reasonable certainty. The issue has arisen most frequently in connection with lost profit claims, presumably for the reason that determining the injured party's "profits" entails projections and predictions that are sometimes speculative and conjectural and are almost always open to debate. As in the *Village Plaza* case, discussed below, each of the parties is likely to produce an expert, often more than one, to testify in his behalf. Hired for the purpose, the experts are virtually certain to disagree with one another, and to do so at length and in the most positive terms, leading an exhausted court or jury to view the whole process with skepticism verging on mistrust. In the end, as the Restatement observes, reasonable doubts are likely to be resolved against the party in breach, since it is he who is responsible for generating the problem to start with.

In *Fera v. Village Plaza, Inc.,*[16] the Supreme Court of Michigan affirmed a jury award to the plaintiffs of $200,000 for lost profits.

15. Goldberg, *Relational Exchange, Contract Law, and the Boomer Problem* (in Goldberg ed., Readings in the Economic of Contract Law, 1989, p. 71). And see, Posner, *Economic Analysis of the Law* 107 (3d ed. 1986).

16. 396 Mich. 639, 242 N.W.2d 372 (1976). And see Restatement Section 352.

The plaintiffs had leased store-space in a shopping center, the lease to run for 10 years at a stated monthly rental plus a percentage of sales. The leased space was to be used by the plaintiffs as a "book-and-bottle" shop, whatever that may be, but through neglect or confusion on the part of the managers of the shopping center the space was leased to another tenant and the plaintiffs were refused occupancy. The Court held that the evidence on lost profit presented at the trial—after "days and days of testimony" from experts on both sides—was sufficient to sustain the jury's verdict. This was true even though the book-and-bottle shop was a new business with no past-earnings history on which to base an estimate of future earnings, even though it appeared doubtful that the lessees would ever have obtained a liquor license, and even though the Court itself "might have found plaintiffs' proofs lacking had we been members of the jury". Mathematical precision was not required in cases where precision is unattainable, said the Court, particularly when "it is the defendant's own act or neglect" that has created the problem.

Although it upheld the jury's verdict, the Court in *Village Plaza* may have been troubled by a sense that the award was exaggerated and perhaps vindictive. We are told next to nothing about the lessees' business outlook, yet $200,000 does seem rather a large number to attach to the "lost profit" of a humble book-and-bottle shop, and I suppose we might wonder how the jury arrived at that figure. My own suspicion—just a guess and admittedly unprovable—is that, in calculating the lessees' damages for lost profit, the jury, or the trial court, overlooked two important financial elements that should have been taken into account and that might well have reduced the award in size. The first such element concerns the definition of "profit", especially relevant here because the shop was a new business to which the plaintiffs had as yet committed neither services nor funds. The second concerns the purely mechanical process of discounting future earnings to present value.

First, then, what should we understand by "profit"? For accounting and tax purposes, the answer would be: total returns from the sale of books and bottles minus the firm's actual business outlays, which would typically include payments for inventory (the books and bottles), employees' wages, rent, utilities and various other "inputs" purchased from third parties. But while the balance—revenues less business expenses—is certainly "net income" in an accounting sense, it is not economic "profit". Thus, an economist would presumably argue that the accountant's "net income" is just a preliminary or midway figure and needs to be reduced by "implicit costs"—costs for which no obvious money payments are made—in order to determine whether the firm has truly realized a profit from operations. Such implicit costs would chiefly include (a) the value of the individual plaintiffs' services in running the shop (that is, the salaries they would be entitled to if they worked for an outside employer instead of for themselves) and (b) a normal return on the plaintiffs' invested capital (that is, the interest they would earn if the plaintiffs put their money in a savings account instead of in their own business). In economic terms, "profit" is what is left after deducting these implicit costs from accounting net income. My hunch (unprovable, etc.) is that the jury in the *Village Plaza* case calculated the shop's "lost profit" by deducting money outlays only and ignoring implicit costs—and further, that if implicit costs *had* been taken into account the "profit" figure would have been pretty close to zero.

If that hunch is correct, then the effect of the jury's action would be not only to overstate the plaintiffs' loss, but—equally important for our purposes—to disregard the plaintiffs' legal duty to mitigate damages. Thus, once aware that the defendants had breached, the plaintiffs must be assumed, as a matter of law, to have sought substitute (non-inferior) employment as managers of somebody else's liquor store and likewise to have invested their capital in some other income-producing asset. The Shirley Mac-Laine case shows that the duty to mitigate is not always the same as the economist's notion of implicit opportunity cost; but where, as here, the injured party's service skills are routine in nature, the two constructs are very much alike and omitting one is roughly equivalent to omitting the other. To be sure, the State liquor license for which the plaintiffs had applied would have no close economic substitute, and I concede that the license (if it had ever been granted) would be an asset of premium value in the plaintiffs' hands. In addition, I suppose that the idea of combining books with bottles might have seemed to the jury to be an innovative marketing concept from which the plaintiffs were entitled to expect an unusually high return. Still, it is hard to believe that either the liquor license or the marketing concept could have been worth as much as $200,000 in the year 1965, and of course the Court did not suggest they were.

The other question that comes to mind is whether the jury's $200,000 figure represented the discounted value of 10 years' future earnings or was simply the *sum* of such earnings, that is, 10 times average earnings of $20,000. If the former, and if we assume a discount rate of (say) 15% on liquor store investments, then, to generate a present-value figure of $200,000, the expected annual earnings of the book-and-bottle shop would have to have been about $40,000. The number $40,000 seems rather high, however, and my suspicion is that the jury simply multiplied expected annual earnings by 10. If so, the result would be a substantial measure of over-compensation, but there would be nothing on the face of a general verdict that would tell you which "methodology" the jury had actually employed.

5. *UCC 2–106 and 2–713.* The "cover" rule in the case of an injured buyer and the "resale" rule in the case of an injured seller generally work well and without undue complications. As a brief exercise for the reader, how would the following come out? Assume Seller contracts to sell Buyer goods for $50,000. Seller then makes a contract to purchase the goods from a supplier for $45,000, intending to net $5,000 on the resale to Buyer. The market price for the goods promptly falls to $35,000 and Buyer repudiates the contract. How much should Seller recover from Buyer if Seller, having received the goods from his supplier, resells the goods for $35,000? Easy answer: $15,000. Does $15,000 overcompensate Seller, who looked forward to a profit of only $5,000? Obviously not. UCC 2–706(1) provides, in effect, that where the buyer repudiates, the seller may recover the difference between the contract price, $50,000, and the resale price, $35,000. The fall in the market value of the goods is at Buyer's expense, just as a rise would be at Seller's.

Is "expected profit" ever a limitation on the injured party's recovery claim under the UCC? In *Tongish v. Thomas*[17], Tongish (a farmer and the defendant) entered into a contract with Decatur Coop Association (the plaintiff) to sell the latter 116 acres worth of sunflower seeds at $13 a hundredweight. Coop had a contract to deliver the seeds at the same $13 price, plus a 55–cent per hundredweight handling fee, to Bambino Bean & Seed Company. Owing to bad weather and other factors, the market price for sunflower seeds nearly doubled. Tongish thereupon halted its deliveries to Coop and sold the remaining seeds to another buyer for $20, which was $5,153 more than the Coop contract price.

Coop sued Tongish for $5,153. Tongish conceded its breach but contended that its liability to Coop was limited to Coop's "expected profit," namely, 55 cents—Coop's handling fee—times the quantity of undelivered hundredweights, or $455. In particular, Tongish pointed to UCC 1–106, which states that "The remedies provided by this Act shall be liberally administered to the end that the

17. 251 Kan. 728, 840 P.2d 471 (1992).

aggrieved party may be put in as good a position as if the other party had fully performed...." Full performance, Tongish argued, would have earned Coop its expected $455 handling fee but *not* the market/contract difference of $5,153.

Reversing the trial court, which found for Tongish on the damage issue, the Kansas Supreme Court held that UCC 2–713 properly governed the damage calculation. That section provides, in the case of an injured buyer (Coop), that "the measure of damages for non-delivery or repudiation by the seller is the difference between the market price at the time when the buyer learned of the breach and the contract price"—here the sum of $5,153. The clincher in the Court's view, apparently, was the obvious point that if the measure of damages were limited to 55–cents per hundred-weight, Tongish could then consider the Coop contract price of $13 plus 55–cents to be "the floor price for his seeds, take advantage of rapidly escalating prices, ignore his contractual obligation, and profitably sell to the highest bidder." Protected on the downside but free to profit on the upside, any substantial rise in the market price for sunflower seeds must inevitably lead Tongish to breach. Computing damages under UCC 2–713, by contrast, will "encourage the honoring of contracts and market stability...."

The decision in *Tongish* is easily approved if we accept that Coop made a resale contract with Bambino in reliance on its supply contract with Tongish. If the decision had come out the other way, with Coop recovering nothing more than its 55–cent handling fee but having a legal obligation to resell to Bambino at $13, then, in the future, Coop would have to hedge its position in both directions to avoid the possibility of a heavy loss in case of a sharp rise or fall in the market for sunflower seeds. Assuming sunflower seeds (like wheat, cattle, etc.) are an actively traded commodity, the hedge would presumably take the form of offsetting options—a "call" at the contract price to protect against a market rise and a "put" at the contract price to protect against a market plunge. Options cost money, however. That cost would undoubtedly be passed on by Coop to Tongish (the call) and Bambino (the put). The Court's decision in *Tongish* eliminates the need for Coop to hedge in this fashion, and thus presumably has the virtue of reducing transaction costs for the parties themselves.

C. Reliance and Restitution

While damages for breach of contract are generally based on the injured party's expectations, there are two well-recognized alternatives to the expectations measure; namely, reliance and restitution. The alternatives are elective in the sense that the injured party may choose to seek reliance damages or restitution instead of expectation damages, but as a matter of pleading and case-presentation there is nothing binding about the choice and a plaintiff may present his claim *in* the alternative—that is, under more than one heading—or may shift from one to the other if the defendant is not misled thereby.

Actually, expectation and reliance are not true alternatives since both assume that the contract is to be enforced against the promisor in accordance with its terms. The promisor being bound by his promise to perform and having breached, the remedy is money damages and the question becomes one of how best to measure the promisee's loss, that is, whether with respect to reliance only or with respect to expectations as well. Restitution, by contrast, though a fairly frequent form of relief in contract cases, is based upon the quite separate concept of unjust enrichment; recovery is measured by the value of the benefits conferred upon the promisor by the promisee rather than by reference to the loss resulting from the promisor's failure to meet his obligations under the contract as such.

What follows is a very brief discussion of the reliance and the restitution interests, with the latter being further divided into two sub-topics, namely, restitution for a breaching plaintiff and restitution for the injured party to a "losing" contract.

1. *Reliance Damages.* As amply noted, the customary damage claim for breach of contract seeks compensation both for the injured party's expenditures in reliance and for his lost profit. In some instances, however, the lost profit element may be uncertain or, at least, very difficult to establish, and the injured party may find it simpler and less burdensome to limit his claim to his expenditures. Expenditures in reliance would include outlays made in actual performance of the contract itself—the $1,900 spent by Luten prior to the County's repudiation, for example—and also amounts spent on items that are incidental or collateral to the contract—the cost of advertising and promotion, say, incurred by the disappointed lessees in *Village Plaza*. Damages recovered under a claim of promissory estoppel as in the *Red Owl* case (supra, p. 61) may similarly be based on the injured party's reliance, though the claim itself need not, strictly speaking, seek contract enforcement in conventional terms.[18]

---

18. *See generally*, Birmingham, *Notes on the Reliance Interest,* 60 Wash. L.Rev. 217 (1985).

Damages based on the reliance interest bear an obvious resemblance to damages for tort since the effect under either approach is to restore the victim to the position he would have occupied if the event or transaction had never occurred. While overlapping circumstances would be rare, there may be instances—*Sullivan*, below, is evidently one—in which an injured party can frame his complaint both in tort *and* in contract. But why would he bother to do that— why would he add a contract claim to a tort claim if his potential damage recovery is the same whether he is found to be the victim of a breach or is found to be the victim of a tort? The answer, presumably, is that the injured party's legal burden becomes considerably easier to carry if the existence of a contract can be established. The reason, once again, is that contractual obligation is a form of absolute liability. The injured party—now a promisee— establishes his claim to damages by showing merely that the wrongdoer—now a promisor—failed to perform. That done, and the failure being unexcused, the case for liability is complete. Fault, in the technical, tort-related sense of wrongful or negligent conduct, is irrelevant and need not be proved.

In *Sullivan v. O'Connor,*[19] the Supreme Court of Massachusetts was obliged to review a jury verdict awarding contract damages to the plaintiff, a self-styled professional entertainer, in connection with an unsuccessful effort by the defendant, a plastic surgeon, to reduce the length of the plaintiff's nose. The entire procedure was expected to require two operations, but when the second was completed the result was apparently so disappointing that a third operation had to be undergone in an effort to undo the effects of the first two. The third operation, however, made matters still worse: the plaintiff's nose "now had a concave line to about the midpoint, at which it became bulbous ... flattened and broadened ..." and somehow asymmetrical. For all this misery the plaintiff paid $622 in fees and hospital expenses.

In her suit against the doctor, the plaintiff sought damages principally on grounds of medical malpractice. As an alternative cause of action, she asserted that there had been a breach of contract by the defendant for having failed to improve the appearance of her nose as promised. The jury found for the defendant on the malpractice count, apparently concluding that there had been no negligence in the way he performed the several operations. On the contract count, however, it found for the plaintiff and awarded damages of $13,500, having been instructed by the trial judge that such a finding would entitle the plaintiff to recover:

19.   363 Mass. 579, 296 N.E.2d 183 (1973).

(a) the $622 of out-of-pocket expenses,

(b) compensation for the *worsening* of her appearance (i.e., the difference between the mildly regrettable "before" and the perfectly ghastly "after"), including the mental anguish she felt as a person with a professional stake in how she looked, and

(c) compensation for the pain and suffering she experienced by reason of the third operation, though not the first two, but

(d) nothing whatever for lost earnings, because there had been no proof that the plaintiff actually lost any.

The trial judge refused the plaintiff's request to instruct the jury that she could also recover for the difference in value between the beautiful nose that the defendant had promised and the nose as it appeared before the operations. Both plaintiff and defendant appealed.

Sustaining the verdict and the damage award, the Supreme Court held that there had been no error in the trial court's jury instructions. In a carefully developed opinion, the Court apparently agreed that there was sufficient evidence of an exchange of promises between the doctor and his patient to justify an award of damages for breach of contract. To be sure, physicians would "seldom" be found to have made binding promises (as opposed to mere encouraging noises), and it would be appropriate to instruct juries that "clear proof" was required before a doctor could be held to have entered into a contract with his patient to achieve a particular result. "On the other hand," said Justice Kaplan, "if these actions [for breach of contract] were outlawed, leaving only the possibility of suits for malpractice, there is fear that the public might be exposed to the enticements of charlatans, and confidence in the profession might ultimately be shaken."

With respect to damages, the Court apparently rejected both "restitution" and "expectations" as the proper measure of the plaintiff's claim. Restitution would entitle her to recover no more than the $622 that she had paid to the doctor and the hospital, and this was "plainly too meager". By contrast, expectations would entitle her to the difference in value (net of the surgeon's fee) between a beautiful nose and the nose she started with. To this would be added the plaintiff's consequential damages, to-wit, the loss caused by her worsened appearance plus the pain and suffering associated with the third "unnecessary" operation. While the consequential figure was capable of jury determination (just as it would be in a tort-malpractice action), the Court agreed that the expectations element was indeterminable. What a beautiful nose is worth in general, or what it might have been worth to an aspiring entertainer, was presumably beyond reliable calculation. There was, moreover, a danger that a compassionate jury, if allowed to compensate for expectations, would heave up a very large damage figure and thus, despite the absence of negligence, impose a liability out of all proportion to the fee the doctor had received for his services. One supposes, also, that breach of contract damages would not have been covered by the doctor's malpractice insurance, which normally extends to tort claims only. A large award for lost "expectations" might thus have wiped him out completely.

On the whole, therefore, although not obliged to rule finally on the issue (owing to the posture of the appeal), the Court appeared to view "reliance" as the best measure of the plaintiff's loss. This, in turn, meant that the plaintiff was entitled to recover her "detriments", that is, to be put back in the position she occupied before the parties made their contract. The trial court was therefore correct in instructing the jury that the plaintiff was entitled to the $622 paid out in fees, plus the loss caused by her worsened appearance, plus the pain and suffering associated with the third operation. Probably, it would have been proper to award damages for the pain and suffering she experienced from the first two operations as well since there would have been no pain and suffering at all if there had been no contract and hence no surgery; in effect, limiting P & S to the third operation was not consistent with the reliance measure, because the suffering associated with the first two was similarly "wasted" when the contract failed. As the plaintiff had not appealed with respect to that issue, however, the verdict as rendered could be sustained.

Having labored through this wearisome dissection, I think we might return again to consider the Court's larger premise, namely, that the doctor-patient relationship can sometimes, even if only seldom, be regarded as a contract with result specified. Thus, why should the Court have accepted the jury's finding that this—out of the multitude of malpractice suits that sound in tort only—was the seldom-occurring case? The Court made no effort to review the evidence on the contract question, and perhaps the opinion can be faulted on that ground. In the end, however, I suspect that the Court's attitude and sense of the situation was revealed by its rather startling reference to "the enticements of charlatans". Almost everybody feels aggrieved about some aspect of his or her appearance and most people are prepared to spend small amounts of money on remedial devices in an effort to feel a little better. If you feel bad to the point of despair, however, you are likely to be willing to spend a great deal more; and I suppose nothing is quite so enticing as the sudden magic of a surgical procedure that promises to change one's life completely—for example, by turning one's fantasy about being a professional entertainer into a dream-come-true. Sensitive to the pathos of it all, the Court in *Sullivan* no doubt wished to establish a constraint in this connection by warning practitioners that their promotional efforts might ultimately come back to haunt them as contractual obligations, particularly when, in the view of a sympathetic jury, the promotion or "enticement" had been too aggressive.

The Court in *Sullivan* expressly declined to follow the reasoning in the (even more famous) case of *Hawkins v. McGee*[20], in which the New Hampshire Supreme Court ruled that "expectation" was the proper measure of recovery for a plaintiff who had been "guaranteed" by his surgeon that a skin graft would restore his badly scarred hand to "a hundred percent perfect hand ... a hundred percent good hand". The skin graft failed miserably and in fact made the plaintiff's hand even worse and less functional than it had been before the surgery. The trial court in *Hawkins*, while holding that there was a breach of contract by the surgeon, limited the plaintiff's damages to the pain and suffering of surgery plus the "ill effects" of the failed operation—a damage measure very similar to the "reliance" measure approved in *Sullivan*.

Reversing the trial court on the question of damages, the Supreme Court said:

"The present case is closely analogous to one in which a machine is built for a certain purpose and warranted to do certain work. In such cases, the usual rule of damages for breach of warranty in the sale of chattels is applied and it is held that the measure of damages is the difference between the value of the machine if it had corresponded with the warranty and its actual value.... We therefore conclude that the true measure of the plaintiff's damage in the present case is the difference between the value to him of a perfect hand or a good hand ... and the value of his hand in its present condition...."

Was the plaintiff's scarred hand analogous to a "machine" or a "chattel"? Was it, in effect, a "productive instrument," necessary or essential to whatever work he did on a daily basis? Or was the skin graft undertaken solely for cosmetic purposes? Since the original scarring was "the result of a severe burn caused by contact with an electric wire," I suppose it is possible that Hawkins was an artisan of some kind—an electrician?—and that the scarring had an

20.   84 N.H. 114, 146 A. 641 (1929).

adverse effect on his professional skills. If so, his "expectation" may have been related to his future earning capacity, which would be a measurable quantity, and not merely to his comfort and appearance. We never learn about that, and the *Sullivan* Court apparently did not consider the question (if there was one) relevant.

Somewhat ironically, the plaintiff in *Sullivan* actually did make a claim that the botched rhinoplasty damaged her career as a professional "entertainer," presumably including future employment opportunities on the stage and silver screen. The difficulty with this, from her standpoint, was that there was no evidence whatever that Ms. Sullivan had ever "entertained" anybody outside her family circle or had any offers of future employment as such. Almost certainly, as the Court knew very well, the "commercial" value of the surgery was a fantasy at best and most probably an invention of counsel. Like anyone getting a nose job, what Ms. Sullivan really sought (perhaps in contrast to poor Hawkins) was the enhanced self-esteem and social acceptance that she hoped the purchase of a new nose would bring her. Then, however, her true "expectation" was the difference between her "cost" (the Doctor's fee and hospital expense plus the pains of surgery) and the much greater value, *to her*, of improved appearance, otherwise known as "consumer surplus". But that loss, or disappointment, is not compensable. A retail buyer (Ms. Sullivan) of defective merchandise is of course entitled to a replacement. In the less common case where the defective item (Sullivan's nose) is not replaceable, the buyer would get a refund of her cost, her "reliance," which is roughly what the Court awarded Ms. Sullivan. But the "surplus", the difference between cost and anticipated psychic benefit, is obviously subjective and incapable of measurement. Restatement Section 352—limiting damages to an amount "established with reasonable certainty"—can be cited for this proposition, as well as the *Hadley* principle, if any cite is needed.

2. *Restitution.* As noted, while restitution is a claim that is based on a concept of unjust enrichment rather than contractual obligation, it does serve on occasion as an appropriate remedy in the contract setting. One situation in which restitution rather than contract damages might be sought would be that of a buyer who has paid in advance for undelivered property or services. Logically, the choice of restitution would be made only if the market value of the property or service had fallen well below the contract price, although in such event, apart from special circumstances, one assumes that the seller would be eager to perform and unlikely to breach. If the property or service was clearly worth more than the contract price, then, restitution being the lesser claim, the injured

buyer would presumably seek contract damages in the usual manner. However, establishing expectation damages through detailed proof can be a burdensome exercise, so that even in the latter case the injured buyer might find it simpler and less costly to claim restitution and, in effect, settle for his money back.

The discussion following takes up two problems in the restitution field that are of special note. The first is relatively uncomplicated and the solution is straightforward; the second is somewhat knottier and, in the words of the Restatement, "has engendered much controversy".

(a) *The breaching plaintiff.* We would not ordinarily think of the party in breach as having a right of recovery against the injured party, but on second thought it becomes apparent that such a right is built into the damage calculation itself. Thus, suppose S agrees to deliver a carload of widgets to B at a price of $1 a widget and delivers on schedule. B pays S at the contract rate but subsequently discovers that the widgets do not conform to the contract description—too small, let's say—and as such are worth only 90 cents apiece. B nevertheless elects to accept the non-conforming goods and sues S for damages. Under UCC 2–714(2), the measure of such damages is the difference between the value of the goods if they had been as warranted and the value of the goods as actually delivered—10 cents a widget, obviously, assuming no change in the market price of widgets between the contract and delivery date. In effect, although S is the party in breach, he gets credit for the value of the non-conforming goods and is liable only for the shortfall. One way to explain (really, over-explain) the result would be to say that it reflects two separate computational steps, the first being B's claim to recover the contract price ($1) of the widgets paid for but never delivered, the second being S's claim to restitution for the value (90 cents) of the non-conforming goods which B accepted and placed in inventory. The conclusion—that B's damage claim nets down to 10 cents a unit—is so plain that a two-step computation is unnecessary. Yet it (the conclusion) does embody a legal principle of sorts; namely, that a party's right to restitution may survive his own performance deficiency, or, to put it differently, that breach of contract does not validate unjust enrichment.

In *Britton v. Turner,*[21] decided by the Supreme Court of New Hampshire in 1834, the plaintiff agreed to work for the defendant for one full year—March to March—for a salary of $120, the entire salary to be paid at the *end* of the 12–month period rather than at weekly or monthly intervals. After about 9½ months the plaintiff

21. 6 N.H. 481 (1834).

quit his job for "no good cause" and the defendant refused to pay
him anything. The plaintiff sued in *quantum meruit* for the value of
9½ months work and was awarded $95 by the jury, which obviously
prorated his annual compensation over the 9½–month period. On
appeal, the Court sustained the jury's verdict, holding that as the
defendant had realized an economic benefit from the plaintiff's
services which obviously couldn't be rejected or returned, the
defendant was bound to pay for the value of those services even
though the plaintiff had breached the employment agreement by
quitting early. The defendant would be entitled to counterclaim for
any damages he had sustained by reason of the plaintiff's breach—
e.g., hiring another man at a higher salary for the 2½ months
remaining—but in fact "no evidence [was] offered of any damage
arising from the plaintiff's departure". Finally, since the plaintiff's
claim was in *quantum meruit* rather than for contract damages, the
defendant was liable for the "reasonable worth" of the plaintiff's
services, which the jury might have found (but didn't find) to have
been less than the contract rate. The defendant could not, of
course, be liable for an amount in excess of the contract rate, since
the plaintiff would then have succeeded in breaching the contract
to his own advantage.

The rule of the *Britton* case—that restitution can be claimed by
the party in breach—is obviously correct and is reflected in Restatement Section 374, which apparently also approves the Court's
approach to the calculation of damages. Thus, Section 374(1) provides that the breaching party is entitled to restitution for "any
benefit that he has conferred" on the injured party through part
performance "in excess of the loss that he has caused by his own
breach".

Damage calculation aside, the *Britton* opinion tells us nothing
directly about the nature of the plaintiff's employment or the
reason for the once-a-year payment arrangement, and I suppose we
might wonder how the plaintiff, who must have been an ordinary
farm-hand, could have met his daily living expenses for 12 long
months without pay. The explanation, no doubt, is that he did get
paid for the day's work, not in cash, to be sure, but in the form of
room-and-board and other necessaries which the defendant would
have supplied to him and to the other workers on the farm. But of
course farm-hands were wanderers—rootless non-cosmopolites—
who came and went more or less at will in those days, and unless
their shiftless habits could be restrained somehow the effect might
be to disrupt the operation of the farm by confronting the defendant with a manpower shortage during harvest season or some
other critical period. Slavery having been ruled out, the 12–month

payment arrangement may have been designed to promote job-loyalty and discourage abrupt departures. From that perspective, instead of being regarded as pro-ratable wages, the deferred payment could be looked at as a standard length-of-service award that was subject to a 1–year "vesting" requirement. A modern analogue would be the corporate employee's pension rights, which begin to build when employment commences but are forfeited if the employee fails to complete a stated period of service. No "restitution" or *quantum meruit* recovery is allowed to an employee who quits before his pension rights have vested, it being understood that the employer's aim is not (or not only) to compensate daily services as such, but to encourage continuity and minimize employee turnover.

The Court in *Britton,* which knew at least as much as the writer knows about the conditions of New Hampshire farm labor in 1834, certainly understood all this. Plainly also, however, it felt concern—probably more than a little—for the vulnerability of ordinary farm workers to oppressive tactics on the part of their employers. Thus, why *did* the plaintiff quit his job so near to the end of the 12–month period? Maybe he was just a heedless fellow, indifferent to his obligations and quite prepared "to desert his service before the stipulated time". On the other hand, perhaps the defendant cruelly "[drove] the laborer from his service, near the close of his term, by ill treatment, in order to escape from payment. . . ." Which of the parties was at fault in this context, and where to place the blame, might be a close and complicated question. Looking for some way to balance interests, the Court conceded that the parties *could* "provide by an express agreement that nothing shall be earned if the laborer leaves his employer . . . before the expiration of the time" agreed upon. But in the absence of such "express agreement" the legal presumption would be otherwise, because the Court had "abundant reason to believe that the general understanding of the community is that the hired laborer shall be entitled to compensation for the service actually performed".

Just why "express agreement" was deemed lacking where the employee had been told that he would be paid *only* on the completion of 12 months' service, the Court in *Britton* did not say. Presumably the defendant failed to prove by sufficient evidence that the "general understanding" had been overcome in the present case; he probably did not realize he had to. This, however, left the Court free to extend some measure of protection to the plaintiff (and others in his position) by giving notice to employers who sought to tie their workers to the land through deferred payment arrangements that the burden would be on them to show (a) that the employee had expressly agreed to the conditions of vesting and

(b) equally important, that the employee had not been driven from his job "by ill treatment" just as the term was coming to an end.

(b) *Losing contracts.* Damage claims for breach of contract normally arise in a setting in which the injured party expects to make a profit from completing the contract, while the party in breach anticipates a loss. The injured party's claim, under the customary formula, is equal to the sum of his expenditures in reliance plus his disappointed profit expectation. But suppose that the injured party *himself* anticipates a loss. A builder, for example, having done a portion of the work called for by a construction contract, realizes that his expenditures *already* exceed the contract price and that completion of the job will simply mean a further deficit from his standpoint. At this point, the owner—for its own special reasons—elects to repudiate the contract and directs the builder to discontinue his work. How should the builder's damages be calculated? Should the expenditures made up to the date of the breach be recoverable by the builder in full, or should the builder's recovery be reduced by his anticipated loss? Or is there some other measure? A completely satisfactory answer, as will be seen, is not so easy to come by.

An illustration—drawn from the venerable *Kehoe* case[22]—will be useful. Assume a builder-plaintiff agrees to pave a street for a price of $2,700. Having completed 60% of the work, the builder finds that his costs already amount to $3,000—$300 more than the contract price—and he estimates that he will have expended $5,000 by the time the job is done. The builder thus expects to incur a loss of $2,300 ($5,000–$2,700) overall. The owner-defendant, a municipality, suddenly decides to terminate the paving project and tells the builder to stop working. How much in damages can the builder recover from the municipality?

The Restatement and the decided cases offer a number of alternative solutions—three plus a variation, actually—and this in turn suggests that the problem here addressed is a bit more complicated than most. While each of the alternatives has some measure of plausibility, in the end (as shown below) one realizes that the differences between them relate chiefly to the question of which of the two parties—builder or municipality—the inevitable loss falls on *first*. Our choice of rule might then boil down to a judgment as to whether "we" are better off if one party to a losing contract rather than the other takes the first hit or if they share the misery somehow.

22. Kehoe v. Rutherford, 56 N.J.L. 23, 27 A. 912 (1893).

Rule # 1: Restitution. Restatement Section 373 would apparently support recovery by the builder of the entire value of his work up to the date of breach. That amount—$3,000—necessarily equals the builder's reliance interest, though here expressed in terms of restitution of the benefit received by the municipality. Recovery is under *quantum meruit* rather than the contract, so that the builder's prospective loss becomes irrelevant. In effect, the contract is discharged in view of the municipality's breach, and the builder's recovery is measured by the market value of the services rendered. As stated in a leading case,[23] "The measure of recovery for quantum meruit is the reasonable value of performance ... undiminished by any loss which would have been incurred by complete performance."

Treating the builder's claim as independent of any contract limitation means not only that his loss expectation is disregarded, but also that his recovery will exceed the contract price itself. Thus, the restitution damage measure is $3,000, while the total contract price—the amount the defendant would have had to pay if it hadn't breached the contract—is only $2,700. The result (as has often been noted) is odd and anomalous. Since the builder thus recovers more in damages than the payment he would be entitled to under the contract itself, the municipality, once aware of the rule, would apparently be prompted to engage in "strategic" behavior in order to contain its own liability. If, instead of terminating the project at the time its undesirability became apparent, the municipality simply allowed the builder to go on and finish the job, the builder's entitlement would obviously be limited to $2,700. There would then be no breach and no damage claim—merely an obligation to pay the contract price. In effect, the municipality's potential liability for the unwanted paving work rises to a high of $4,999 just before the contract is completed, and then abruptly drops to $2,700 when the job is done. Although $2,000 ($5,000 – $3,000) of wasted expenditures are avoided if the contract is promptly terminated, the municipality can save $300 for itself alone if it permits the work to grind along pointlessly to completion.

To avoid this wasteful consequence, it might be best, in these special circumstances, to limit the measure of restitution damages to an amount not in excess of the contract price. The builder is still permitted to disregard his expected loss in calculating his restitution claim, but outlays above the contract price would be excluded from such claim and would not be reimbursed. The result, admit-

23. United States v. Algernon Blair, Inc., 479 F.2d 638 (4th Cir.1973). *See* Wolcher, *The Accommodation of Regret* *in Contract Remedies*, 73 Iowa L.Rev. 797, 809 (1988).

tedly, is something of a conceptual hybrid, but perhaps we can give it dignity by calling it "constrained restitution". Taking this approach, the municipality in my illustration would be liable for only $2,700, with the builder being left to absorb the $300 balance.

The important thing to observe—especially in comparing the capped version of Rule # 1 with the alternatives described below—is that using restitution as the measure of damages in this context means that the *first* $2,700 of loss incurred by the parties falls on the municipality alone rather than on the builder or on both parties proportionately. The municipality is thus encouraged to minimize social and private costs by terminating the unwanted paving contract at the *earliest* possible date—that is, presumably, before the $2,700 outlay figure is reached. Given the cap, moreover, the municipality would have somewhat less inducement to engage in strategic behavior by allowing the work to continue beyond the point at which the project would otherwise be brought to a halt.[24]

Rule # 2: Contract Damages. Though unlikely to be elected by a losing-contract plaintiff, Restatement Section 349 offers a damage measure that permits the injured party to recover his reliance costs, reduced, however, by any loss that the injured party would have suffered had the contract been fully performed. As applied in my illustrative case, a reliance-minus-negative-expectations rule would entitle the builder to recover $700—$3,000 of actual outlays less $2,300 of anticipated loss. In effect, the first $2,300 of loss falls on the builder, with the balance—here $700—being absorbed by the municipality. Since the builder takes the first hit, the municipality has less incentive than it does under the restitution measure to effect an early termination of the contract. For the same reason, perhaps, the builder is encouraged to make a more careful estimate of his own costs and risks when he submits his original bid; yet it seems unlikely that the builder would be led to relax his customary degree of care in the hope that an act of breach by the municipality might rescue him from error.

Rule # 3: Loss Sharing. Apparently alone among the decisions in this field, *Kehoe v. Rutherford,* mentioned above, permits the plaintiff to recover in damages a proportion of the original contract price equal to the percentage of the contract completed at the date

---

24. But, I admit, only somewhat less. Once the builder's outlays had passed the $2,700 level, the municipality would have no further inducement to terminate and, indeed, could threaten to keep the contract going unless the builder agreed to settle on a favorable basis. Rule # 3, under which the loss is shared between the parties at all stages, avoids this defect, but by sharing the loss it provides less inducement to terminate the project early. While the choice is hard to make, as suggested below either approach seems better than that of Restatement Sec. 373.

the breach occurs. Having expended \$3,000 out of a total foresee-able cost of \$5,000, the builder's recovery would be \$3,000/\$5,000 × \$2,700, or \$1,620. The balance of \$1,380 (\$3,000 − \$1,620) would be absorbed by the builder himself.

It will be recalled that the builder's total loss expectation is \$2,300, while the municipality's total contract obligation is \$2,700. Since the fraction \$1,380 (builder's loss)/\$1,620 (municipality's loss) is the same as the fraction 2300/2700, the effect of the *Kehoe* "principle" is simply to divide the burden between the two parties on a ratio of 23:27 throughout the entire term of the contract. In some cases—for example, where the defendant is a governmental agency whose appropriations have unexpectedly been terminated by the legislature—the act of breach might be viewed as faultless or as a kind of quasi-impossibility event, so that a sharing concept has some equitable appeal. The plaintiff would still have reason to make a careful estimate of costs and the defendant would still have an incentive to avoid delay in terminating the project, but now both parties take the risk of an abrupt change in underlying circumstances.

Which of the damage rules that have been described is best? Solely from the standpoint of fairness, the question seems rather evenly balanced. On the one hand, no very good reason exists for relieving the builder of the consequences of his bidding error. The municipality's breach is fortuitous as far as the builder is concerned and it is not obvious why that chance event should generate a windfall for him. On the other hand, the municipality's action in terminating the contract is "willful" in the sense of being deliberate and perhaps for that reason the financial consequences should fall more heavily on it. In the end, however, as suggested, our choice may depend less on fairness considerations than on what we want the damage rule to do in practical terms. Viewed from that standpoint, I think "constrained restitution"—the capped version of Rule # 1—can be seen as marginally preferable to any of the alternatives. Under this approach, as noted, the loss falls first on the municipality, which is presumably in the best position to bring what has become a wasteful undertaking to a speedy end. The street-paving job is a dead loss to everyone—unprofitable to the builder and unwanted by the municipality—and hence a damage rule that encourages early termination is clearly desirable. As conceded, there is an element of windfall to the builder under the restitution measure which one might otherwise prefer to withhold, but the fact is that a complete integration of goals is impossible and on balance the former objective—encouraging early termination—seems the more important of the two.

D.   Liquidated Damages

As an original matter, we might think it doubtful that the courts would ever be willing to give up the damage-setting function to the contracting parties themselves. It is true, as has been stated, that contract rules largely operate as default provisions in lieu of express provisions, and that the parties are free to contract around the legal rules if it suits their interests to do so. Still, we might suppose that the freedom to "contract around" would be denied when it comes to damage rules. Awarding damages is the principle means by which courts exercise their enforcement authority. Allowing the parties to agree upon their own damage award might be thought equivalent to allowing private persons to preempt that authority.

As it turns out, the law has taken a kind of mid-way approach in this area. Recognizing that a prior agreement on damages may avoid litigation costs and save the time of courts and juries, the rule in most jurisdictions, as reflected in Restatement Section 356(1), is that damages for breach may be "liquidated", that is, pre-determined by the contract. The amount of such liquidated damages, however, cannot exceed a figure "that is reasonable in the light of the anticipated or actual loss caused by the breach and the difficulties of proof of loss." If excessive, the liquidated damage provision may be deemed unenforceable as a "penalty", in which event, presumably, the injured party's damages will be determined under customary standards. In effect, the contracting parties may agree on damages in advance of the event and create their own "rule" in that respect. But unlike other self-created rules, this one is subject to review and to possible rejection on the ground that public policy prohibits private parties from imposing penalties on one another for breach of contract.

A very common illustration of liquidated damages would be a provision requiring a builder to pay a stated amount for completion delays. Thus, a contract to construct a store-building might provide that the builder shall pay the owner $1,000 for every day completion is delayed beyond a specified date. If $1,000 reasonably approximates the owner's anticipated loss of net rents, and if the actual loss would be difficult to prove, the contract provision fixing damages will be enforced. On the other hand, if the construction delay is harmless because the owner is obliged to delay renting the facility for some other reason—denial of an occupancy permit, say— or if the loss of rents is plainly less in amount than $1,000 a day, then the liquidated damage term is likely to be treated as a penalty and for that reason held unenforceable.

Lake River Corp. v. Carborundum Co.,[25] decided by the Seventh Circuit in 1985, offers a full work-out of the rules on liquidated damages (together with a brief lecture by Judge Posner on the infirmities of paternalism). In 1979 Lake River and Carborundum entered into a three-year contract for the local distribution of an abrasive powder used in making steel. Lake River would receive the powder in bulk from Carborundum, bag it, and then ship the bagged material to Carborundum's customers. Carborundum would pay Lake River a stated price per unit for this service. At Carborundum's insistence, Lake River purchased new bagging equipment at considerable cost. Carborundum then promised to ship not less than 22,500 tons of powder to Lake River for bagging over the three-year term and agreed also that "if, at the end of the three-year term, this minimum quantity shall not have been shipped, Lake River shall invoice Carborundum at the then prevailing rates for the difference between the quantity bagged and the minimum guaranteed."

Demand for domestic steel declined sharply during the period covered by the contract, so that by the end of the three-year period Carborundum had shipped and paid Lake River for only 12,000 of the guaranteed minimum of 22,500 tons. Lake River thereupon sent Carborundum a bill for the balance of the amount guaranteed—$241,000, the contract price for bagging an additional 10,500 tons—and sued when Carborundum refused to pay. Carborundum's defense was that the above-quoted contract formula imposed a penalty and was therefore unenforceable under applicable Illinois law.

The Court, finding that "Illinois, untroubled by academic skepticism . . ., continues steadfastly to insist on the distinction between penalties and liquidated damages", held for Carborundum on this issue. The reason, fairly obviously, was that the amount claimed as liquidated damages failed to reflect the cost avoided by Lake River in not having been required to process the omitted 10,500 tons. Carborundum's breach at any point in the life of the contract, whether early or late, necessarily meant that Lake River would be spared the expense (labor, materials) of bagging from that point forward. A damage formula based on the full contract price would therefore compensate Lake River for costs that it would never incur. Since damages so calculated must exceed Lake River's actual loss (the earlier the breach, to be sure, the greater the excess), the

25.   769 F.2d 1284 (7th Cir.1985).

formula was a penalty provision and could not be enforced. Lake River was still entitled to its common law damages, however—$241,000 minus "cost avoided"—and that figure would be determined by the trial court on remand.

The basis for "academic skepticism"[26] regarding the wisdom of the prohibition against penalties in this context can probably be surmised. Carborundum was a seasoned and sophisticated business organization amply provided with legal and financial counsel when it entered into the distribution contract with Lake River, so that considerations of duress, capacity, adhesion and the like obviously have no application. If it was willing to commit itself to a damage obligation equal to the full contract price in the event it failed to deliver the minimum tonnage—without reduction for "cost avoided"—then the very strong presumption is that it saw an advantage to itself in making that commitment. The advantage, presumably, as the Court observed, lay in providing a "credible assurance" to Lake River—which was being asked to purchase new equipment and perhaps also to redirect other resources such as warehouse space and docking facilities—that the contract would be performed. To be sure, non-performance would entitle Lake River to damages for its reliance plus lost profits, but for various reasons it might well have seemed to Lake River that the customary damage measure would be inadequate and that it needed a promise of premium damages before it could accept the risks involved. For its part, Carborundum probably foresaw little likelihood that it would breach and in any event deemed the additional risk worth taking when compared with the certain costs that it would incur if it had to develop its own distribution services. Had the parties known at the time the contract was being negotiated that the liquidated damage provision would be rejected by a court, then either the contract price would have had to be increased in Lake River's favor or there would have been no deal at all. Neither of the latter alternatives, however, would then have seemed as desirable to Carborundum as its apparent obligation to pay premium damages if it should later choose to withhold performance.

Carborundum made a bet on the three-year market for domestic steel when it entered into the distribution agreement with Lake River. The bet turned out to be a loser but the Court's decision eliminated much of the adverse consequences. In effect, "public

---

26. *See* Clarkson, Miller & Muris, *Liquidated Damages versus Penalties: Sense or Nonsense,* 1978 Wis.L.Rev. 351 (1978); Goetz & Scott, *Liquidated Damages, Penalties and the Just Compensa-* *tion Principle,* 77 Columbia L.Rev. 554 (1977). And see, Epstein, *Beyond Foreseeability: Consequential Damages in the Law of Contract,* 18 J. of Legal Studies 105 (1989).

policy" produced a windfall to Carborundum and a penalty to Lake River, which is kind of an ironic reversal, and perhaps it is this that explains why some observers have been skeptical. There may be instances in which liquidated damage provisions are so extreme as to shock one's conscience, but by and large such instances are likely to involve individual consumers (see the *Walker–Thomas* case, supra p. 94) and are probably best dealt with through an application of the unconscionability doctrine. Carborundum, by contrast, breached its contract with Lake River because it chose to allocate its resources in a different way, and it was therefore hardly a candidate for special mercy.

What is/are "liquidated damages"? In *Wasserman's Inc. v. Middletown,*[27] the plaintiff, owner of a general store, in 1971 entered into a 30–year lease for a tract of municipally-owned property—valued by the Township at $47,500—on which the plaintiff made various improvements. The lease called for a fixed rental of only $450 a month. As a measure of self-protection, however, the Township reserved a right to cancel the lease at any time on short notice. If the cancellation right were exercised, the Township would (i) reimburse Wasserman's for the unamortized cost of the leasehold improvements and (ii) pay Wasserman's twenty-five percent of its average gross receipts for one year, presumably to reflect the going concern value of Wasserman's store business.

In 1987, the Township gave notice to the plaintiff that it was exercising its option to cancel the lease. Recognizing the Township's right to cancel, Wasserman's vacated the premises, apparently without objection. Shortly afterwards, the Township sold the property for $610,000 at public auction. But the question then was how much the Township owed Wasserman's under the terms of the lease described above. Contending that the gross receipts formula was invalid, the Township refused to pay anything and Wasserman's sued.

The trial court awarded Wasserman's $56,000 for the improvements plus $290,000 under the gross receipts formula, for a total of $346,000. The Township evidently accepted the $56,000 number, but it appealed all the way to the New Jersey Supreme Court with respect to the $290,000. It did not dispute the calculation— $290,000 was correct under the formula provision. The question raised on appeal was whether, in the Supreme Court's words, "that provision is an enforceable liquidated damages provision or is an unenforceable penalty clause." If an unenforceable penalty, much the greater part of the sale proceeds—$610,000 minus $56,000 =

27. 137 N.J. 238, 645 A.2d 100 (1994).

$554,000—would belong to the Township. If enforceable, nearly 57% ($346,000/$610,000) would belong to Wasserman's.

Stressing the long-standing prohibition against the assessment of penalties under the guise of liquidated damages, the Court reversed and remanded for a determination of the "reasonableness" of the $290,000 figure. Among other matters, the trial court was directed to take account of the plaintiff's *net* profits (it reported a $323 loss for the preceding year) as opposed to its much larger gross receipts, and to consider as well the plaintiff's duty to mitigate by finding comparable rental space. If $290,000 substantially exceeded the plaintiff's damages computed under conventional damage standards, then $290,000 would be viewed as a "penalty" and would be disallowed in favor of some other number, obviously a lot lower, that would be calculated with reference to the injury actually sustained.

The New Jersey Court, in its long and leisurely opinion, treats us to an interesting historical review of liquidated damages and the penalty prohibition. But the question, I think, is whether all that scholarly research was truly relevant. Was there a breach of contract by the Township? Was Wasserman's an "injured party" and did it claim "damages"? The answer to both questions is no. The Township was legally free, and had a perfect right, to terminate the lease at any time it chose; that is, whenever it appeared economically advantageous to do so. Indeed, the option to terminate was a feature of the lease on which the Township, not Wasserman's, had insisted at the time the lease was entered into. Wasserman's could not and did not claim that exercise of the option to terminate was a breach of the lease agreement; and, of course, it wasn't. But if there was no "breach," then "damages," liquidated or otherwise, should not have been at issue, and apparently *weren't* at issue in the trial court. Having exercised its option to terminate, the only proper question was how much money the Township owed Wasserman's under the stated payment formula.

The Supreme Court converted the option exercise into an act of breach and the option price into liquidated damages; in fact, it was neither.

But even if we accept the breach-and-damages analysis, what the Court seems to have overlooked in rejecting the $290,000 number is the fact that Wasserman's, as a long-term lessee, had an equitable interest in the property, *i.e.*, a 30–year leasehold. If the Township had attempted to evict Wasserman's—if it had *really* breached the contract by barring access to the premises—it would at once have been met with a restraining injunction, just as the shopping-center owner was in the *Walgreen* case discussed at p. 197. Once enjoined, the next step for the Township would be to negotiate with Wasserman's for a buy-out of its property interest, that is, for dissolution of the injunction. Wasserman's would of course demand, and would undoubtedly get, a share of the property appreciation—why else should it consent to vacate? The price on which the parties might finally settle would, as usual, depend on which was in the better position to haggle (Wasserman's, one would think) and which had the most to gain or lose by holding out.

The Township's contractual option simply took the place of such settlement negotiations. In agreeing to a payment formula in advance, the parties in effect pre-negotiated a buy-out price—expressed, not unreasonably, as a percentage of Wasserman's gross receipts. By so agreeing, they avoided the cost of a drawn-out, time-consuming bargaining process, as well as the possibility that Wasserman's might prove unreasonable and force an impasse. Perhaps the option should have had a scale-down feature to reflect the progressive expiration of the lease, and in that sense it was poorly formulated from the Township's standpoint. But the Township was entirely free to decide when, or whether, to exercise its termination right, and no doubt it would choose to wait rather than pay the option price if the lease had only a year or two remaining.

Chapter 9

THIRD PARTY BENEFICIARIES

Commencing with the New York Court of Appeals' decision in *Lawrence v. Fox*,[1] the courts in this country, with support from successive Restatements, have exhibited a general willingness to recognize the contract rights of third party beneficiaries. The concept is easily expressed: where A, for a consideration, promises B to pay money or transfer property to C, then, in the name of procedural economy and convenience of remedy, C, no less than B, should be able to sue for damages if A fails to perform. To be sure, C has furnished no consideration to A (though, of course, B has), and C is not a party to the contract between A and B. But these shortcomings would appear to be largely formal. Thus, A's obligation to perform is the same whether it is B or C who receives the benefit, and A's exposure to liability for non-performance is the same whether it is B or C who asserts a claim against her. Given the simple outlines of the problem, perhaps the real question is why there should ever have been any hesitation about accepting the idea of third-party contract rights. In the alternative, one wonders whether the situation is really as straightforward as it appears.

In *Lawrence v. Fox,* the defendant, Fox, borrowed $300 from an acquaintance named Holly. As Holly owed the same amount to Lawrence, Fox promised Holly that on the very next day he would repay Holly, in effect, by paying Holly's debt to Lawrence. What all this was really about remains something of a mystery, though it has been suggested that the loans in question—Lawrence to Holly and Holly to Fox—were actually gambling debts which, as a matter of public policy, could not have been enforced directly.[2] Whatever the case, Fox ultimately refused to pay Lawrence and Lawrence sued. Fox defended on the ground that his promise had been addressed to Holly alone and not to Lawrence: while Holly (the promisee) might claim against Fox (the promisor) if he chose, Lawrence had no equivalent right. Fox, after all, had received no consideration from Lawrence, and as Lawrence was not a party to the contract between Fox and Holly, he (Lawrence) lacked standing to seek enforcement.

1. 20 N.Y. 268 (1859).

2. Waters, *The Property in the Promise: A Study of the Third Party Beneficiary Rule,* 98 Harv.L.Rev. 1109 (1985).

The New York Court of Appeals held for Lawrence. While Lawrence could not, in traditional terms, be regarded as Fox's promisee, the fact was that Fox had received ample consideration from Holly and in return had made an unequivocal promise to repay the amount borrowed in accordance with Holly's direction: "... the consideration received and the promise to Holly made it as plainly his [Fox's] duty to pay the plaintiff as if the money had been remitted to him for that purpose...." It might be true (as fervently stressed by a dissenting judge) that Holly at some stage could have discharged Lawrence's claim against Fox either by settling with Fox directly or by assigning Fox's debt to someone else—say an even more insistent creditor of his own. In that sense Lawrence's claim, unlike that of a conventional promisee, could be divested by action of other parties and perhaps even without his knowledge.[3] This, however, in the Court's view, was not a damaging anomaly. Once Lawrence had recovered a judgment against Fox, Holly's legal power to make an independent settlement with Fox would disappear; indeed, such power might have disappeared when Lawrence commenced the present action, or even, possibly, at some earlier point. In effect, the danger that recognition of third-party rights might generate legal confusion—overlapping claims, say, or settlements without the consent of the affected party—seemed to the Court majority to be a manageable risk. In hindsight, as suggested below, the Court's confidence has largely proven to have been justified. On the other hand, the problems and difficulties that might have been foreseen were certainly not fully debated by Court or counsel, and hence the decision in *Lawrence v. Fox* must be admired (from one standpoint) as a leap of faith.

Having determined that Lawrence, whom we may refer to now as a "creditor beneficiary", possessed enforceable rights under a contract entered into by two other people, the New York Court had relatively little difficulty in according the same enforcement rights to contract beneficiaries occupying the status of "donee". In *Seaver v. Ransom*,[4] the plaintiff was the "beloved niece" of old Mrs. Beman, who, on her deathbed, was asked by her husband, the Judge, to sign a will leaving her property, a house and lot, to him for life, remainder to the ASPCA. Mrs. Beman feebly objected that she wished to give the remainder interest to her niece rather than the ASPCA, whereupon the Judge, with upraised hand, took a

---

3. Lawrence's claim against Holly is, of course, unaffected by Holly's arrangement with Fox: if Fox fails to pay, Lawrence can still recover from Holly as Fox's "surety". *See* Restatement Section 304, Comment c. If Fox does actually pay Lawrence, then Holly's debt to Lawrence is obviously satisfied—Lawrence can't collect from both.

4. 224 N.Y. 233, 120 N.E. 639 (1918).

mighty oath that if Mrs. Beman would sign the will already prepared, he would leave enough to the niece in his own will "to make up the difference". Mrs. Beman did as requested, then expired. When, however, the Judge himself later "came to die", it was found that he had left the niece nothing whatever. The latter, claiming breach, brought suit against the Judge's estate for the value of the real estate, which was found to be $6,000.

Echoing the proposition that the rule of *Lawrence v. Fox* was "progressive, not retrograde", the Court held for the plaintiff. The Judge had made "an unqualified promise on a valuable consideration" which the plaintiff, as "donee beneficiary", had standing to enforce in a suit for contract damages. The case would be clear, said the Court in effect, had the gift to the plaintiff been wholly testamentary. If Mrs. Beman had made a will leaving the house to the Judge on condition that he assume a debt to the plaintiff of $6,000, then the Judge's "debt" would be an asset of Mrs. Beman's estate and would simply be a bequest to her niece from Mrs. Beman herself. The distinction between the latter arrangement and the contractual obligation to which the Judge agreed was "discernable, but not obvious"; if one was enforceable, the other should be as well. The Court therefore approved the "tendency of American authority ... to sustain the gift in all such cases and to permit the donee beneficiary to recover on the contract."

The outcome in *Seaver,* insofar as it confirms the extension of third-party rights to donee beneficiaries, is hardly debatable. On the other hand, drawing an analogy, as the opinion does, between a testamentary gift and an oral contract for the donee's benefit is itself slightly breathtaking. Testamentary gifts (i.e., wills) are required by statute to be in writing and to be dated, executed and formally witnessed; oral dispositions made at the last gasp generally wouldn't, and I suppose shouldn't, qualify as legally effective substitutes. The Court's willingness, here, to give effect to a hasty, deathbed agreement—neither promisor (Judge) nor promisee (Mrs. B) being available to verify it—suggests either that the evidence in support of that agreement was powerful indeed[5] or else, perhaps, that the beloved niece made an eye-moistening appeal to judicial sentiment which the alternate takers under the Judge's will (who-

---

5. In addition to some rather shaky testimony from the attending physician, such "evidence" consisted of the lower court's finding that Mrs. Beman was simply not a pet-lover: "It does not appear that a dog, a cat, a bird or any animal at any time had a home in the Beman house, or that she ever showed any particular interest in animals. Unexplained, we cannot understand why she should ... practically overlook her favorite niece ... and throw her property to the dogs." Seaver v. Ransom, 180 App.Div. 734, 168 N.Y.S. 454, 456 (1917).

ever they were) just couldn't match. Whatever the case, resort to third-party beneficiary "law" enabled the Court to make an end-run around the much stricter rules and requirements that otherwise apply to testamentary dispositions.

As indicated immediately below, the "tendency of American law" has been to expand the category of third-party beneficiary to include any person *intended* to be benefited by the contracting parties, whether or not such person would otherwise fit within the definition of "creditor" or "donee". Reflecting this approach, Section 302 of the Restatement distinguishes between "intended" and "incidental" contract beneficiaries, defining the former (somewhat tautologically) as anyone intended by the promisee to be benefited by the promisor's performance and the latter as anyone who is not the former. Section 304 then provides that a promise creates a duty in the promisor which an "intended beneficiary" may enforce. The aim, presumably, is to confirm that the parties to a contract shall be free, if it suits their interests, not only to confer economic benefits on non-parties but also to extend enforcement rights against the promisor to such non-parties, always assuming the promise is otherwise binding.

Broadly speaking, the problems of interpretation that arise under the Restatement and its common-law counterpart are two. The first, and perhaps the more challenging, is simply how to apply the terms "intended" and "incidental" where the promisee's aims are less explicit than they were in *Lawrence v. Fox* and *Seaver v. Ransom*. Having moved beyond "creditors" and "donees", the question, essentially, is who else might qualify as a contract beneficiary and whom to regard as a mere outsider. The second set of problems, as suggested, concerns the scope of the promisor's defenses to third-party claims and the ability of the contracting parties to terminate the beneficiary's claims without the beneficiary's consent.

1. *Intended Beneficiaries.* In *Lawrence* and in *Seaver* the third-party beneficiary was designated by name in the agreement between the contracting parties; hence there could be no doubt as to either (a) the intention of the promisee (Holly, Mrs. Beman) to give the beneficiary (Lawrence, the niece) the benefit of the promised performance or (b) the willingness of the promisor (Fox, the Judge) to assume an obligation to such beneficiary. The Restatement, however, does not restrict the status of "intended beneficiary" to persons named or otherwise specifically designated by the promisor and promisee. Rather, the beneficiary of a promise is to be recognized as an intended (not merely an "incidental") beneficiary if such "recognition . . . is appropriate to effectuate the intention of

the parties" and if "the circumstances indicate" that the beneficiary was expected by the promisee to receive the benefit of the promised performance. The implication, borne out, it would seem, by the decisions in the field, is that the question is one of interpretation and case-by-case analysis.

Third-parties who are money-creditors or donees obviously qualify as intended beneficiaries and presumably stand at one end of the spectrum. At the other end would be those individuals for whom the contract between promisor and promisee may have important consequences, but whose interests were simply not within the contemplation of the contracting parties at the time they made their agreement. Thus, suppose A agrees to erect an improvement on B's land which, if completed, will enhance the value of an adjoining tract that happens to belong to C. C licks her chops in anticipation of a windfall, but if A (for example) breaches the contract and the project fails there is obviously nothing that C can do about it as a matter of legal right. C cannot invoke A's contract duties as if she (C) were the intended beneficiary of A's promise, even though C would in fact have benefited had A performed her obligations. The reason, if any is needed, is that A and B could not have considered the expectations of myriad unnamed persons (C and other neighboring landowners) when calculating the risks of their original undertaking; nor, indeed, would they have worried much about the financial impact on such persons of any subsequent decision to breach. Generally, and as already much noted, contract law provides an enabling framework within which the contracting parties can generate financial benefits for themselves; it is not, however, directly concerned with the wealth effects on *non*-parties.

The hard case in this area—one that falls somewhere towards the middle of the spectrum—would seem to be that of a third party whose primary claim against the promisee depends, as a practical matter, on the promisor's willingness to perform her duties to the promisee under a separate but related agreement. By way of common illustration, suppose G, a general contractor, agrees to construct a building for O, the owner. G then subcontracts with P to do the plumbing. Is P an intended beneficiary of G's contract with O? If O terminates the contract—say before any work has been done—can P recover lost profits from O? The answer—at least the answer given by the Restatement[6]—is no: O's obligation as promisor is to pay G for the construction of the building, but not to discharge G's obligation to P. O would have had no knowledge of the costs and profit-expectations of G's subcontractors (P and

6. Restatement Section 302, Illustration 19.

dozens of others perhaps) and might not even know the subcontractors' identity in many cases. O knew she might be liable for G's costs and profits when she entered into the original contract with G; but the liability *then* within O's contemplation would be different in amount from that claimed by P and other disappointed subs.[7]

Presumably the same answer and the same reasoning would apply if P failed to perform her contract with G, and O attempted to recover from P on a third-party theory. Thus, P's obligation as promisor is to do the plumbing, but not to erect an entire building. Hence P's work, even if completed, would not discharge G's duty to O. P would properly be liable to G for the difference between the price to which she had agreed and any higher price that G might have to pay for the same plumbing work, but P would not have assumed liability for O's profit expectations or other incidental costs, which would presumably exceed the value of the plumbing contract itself.

In effect, recognizing third-party claims in either of the above cases is objectionable because doing so would impose risks on the promisor which the latter would not and probably could not have taken into account when the terms of the primary contract (between O and G in the first case, between P and G in the second) were negotiated and agreed upon.

Yet despite this rather cautious approach to third-party rights, the courts in some instances have gone beyond the manifest objectives of the contracting parties and have found the requisite "intention to benefit" even though the promisor (at least) may have been wholly indifferent to the third party's interest. In the *Septembertide* case,[8] for example, the plaintiff, Patterson, entered into a conventional author's contract with a publisher, Stein & Day, for the publication of the plaintiff's new novel, "Confessional". The plaintiff was to receive a cash advance of $375,000 against future royalties, payable in three annual installments, plus two-thirds of the proceeds of any sale of paperback publishing rights in excess of the royalty advance. To finance the advance, Stein & Day on the same date sold the paperback rights to another publisher, New Library, for $750,000, also to be paid in annual installments.

---

7. State statutes, however, protect laborers and suppliers by allowing them to place so-called mechanics' liens on the owner's property in order to secure their rights to payment for services actually performed. To free her property from lien, the owner, in turn, may require the general contractor to furnish a payment bond obligating the issuing surety company to pay all debts owed to sub-contractors if the general fails to do so. The subs, presumably, are "intended beneficiaries" of the surety's promise to the owner.

8. Septembertide Publishing, B.V. v. Stein & Day, Inc., 884 F.2d 675 (2d Cir.1989).

About a year later, urgently needing funds, Stein & Day assigned all of its publishing contracts, including the agreement with New Library, to a financier, Bookcrafters, as security for a substantial loan. Bookcrafters, which evidently specialized in making secured loans to commercial publishers, was unaware of the plaintiff's two-thirds interest in the paperback sale. More particularly, a search of UCC filings by Bookcrafters uncovered no evidence of the plaintiff's interest. Some $385,000 was currently due and payable from New Library at the time the present lawsuit was commenced.

Arguing that he was an "intended beneficiary" of the contract between New Library and Stein & Day, the plaintiff insisted that the amounts due from New Library be paid to him, not to Bookcrafters. Bookcrafters, contending that the plaintiff's only legal claim was against Stein & Day (which was, alas, insolvent), asserted that its own rights as a secured creditor were prior and superior to the plaintiff's. New Library deposited the funds it concededly owed into court.

The district court, holding for the plaintiff on this issue, divided those funds two-thirds to the plaintiff and one-third to Bookcrafters. On appeal by Bookcrafters, the Second Circuit affirmed. Stating that Restatement Section 302 "captures the essence of New York law," the Court held that the plaintiff was indeed an "intended beneficiary" of the agreement between Stein & Day and New Library. To be sure, New Library's only obligation under that agreement was to pay $750,000 to Stein & Day; the contract between New Library and Stein & Day apparently contained no mention of the plaintiff's interest or of any obligation to the plaintiff on New Library's part. Nevertheless, the requirement of Section 302(1)—that "recognition of a right to performance in the beneficiary is appropriate to effectuate the intention of the parties"—was found by the Court to be met. New Library was aware, based on normal practice in the publishing industry, that an author shares in the sale of paperback rights; and in this case New Library had some particular knowledge of the agreement between the plaintiff and Stein & Day because the two contracts had been executed simultaneously. That awareness and that knowledge, in the Court's view, were sufficient to constitute "recognition" by New Library for purposes of Section 302(1) and thus to impart the status of "intended beneficiary" to the plaintiff.

Though a bit tough on Bookcrafters, sustaining the plaintiff's right to share in the paperback proceeds seems reasonable on the whole, and it was of course harmless to New Library whose payment obligation was fixed and limited to $750,000 at all events.

On the other hand, the decision does, obviously, entail something of a stretch as far as the language of Section 302(1) is concerned. New Library's "intention to benefit the plaintiff," as the Court conceded, "is not quite so clear."

But was the issue really as presented, or might we now be witnessing yet another end-run, this time around the purported filing requirements of the UCC? Just possibly, the Court may have been moved by a sense that Bookcrafters had acted carelessly, even negligently, when it took assignment of the New Library contract from Stein & Day. Like New Library, Bookcrafters had ample knowledge of industry practice and either was or should have been aware that the author of "Confessional" would be likely to have a percentage interest in the sale of paperback rights. The Court may have felt that a routine search of UCC filings was simply insufficient, and that Bookcrafters itself was at fault for ignoring or neglecting to make relevant inquiries about the plaintiff's interest. The question then was whether the plaintiff or Bookcrafters should have to take the consequences, and if the latter, how to justify that result in strictly legal terms. Once again, third-party beneficiary law proved handy for the purpose.

2. *Defenses.* At least at inception, a third-party beneficiary's rights against a promisor (e.g., Lawrence's rights against Fox) derive from the rights of the promisee. In an action by the beneficiary, therefore, the promisor can presumably assert any contract defenses that could be raised against the promisee, unless for some reason the parties have otherwise agreed. In the *Rouse* case,[9] for example, Winston, a homeowner, purchased a furnace from Associated, giving the latter her note for $1,008 payable in monthly installments of $28. The note finally wound up in the hands of the Federal Housing Authority as guarantor. Winston subsequently sold the house to Rouse, the defendant, who (though he didn't sign the note) agreed in the contract of sale "to assume payment of $850 for heating plant, payable $28 per mo." The note being in default, the FHA sued Rouse for $850 as a third-party beneficiary of Rouse's contract with Winston. Rouse raised two defenses: first, that Winston had lied to him about the condition of the furnace, which apparently didn't work; and second, that Associated had failed to install the thing correctly to begin with. The lower court struck both defenses and Rouse appealed.

Reversing in part and affirming in part, the Court of Appeals held that the first defense—that Rouse had been cheated by Winston—should be reinstated. Conceding that the FHA was an intend-

---

9. Rouse v. United States, 215 F.2d 872 (D.C.Cir.1954).

ed beneficiary of the Winston–Rouse agreement, Rouse's liability to a third party could be no greater than his liability to the promisee. If Rouse could raise a fraud defense to a suit on the contract by Winston, then the same defense must be available in a suit by the contract beneficiary; in effect, "one who promises to make a payment to the promisee's creditor can assert against the creditor any defense that the promisor could assert against the promisee." With respect to the second defense—that against Associated for improper installation—the lower court's decision to strike was sustained. To be sure, the promisor (Rouse) would be entitled to show, if he could, that the promisee (Winston) was under no enforceable liability with respect to the heating plant; if Associated (and the FHA as its successor) had no valid claim against Winston, its rights against Rouse would be no greater merely because Rouse had agreed to take over Winston's outstanding contractual obligations. Here, however, the obligation assumed by Rouse was to pay a specific amount of money—$850—rather than to take over a litigable claim. It was as if Winston had *already* settled with Associated and had conceded herself to be indebted in the amount of $850 at the time she sold the house to Rouse. In effect, Rouse assumed the burden of that settlement (which might have subsumed a variety of claims between Winston and Associated and in any case was reflected in the purchase price of the house) and was not at this stage free to reopen it.

The *Rouse* decision thus confirms that a third party's claim is subject, generally, to the promisor's defenses against the promisee and, unless already settled, to the promisee's defenses against the third party. What remains to be considered, briefly, is the related question of *post*-contractual modification or discharge—in effect, the question that seemed to trouble the dissenting judge in *Lawrence v. Fox* itself. As noted earlier, Judge Comstock, the dissenter, objected to the majority decision on the ground, among others, that the third party's claim might be subject to divestment or dilution through separate action of the promisor and promisee and for that reason occupied a sort of legal limbo. The answer given by the majority was that the third party's rights must "vest" at some appropriate point, though whether at the time the third party actually brings suit against the promisor, or earlier, was not made clear. The problem arises (one imagines) because dealings between the promisor and promisee may involve other matters and other issues than those involved in the contract affecting the beneficiary, so that the beneficiary's interest may ultimately be bargained away or compromised as part of a separate settlement or exchange between the primary parties. More simply, the promisor and promisee may decide, for reasons of their own, to rescind their contract or modify it in a way that eliminates the third party's claim.

On the whole, as stated, a third-party beneficiary's rights are derivative and rise no higher than those of the promisee himself. As a result, generally, the contracting parties retain control of their contract and are free to rescind or modify without the third party's assent. There are, however, reasonable and largely expectable limitations on such freedom. If the third party participated directly in the bargaining that led to the agreement, then either expressly or by inference his assent to any variance is likely to be required. Going further, if the third party learns or is advised of the agreement and changes his position in reliance on what he assumes to be the promisor's enforceable duty, modification or discharge without his assent may be precluded. Whether there has been "reliance" depends on facts and circumstances, but as to "creditor beneficiaries"—Lawrence himself—mere notification probably is sufficient.[10] Lawrence, we may assume, would have relaxed his efforts to collect from Holly once he learned that Fox had agreed to pay the debt. Having been told to expect performance from Fox (Holly, perhaps, meanwhile departing for another jurisdiction), the presumption is that Lawrence's rights become fully vested and are thereafter immune from any subsequent attempt by the primary parties to discharge or modify their agreement.

10. Robson v. Robson, 514 F.Supp. 99 (N.D.Ill.1981).

AFTERWORD

Returning to a theme mentioned at the very beginning, it seems to me that Contracts is preeminently a course in facts and circumstances—in effect, "cases"—rather than a course that stresses legal rules as such. The rules themselves, whether contained in the UCC or in the Restatement, are flexible and general; they are not prescriptive, or only mildly so; and on the whole they are non-technical. That, of course, is perfectly consistent with the basic idea that the parties to a contract are free, within the broadest limits, to construct whatever arrangement or relationship suits their own interests. Rules of law, as has been said over and over, are generally viewed as "defaults," meaning that they are designed to complete what is inevitably an incomplete document—the contract—and to do so in a way that is likely to accord with what the parties, acting rationally, would have wanted and expressed in contractual terms had they foreseen the event or the issue in question at the time they made their deal.

In practice, however, that function—supplying the appropriate "default"—is very far from being routine and automatic. Much more often than not, the unexpressed intention of the parties— "what they would have wanted"—is less than obvious and can only be identified through inference and surmise. Any number of cases can be cited for this proposition, among them the well-known Cardozo decisions in *Wood v. Lucy* and *Jacob & Youngs v. Kent*. Assuming those decisions are correct, as almost everyone believes, the great strength of the Cardozo opinions consists not in the application of fixed and overriding rules, but in the Court's acute perception of the local factual setting and the individual aims and attitudes of the parties themselves.

Not all of the cases that we read in the casebooks are the equal of the two just named. Judicial opinions are sometimes incomplete, even hasty, and are often much less than fully informative about the background of the events under consideration. That is to be regretted, I suppose, but from another standpoint it is a useful shortcoming because it invites us, as critics, to engage in a little worldly speculation about the motives of the parties and the business context in which the present litigation apparently took place. Indeed, what keeps (or should keep) the Contracts course interesting are the opportunities we get to reassess or re-imagine the circumstances out of which a particular dispute has arisen, and

251

having done that, to make a judgment about whether the result that has been reached is wise and sensible or the reverse.

Such speculation, I think, is a worthwhile exercise for first-year law students. Being new at the game, they might otherwise be inclined to take what they read at face value and innocently believe what they are told. If nothing else, the Contracts course should be the occasion for a loss of innocence. The cases are full of self-serving stories, some funny, some sad. Many of those stories, however, perhaps most, are either partly false or (more often) true as far as they go but not the whole story by any means. Students should learn skepticism from this, call it healthy skepticism if you like, and while that is rather a sour habit of mind to go about the world with, I think it is a necessary component of the professional outlook.

TABLE OF CASES

References are to Pages.

253

INDEX

†